FRAGILE MAJORITIES AND EDUCATION

Fragile Majorities and Education

Belgium, Catalonia, Northern Ireland, and Quebec

MARIE MCANDREW

Translated by Michael O'Hearn

McGill-Queen's University Press
Montreal & Kingston • London • Ithaca

© McGill-Queen's University Press 2013

ISBN 978-0-7735-4090-3 (cloth)
ISBN 978-0-7735-4091-0 (paper)

Legal deposit first quarter 2013
Bibliothèque nationale du Québec

Printed in Canada on acid-free paper that is 100% ancient forest
free (100% post-consumer recycled), processed chlorine free

This book has been published with the help of a grant from
the Canadian Federation for the Humanities and Social Sciences,
through the Awards to Scholarly Publications Program, using funds
provided by the Social Sciences and Humanities Research Council of
Canada. We acknowledge the financial support of the Government
of Canada, through the National Translation Program for Book
Publishing for our translation activities.

McGill-Queen's University Press acknowledges the support of the
Canada Council for the Arts for our publishing program. We also
acknowledge the financial support of the Government of Canada
through the Canada Book Fund for our publishing activities.

Library and Archives Canada Cataloguing in Publication

McAndrew, Marie, 1953–
    [Majorités fragiles et l'éducation]
    Fragile majorities and education: Belgium, Catalonia, Northern Ireland,
and Quebec / Marie McAndrew; translated by Michael O'Hearn.

    Translation of: Les majorités fragiles et l'éducation.
    Includes bibliographical references and index.
    ISBN 978-0-7735-4090-3 (bound). – ISBN 978-0-7735-4091-0 (pbk.)

    1. Minorities – Education. 2. Linguistic minorities – Education. 3. Ethnic
groups – Education. 4. Cultural pluralism. 5. History – Study and
teaching – Social aspects. 6. Comparative education. I. McAndrew,
Marie, 1953– . Majorités fragiles et l'éducation. II. Title.

LC3715.M3313 2012   370.89   C2012-906313-4

This book was typeset by Interscript in 10.5/13 Sabon.

Contents

Acknowledgments

We would like to thank the following organizations, whose support allowed us to complete this volume: the Social Sciences and Humanities Research Council of Canada (SSHRC), the Endowment Fund of the Chair in Ethnic Relations of the University of Montreal, the Quebec Research Fund on Society and Culture (FQRSC), and the Ministry of International Relations of Quebec.

The support of various colleagues and collaborators also needs to be highlighted: Professors Johan Leman (Catholic University of Leuven), Xavier Vila (University of Barcelona), Jordi Garetta (University of Lleida), and Alan Smith (University of Ulster, Coleraine) welcomed us into their respective universities and commented on the various sections of this book.

Alice Martin (M.Ed., Faculty of Education, University of Montreal) collaborated closely in researching documents and finalizing the bibliography. She was preceded in this task by Émilie Boileau, then an MA student in the same faculty.

Finally, Marie-Claire Légaré and Louise Simard, respectively, did the linguistic revision of the first French-language draft and assured the word processing of the manuscript's several versions in its original language.

We also benefitted from the help of many decision-makers, researchers, and stakeholders in the various societies studied, especially the Cultural Communities Directorate of the Ministry of Education, Recreation, and Sport of Quebec, whose collaboration was greatly appreciated.

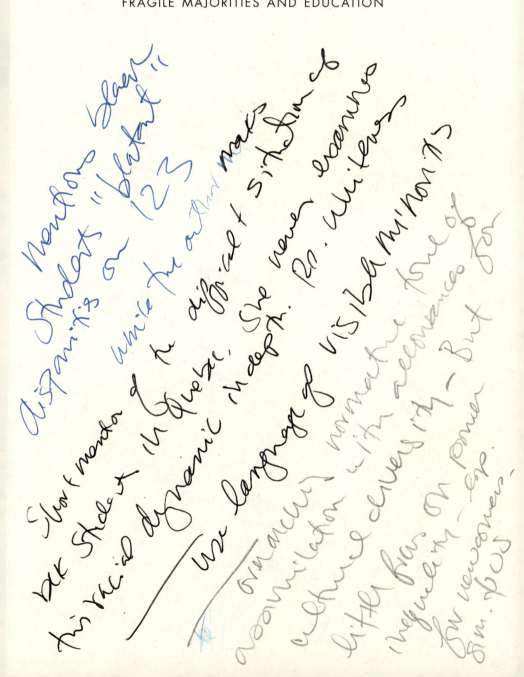

au. critiques dualistic model of
understandj ethnic relations b/c
they "assume the existence of a
clearly dominant majority that
consistently exerts its demographic,
economic, linguistic & socio cultural
power of minority Inferiorstates"[1]

Au. wants to tackle this points from [2]
examination of societies-y fragile
majorities — aby Pg 3

? = pg 6 / Pg 45 - contribution re: ed. models.

[hegemony? ideology?]   contributes to
                    shaptly division
                & is shapatly among groups in oct
                                        presence of a
                                        fragile
                                        min. 10%

Contribution —
how the teachers of historns
important Intervention =
within they developed in US context Campbell
        Short mother contexts   if min.
clunky companion   Inter group context theory
wantymore general holistic approach
                Relationships to
                    "clear minorities"
                        if you in !(....
                    mixtures?   Antram
                            francophones?

Introduction

FRAGILE MAJORITIES, PLURALISM, AND EDUCATION

Ethnic relations is a field of study that has seen some very interesting developments in the last thirty years, including the role of education. First, researchers have critiqued reification, or the tendency to treat cultures and ethnic groups as if they were concrete things, and insisted on the importance of developing a more nuanced view of the dynamic character and multiplicity of identities. Second, researchers have somewhat abandoned, perhaps unduly, the traditional focus on education as a tool for the maintenance of minority cultures and identities in favour of studying its role in the transformation of relations and boundaries between groups. The issues now most debated and explored are the extent to which a shared socialization, defined more or less in a pluralist sense, is carried out in common institutions and the attainment of equal opportunity for students of all backgrounds.[1] Most of these analyses are implicitly or explicitly dualistic. They assume the existence of a clearly dominant majority that consistently exerts its demographic, economic, linguistic, and socio-cultural power over minorities with inferior status. This tendency is influenced by two realities: first, the massive presence of American and, to a lesser extent, English Canadian researchers in this field of study and, second, since the early twentieth century, the marked move away from the study of national minorities to the study of immigrant groups.[2]

However, such situations, which in sociological jargon constitute examples of clear ethnic dominance, are seldom found in the real world. In fact, in many societies, the identification a single majority group is nearly impossible, or the group's status is at least ambiguous enough to raise conceptual dilemmas.

We will examine this phenomenon by looking at four examples drawn from Europe and North America.[3] Sometimes several groups, with differing identities and political agendas, share a more or less equal balance of power, rendering them equally capable or incapable of controlling the state and imposing their definition of the nation. This is the case, for example, with the Flemings and Walloons in Belgium and the Catholics and Protestants in Northern Ireland. Organizing on a territorial basis, or territorialization, made a relatively harmonious coexistence in Belgium possible, but not in Northern Ireland, where reduced space did not foster cohabitation. Conversely, other countries such as Canada and Spain, which have a clearly identifiable majority community, are familiar with the ambiguity of ethnic dominance in regions where another group constitutes the demographic majority. In effect, francophones in Quebec and Catalan-speakers in Catalonia enjoy important political and educational power, which allows them to influence significantly their own development and that of other communities living in their province or state.

In contexts such as these, concepts like *majority* or *minority* are hard to do without, but they must always be nuanced and used with care. Due to the ongoing dynamic of ethnic relations as well as the history of inequality between the groups, so-called "fragile" majorities enjoy a power that is more shared and less consistent in many social settings. Many minorities, notably those consisting of persons who belong to the majority group on the national level, often enjoy in such contexts a status unusual in societies marked by clear ethnic dominance.

What are the consequences of this ambiguity for educational policies, programs, and debates? At first glance a striking feature of societies with fragile majorities during the past thirty years is the dynamism they have displayed in using education as a strategy to transform ethnic relations. Social engineering in the area of education has ranked high in the public agenda, whether in Quebec or Catalonia, to promote a language once accorded minority status, or, as in Northern Ireland, to fight against inter-ethnic tensions.[4] One may think that it is precisely because these power relations were unstable that various groups wanted to get involved in bringing about social change. For decision-makers and researchers of all origins, societies with fragile majorities or ambiguous dominance thus represent extremely interesting cases where the links between educational reform and the transformation of ethnic relations can be explored and the limits to action better identified.[5]

Nevertheless, when viewed from a larger perspective, the extreme resilience of ethnic boundaries and educational divisions reveals a very different reality, especially as regards relations with the majority Other. The existence of distinct national groups is often closely tied to the control these groups were able to obtain and keep in specific institutions. For the most part, fragile-majority societies are also societies *divided* in various areas of social life, such as education. The emotional intensity arising from reform projects likely to affect the status of one competing group or the other largely explains the resistance to change that coexists with a more recent activism. Such controversies frequently reveal the extremely fraught character of *deep diversity,* as well as its history of contradictory myths and mutual distrust.[6]

When fragile-majority societies open their doors to immigrants, they provide us with a fascinating opportunity to observe multilingual practices, the interpenetration of multiple identities, and the potential to transform newcomers into scapegoats for old conflicts. The choice of immigrants for one competing system of schooling over another can become an issue of heated public debate and give rise to tensions and conflicts. In less polarized contexts, newcomer students experience challenges unknown to their peers living in single-majority societies, such as mastering two or more host languages, grasping the complexity of more than one version of national history, or being exposed to policies and programs offering diverging definitions of integration.[7]

Over the longer term, immigration also implies the transformation of interacting groups' traditional identities when education is called upon to play a central role. However, this task can be complex in fragile-majority societies where multicultural, intercultural, and anti-racist education must absolutely take into account the complex dynamic of the prevailing power relations. Policymakers and educators thus have to devise new formulas to reconcile the majority group's fight for survival with the need to create a new civic identity that includes both the recently arrived groups and the community with which this fragile majority has historically been in conflict.[8]

Are fragile majorities capable of opening themselves to the ethno-cultural pluralism emanating from the past or recent history of their society? What is the role of education and, more specifically, of the various structural, political, programmatic, and practical arrangements? This is the subject of this study, which is based on ten years of exchanges and comparative work among researchers and policy-makers from Quebec, Catalonia, Flanders, and Northern Ireland in the context of the Réseau sur l'éducation dans les societies divisées (Network on Education in Divided Societies), which coined the term "fragile majority," among others. This approach, and the synopsis I present here, is born of my deep conviction that the educational challenges associated with the multifaceted diversity of my home society of Quebec cannot be fully explained by classic comparisons with immigrant-receiving countries, such as France, England, or the United States. Without disputing the utility of such comparisons, it seems essential that we go beyond this.

First, we want to examine the relationship to the majority Other – francophones in Flanders, Spanish-speakers in Catalonia, Protestants in Northern Ireland, anglophones in Quebec – an often taboo subject in our respective societies. We will analyse this relationship in three steps. In chapter 1, we discuss the relevance and potential impact of different national groups controlling distinct educational institutions. In chapter 2, we examine the motives that impel certain individuals to cross educational boundaries and the conditions that make it possible for such rapprochements, unplanned or structured, to have a positive impact on inter-ethnic relations. Then, in chapter 3, we study the difficult reconciliation of distinct memories, of the complexity of knowledge, and of the new mandate to develop citizenship competencies in the programs and practices associated with the teaching of history.

Second, we want to revisit the relationship to the immigrant Other from a perspective that fully recognizes the impact of the existing division in society on the debates surrounding the integration of newcomers into the school. The degree to which linguistic integration and equality of opportunity, two key goals in the schooling of immigrants, are complementary or opposed in societies where dominance is ambiguous, is the topic of chapter 4. Obstacles to the pluralistic transformation of fragile-majority institutions are explored next in chapter 5, where the extent of the gap between discourse and practice is evaluated in comparative perspective.

THE DYNAMICS OF ETHNIC RELATIONS
IN FOUR SOCIETIES

Before going any further into this study of educational challenges, we need to point out the comparability of the four contexts that we will use as case studies: Belgium (and more specifically Flanders), Catalonia, Northern Ireland, and Quebec. We have no intention of describing in detail either the history of ethnic relations in these societies or the current legal and socio-political situation of the various groups concerned. When required to further our understanding, we discuss some of these elements in one or other of the chapters that follow. Rather, our objective is to identify the dimensions of convergence and differentiation so as to situate the four societies in a more general typology. This approach allows us to understand better how the observed differences in educational challenges came to be. Do these challenges arise first and foremost from an internal logic of the educational system or school practices, or, to the contrary, should we connect them in whole or in part to the dynamics of ethnic relations in each context?

The four societies under consideration all form regions within a larger state and, in three of the four cases, are home to a minority community (Catalonia and Quebec) or to a community historically reduced to minority status (Flanders). The case of Northern Ireland is more complex. First, no consensus exists on which larger entity it belongs to since two governments and two nationalities (British and Irish) coexist there by virtue of the Peace Agreement signed in 1999. Second, as noted above, Protestants and Catholics are not separated along territorial lines.

These four societies also resemble each other in that ethnic dominance is ambiguous. In Canada and Quebec, the francophone community can be simultaneously a minority or a majority, politically and geographically, depending upon the chosen frame of reference. But even in Quebec, no consensus exists as to its majority status linguistically and economically.[9] Despite important progress, many observers would argue that the francophone community is still *in the process of becoming a majority*. Likewise, the English demographic minority would be *in the process of becoming a minority*, rather than being an authentic minority in the sociological sense. In effect, this group still exercises a certain power of attraction over immigrant groups and enjoys a small economic advantage. In this book, we treat francophones as constituting a fragile majority in Quebec, although the degree of fragility varies according to how one looks at their relations with anglophones, immigrants, and the indigenous peoples.

In Catalonia, we can identify native-born Catalan-speakers as a group *in the process of becoming a majority* or of being a fragile majority, but starting from a slightly different dynamic.[10] Catalans have always been the dominant economic group in both Spain and Catalonia. But their clearly less favourable demographic weight, as well as the status of their language, means that their ethnic dominance is much more noticeably ambiguous, in spite of the normalization that is occurring. Paradoxically, Spanish-speakers are clearly a socio-economic minority group, but whose language plays a role that exceeds their status. Just like in Quebec, the fragility of Catalan-speakers appears to be much less when compared with the status of foreign immigrants or the Roma, whose status as a marginalized group of long standing parallels that of Canada's indigenous peoples.

Traditionally, in Northern Ireland, Protestants have been the majority and Catholics the minority, both demographically and in terms of political and economic power. Still, one can see a reversal occurring; the Catholic community is in the ascendant.[11] Its higher birth rate and the out-migration of Protestants favour Catholics demographically, while the economic gap between them and the Protestant community is vanishing. Finally, from a political point of view, even if the 1999 Peace Agreement preserves Protestant dominance in the short term, it has opened up positive possibilities for Catholics in the medium term. Today, then, most analysts think of Catholics and Protestants as having quite similar statuses or, to use our terminology, as forming two fragile majorities.

Finally in Belgium the establishment of distinct territories by the two competing communities and the major redefinition of power relationships during the past thirty years have appreciably reduced the ambiguity of ethnic dominance.[12] The Flemings are now the dominant group in Flanders economically, demographically, politically, and linguistically, as is evident from the power of attraction they exert on immigrant groups moving into this largely unilingual region. Some observers, especially francophones, reckon that they also constitute the dominant group in the whole of Belgium. However, the prevailing sociolinguistic power imbalance in Brussels, the capital of both Belgium and Flanders, renders the respective statuses more ambiguous than initially appears to be the case. The construction of the Flemish community's identity was also mainly influenced, both historically and even today, by the status of the francophone community, which is a minority in the making. Consequently we consider the Flemings to be Belgium's fragile majority. But in order to preserve the comparability of the educational issues being studied, we will pay particular attention to the school situation in Brussels, the contact zone for the two communities.

Other characteristics allow for a more complex analysis of the comparability of the four contexts under study: the extent of division, the markers that define the identity of the competing groups, the role of immigration, and the sense of belonging to a supranational entity.

The first criterion situates Northern Ireland at one extreme of the continuum. Here, the division is not only institutional and political, but also violent. This is the only society in this study where inter-ethnic conflict has created a significant number of casualties, a circumstance that paradoxically has had positive consequences for public authorities' commitment to educational reform. At the other extreme is Catalonia, where widespread bilingualism has resulted in ethnic boundaries that are clearly more porous than in the other societies. The rejection of parallel educational institutions, a subject we will look at in chapter 1, contributes strongly to depolarizing, or neutralizing somewhat, the relationships between the majority and the minorities. Quebec and Belgium, at the middle of the continuum, are societies where institutional segregation is established, but where ethnic relations are characterized by political avoidance strategies and relatively harmonious contacts in civil society.[13]

The dominance of language as the marker of ethnic boundaries unites Quebec, Belgium, and Catalonia, while in Northern Ireland the religious marker dominates. We are using the term *marker*, which comes out of the constructivist perspective in the sociology of ethnic relations, to recall that in these contexts, as in others, inter-ethnic conflict cannot be reduced to language or religion alone. Conflict arises first and foremost out of a system of inequality and divergent interests; linguistic, cultural, and religious differences can play a role, but they are not at the origin of the tension.[14] Also, with the exception of Catalonia, language and religion maintained strong bonds in the history of each of the societies studied.[15] Only as of the early 1960s did language replace religion as the main criterion of identity mobilization in Quebec. Similarly, Gaelic did not lose its central role in Catholic identity in Northern Ireland until the beginning of the twentieth century. Today, Gaelic still plays an important symbolic role in the mobilization of militant nationalists. In Belgium, the two linguistic communities share a common Catholic heritage, but the Flemish attachment to religious belonging and the Walloon affection for secularity have traditionally been an important factor of differentiation. Even though ethnicity markers are perpetually being redefined, we should not assume that their arbitrary character renders them irrelevant, especially when it comes to education. Language barriers are much more difficult to cross than religious ones and much less conducive to common schooling. Conversely, the absolute character of religious beliefs often leaves their adherents less likely to accept educational compromises.

The four societies also distinguish themselves from one another by the different role that immigration plays in each.[16] At one end of the spectrum, only Quebec is politically committed to the active recruitment and selection of immigrants, having developed over thirty years a vast expertise in matters of integration and intercultural relations. Quebec is where the choice of immigrants to integrate themselves into one or other of the competing communities has been much debated, especially in Montreal, where the point of contestation has been the very status of francophones as the demographic majority in the city. The Catalan situation approximates that of Quebec, at least recently. Historically, internal migration from other parts of Spain contributed to Catalans becoming a minority. But today, international migration, especially from South America, is the key issue for public authorities, who are already actively working to create a civic nation, very similar to the Quebec experience. In Flanders, despite migration's importance in public debate, it is a relatively recent phenomenon. As in other European regions, the involvement of the Belgian federal government and the state of Flanders in the selection or even the integration of immigrants is still limited. Nevertheless, immigrants play a key role in Brussels' demo-linguistic and educational balance. The debates generated by their presence are not without parallels to the situation in Montreal, at least before the adoption of the Charter of the French Language in 1977. As to Northern Ireland, more than twenty-five years of armed conflict have served to discourage many immigrants. The situation is evolving, but immigration is not uppermost in the minds of the people there.

Finally, for the three European countries, the fact of belonging to a supranational entity has a definite impact on the depolarization of groups who were once in competition. It is thus more difficult for the Northern Irish, Catholic or Protestant, to maintain that Irish and British identities are antithetical when the border between Northern Ireland and the Republic of Ireland has disappeared. Likewise, partially because of the significant numbers of bureaucrats and immigrants in Brussels, English increasingly functions as a lingua franca, among Dutch- and French-speakers as well. In Spain, however, as in other contexts where minorities are territorialized, the growing identification with Europe has contributed to Catalan dynamism and to its linguistic and identity claims. In other respects, the membership of these three societies in the European Union strongly influences the policies and programs imposed on immigrant populations, especially in the schools. As we will see in part two of this book, the approaches of these societies differ significantly from that of Quebec, which subscribes largely to the North American model for managing diversity.

PART ONE

Deep Diversity: Relations with the Majority Other

1

Controlling One's Own Institutions: Cultural Isolationism or Assurance of Harmony?

In most societies where an historic conflict exists between two groups in competition for majority status, there is little consensus as to the preferred institutional arrangements for the provision of schooling. In contexts such as these, the tight link between educational structures and the maintenance of group identities and loyalties is generally striking. Ethnic boundaries are maintained thanks to community control of a specific educational system or, at the very least, of a subsystem within it. Moreover, this control is often the result of considerable struggle.[1]

Within distinct educational institutions, cultural heritage and historic memory can be passed on to the future generation through formal instruction. Furthermore, the prevailing climate and contacts with peers of the same background assure that informal socialization will contribute to a sense of belonging. In societies where intercommunity coexistence is peaceful, this formula appears to be an assurance of security and harmony, especially for the most vulnerable groups. Any attempt to disturb the balance in this area might arouse opposition, which sometimes turns into educational wars.[2]

Conversely, opponents of this institutional pluralism, which many immigrant communities envy, see it as a form of self-segregation that could lead to cultural isolation. Separate school systems are increasingly criticized, particularly in countries where latent tensions evolved into violent conflict. They are blamed, among other things, for teaching a version of history that encourages the spread of partial views about the other community and for not contributing sufficiently to the development of common civic values, precisely at the age when feelings of belonging are developing. As well, opponents of community-controlled education argue that its popularity and resilience are the result of the vested interests of ethnic or religious elites.[3]

This chapter is comprised of four case studies that follow a fairly similar path, but that are adapted to both the particularities of each society and the availability of research data. The first part describes the historical, political, and legal context that determined the institutional arrangements for the provision and evolution of schooling for competing groups. The second part deals with the spread of educational segregation or, to the contrary, the sharing of common institutions and with the personal and societal factors that may explain the popularity of one option or the other. In the final part, we examine the internal debate, or lack thereof, within each society about the relevance of the chosen way of proceeding and its consequences for the condition of inter-group relations.

The order of presentation takes into account three cases on the *separate schooling / common schooling* continuum. The first, a highly regulated educational market, brings together Quebec and Belgium, where the areas of freedom are communal (anglophones in Quebec) or territorial (Brussels). Northern Ireland, where both communal control and integrated education are open to the two groups, is the second case. Catalonia clearly sets itself apart with a model of common schooling for Spanish- and Catalan-speakers that excludes any separate structure. Following these analyses, I will present a normative reflection on the relevance of the different policy choices.

QUEBEC

Educational Systems and Ethnic Relations: Origins and Evolution

Since the creation of Canada in 1867, and even before, school structures and ethnicity have been closely associated in Quebec. The British North America Act (BNAA), which made education the exclusive prerogative of the provinces, provided protection not to linguistic groups but to religious minorities, such as Protestants in Quebec.[4] The Act's provisions attest to the preoccupations of the French Canadian group who wanted to make certain it controlled education, at least in the province where it was clearly the majority, and to the religious sensitivities of the time. Very quickly, however, the system structured itself on the basis of a dual cleavage that associated language and religion, since these two identity markers were largely congruent. Francophones attended French Catholic schools, almost exclusively, while anglophones attended English Protestant schools. The arrival of immigrants who fit into neither group made the situation more complex. When they were Catholic, they chose the English Catholic schools. Non-Catholic immigrants separated themselves almost evenly between the English Protestant schools and the private ethno-religious schools.

Beginning in the 1970s, the choice of English schools by immigrants and their descendants, formerly encouraged so as to preserve the "French Canadian" character of the French Catholic schools or simply tolerated as a *natural* phenomenon, became identified as a major social problem. A declining birth rate among francophones and the linguistic assimilation of immigrants by the anglophone community seemed to threaten the fragile francophone majority. By now this group saw itself not as a minority group in Canada but as a territorial majority in Quebec. It refused to accept that it did not represent the host community for the newcomers. In this context a package of linguistic laws, particularly the 1977 Charter of the French Language, known more popularly as Bill 101, was adopted by the Quebec government. These laws were principally aimed not at transforming the anglophone community's linguistic attitudes and behaviours but at breaking its monopoly on the integration of immigrants, which was now to become the responsibility of the francophone community.[5]

Bill 101, which made French the common language for the schooling of students, is based on a compromise. It recognized the right of the *historical* anglophone community to control its own school boards and schools and the right of immigrants and their descendants who had already been assimilated by this community to continue attending English schools. Bill 101 thus had a limited impact on the institutional completeness of an anglophone community in the process of becoming a minority, as well as on the degree of educational segregation between the two groups. Anglophones continue to enjoy a schooling situation from pre-school through university that is generally considered more favourable than that which francophone minorities experience in the English-speaking provinces. Even though the two groups benefit from the same protections by virtue on the Canadian Constitution of 1982, the Quebec government is generally more lenient in its interpretation of the clause that calls for the provision of educational services in the minority language where numbers warrant. Further, despite a few exceptions, the anglophone community remains better off socio-economically, which assures it of access to important additional funding for higher education.[6]

Nevertheless, one thing has changed radically – the demographics of the anglophone sector. In 1971, it had 231,815 students. Today it has only 124,757 students, a nearly 50 percent decrease. This trend is not solely because Bill 101 directed newcomers toward the French schools. It also stems from a demographic decline, which anglophones share with francophones, and significant anglophone emigration from the province. During this same period, however, the French sector succeeded, largely because of immigration, in maintaining its student population, which went from 1,178,163 to 989,152. The more militant voices in the anglophone community talked about a slow strangulation of their institutional completeness. This situation was particularly felt in the outlying regions, where close to 10 percent of the anglophone community lived. Given this community's demographic weakness, it often had to rely on a francophone clientele entitled to an English education (as was the case before 1977) to maintain its schools. Nevertheless the English-language school board currently accommodates 11.2 percent of the student population, which corresponds closely to the combined demographic weight of anglophones and the groups anglicized in the past within the province. As well, this percentage has increased slightly in recent years.[7]

Bill 101 had an even bigger impact on French-language schools, especially in Montreal, where the majority of immigrants live. Traditionally there were homogeneous institutions for the cultural reproduction of the French-Canadian community; now these schools are pluralistic centres with the task of creating a new identity and a new culture. In the outlying areas of Montreal, French-language schools are largely the preserve of old-stock francophones (*francophones de vieille souche*), who are now referred to, for reasons of political correctness, as being of *French Canadian ethnicity*.[8]

Until 1998 the religious marker, increasingly criticized as anachronistic by various sectors of the society, continued to structure the school system, contributing to the maintenance of a fragmented educational environment. For the anglophone community this meant that its decreasing student population would be shared between the Protestant school boards, where its majority was rapidly dwindling, and the Catholic school boards, where it had always been a minority.

For the francophone community, this multiplication of structures served to limit its power to attract immigrant groups who were mainly choosing the French Protestant schools, which were considered more neutral culturally and even anglophile by some.[9]

The replacement of the confessional school boards by linguistic school boards ensured that the structures reflected more closely the transformation that had taken place in society as regards power relations and ethnic boundaries. French-language schools are now the common institution, at least in the spirit of compromise of Bill 101, for francophone and recent immigrant students. English-language schools, while still accepting a multi-ethnic clientele who had arrived in the past, have increasingly become minority institutions, preoccupied with their linguistic and cultural survival. These schools are also strongly committed since the early 1970s to innovative and intensive approaches to teaching French. For Quebec as a whole, 50 percent, and for Montreal, 80 percent, of English-language schools have immersion programs, especially in the primary grades. In the French sector it was only in 2006 that the traditional teaching of English from the first year at the primary level was permitted, along with approaches that generally foster an early-stage bilingualism that many francophones still view with much trepidation.[10]

In looking at the evolution of educational structures in Quebec since 1867, it is clear that the boundaries between francophones and anglophones have remained largely unchanged, even though the two communities have seen their respective statuses redefined and have experienced a pluralistic evolution that has made them more alike. As well, the 1998 reform will doubtless contribute in the longer term to accentuating the identity function of education within the two communities. In effect, they now control the parallel structures corresponding to their redefined statuses, but this arrangement is less likely to encourage structured or informal contacts than did the confessional school boards, which they shared in the past.

The Extent of Inter-community Contacts

In such a regulated educational market, one might think that the crossing of school boundaries is impossible. Though long hidden by the high visibility of media debates about immigrant students illegally enrolled in English schools, boundary-crossing does happen, but on a limited scale. It results from three factors: among recent immigrants, students, whose mother tongue is English, who had to enroll in French school; the not insignificant percentage of francophones who studied in English before the adoption of Bill 101 and who passed on this right to their descendants; and, finally, the possibility for anglophones eligible for English schools to enroll in French schools without losing their eligibility for an English education. For this reason, some opponents of Bill 101 argue that it would have a more negative impact on francophones than on anglophones. Indeed, anglophones form the only community in Quebec that enjoys the freedom to choose its language of instruction. Among the students who study in a linguistic sector different from their mother tongue, *new* anglophones subject to Bill 101 and francophones who attended English schools before 1977, are the most numerous. Nevertheless, from a sociological perspective, anglophone students entitled to English schooling but who study in French are more interesting. The fact that they themselves or their parents are freely opting to cross the educational boundaries, thus breaking down traditional sociolinguistic relationships, may point to an evolution in the attitudes and behaviour of a formerly dominant group. As we will see in chapter 2, this casting aside of identity references is not without ambiguity and insecurity, as much for the parents and students as for the schools that accept them.[11]

The number of francophones (21,152) and anglophones (18,684) being schooled in the other language sector is more or less equal. Nevertheless, given the demographic base of the two communities, the percentages differ radically: 19.9 percent for students whose mother tongue is English and 2.4 percent for students whose mother tongue is French. Given the legal constraints that regulate school attendance, the makeup of these crossovers is not at all the same, as is demonstrated by a study of the school years 2000–01 and 2001–02. Francophones, on a massive scale, were the ones who obtained certificates of admissibility to English schools. Conversely, only 4,839 anglophones, about 6 percent of Quebec's English-language students, are rights-holders.[12]

The popularity of choosing a school in the other language sector varies according to the grade level. Among francophones and anglophones subject to the provisions of Bill 101, this popularity declines systematically from preschool to secondary school, whereas among anglophones who are rights-holders the movement over boundaries is stronger at the primary than at the preschool level. It would be tempting to see in the diminished popularity of the crossover at the primary and secondary levels the expression of intention or meaning on the part of students or parents who made this choice. Maybe the children are immersed in the other language and culture when they are young, but at adolescence a crucial step in identity-formation and career choice, loyalty to their own community becomes a priority. However, the available data are not diachronic; in other words, they deal with different students. It would therefore be hazardous to draw conclusions in this regard.

The two groups of parents also have very different strategies for choosing the public or private system. Francophones who choose English schooling are less likely than other francophones to opt for the private system. Conversely, anglophones who choose to be educated in French are more likely than other anglophones to choose a private school. This popularity is particularly pronounced among rights-holders: 42.5 percent of them choose a French education in the private system. These differences may have something to do with the status of public schools in the two sectors: the English schools enjoy a much better reputation than do the French schools.

The educational boundaries thus appear to be more porous than the legal frameworks would lead us to believe. Nonetheless, the impact of students from the other linguistic community on the two sectors is radically different. The 17,412 anglophone students attending French schools are just a drop in the bucket of the 1,000,366 students in these schools (2 percent). Their presence is seldom a subject of debate, all the more so because it largely coincides with the presence of immigrant students who are clearly more numerous. To the contrary, francophones make up 15.17 percent of the student population in the English sector. They are plainly more visible here. In some regions, their presence is deemed essential for the maintenance of the English schools. This is the case in Estrie, for example, where 31.7 percent of the students in the English schools are francophone. This region is an example of interpenetration of the two school systems. In effect 1,294 French-speaking students do their schooling in English while 715 of their anglophone peers, largely rights-holders, choose French schools.[13]

In Montreal, where the anglophone community is concentrated, there is also quite often a significant local impact. For nearly 25 percent of the primary schools, private and public, at least one student in ten comes from the other language group. In the secondary schools, this percentage is lower (19.4 percent), especially in the public system. In certain French-language schools, English-language students represent the majority of the school population, as we will see in the case study in chapter 2. These schools preferred by anglophone parents are becoming bilingual and bicultural environments, often to the satisfaction of the francophones who attend them, which would indicate that both sides want a shared common school.

But for the vast majority of francophones, and a large proportion of anglophones who are not schooled with their peers from the other group, inter-community contacts are very limited. This is demonstrated by a study of 230 school principals of 14 school boards in various regions of Quebec.[14] Isolation was particularly strong among students in French-language schools: 88 percent said they had *no contact* with the other group in educational activities, and 79 percent in extra-curricular activities. As one might expect given their minority status, anglophone students have more ties or, at least, the frequency of students who claim *never* having any ties, is less (58 percent for educational activities and 42 percent for extra-curricular activities). Relations between staff members were equally less frequent, especially in French-language schools. According to school principals, 82 percent of teachers would *never* meet their peers from the other language group, whereas they themselves did so *rarely* (40 percent) or *never* (57 percent). Here again, the data are slightly more positive in the English schools where 19 percent of school principals and 11 percent of teachers *often* get together with their colleagues from the other language sector. These results are linked, in large part, to the presence of immersion programs and, thus, of francophone teachers in these schools. Furthermore, although one would think that the proximity of the schools would have an impact, researchers found no major differences between Montreal and the outlying regions. The latter, in fact, tend to claim slightly more contacts around extra-curricular activities.

If the school does not ensure the development of bonds between anglophones and francophones in Quebec, activities organized by the other entities, or the simple frequenting of various places in civil society, seem to fulfil this role better. Thus, again according to school authorities, francophone and anglophone students meet each other at the arena or the sports field *often* (41 percent) or *very often* (19 percent) and this tendency is more pronounced among anglophones (46 percent *often* and 39 percent *very often*), as well as in

Montreal (42 percent *often*, and 24 percent *very often)*. According to respondents, these contacts are *friendly* (75 percent) or *very friendly* (21 percent). However, respondents from English schools are clearly more optimistic in this regard than are respondents from French schools.

The Impact of Maintaining Parallel School Structures

Within both the anglophone and francophone communities, there seems to be a consensus about the relevance of parallel school structures. This issue has not figured prominently in public debate, nor has it been studied extensively. While they take positions on the structural arrangements relative to schooling, political elites, pressure groups, and professional organizations are more preoccupied by the dynamism of their own community than they are about the quality of inter-community relations. Francophone institutions for the most part are still adapting to their new mandate to integrate newcomers. For anglophones, experiencing the transformation of their institutions from majority to minority has been more difficult. After a period of strong resistance, their main concerns are now the capacity of English schools to turn out truly bilingual young people and to keep them in Quebec.[15]

Thus no one wants to revisit the question of a common educational system or even an increase in structured contacts between the two communities. This is a Pandora's box; opening it would stir up a great deal of resistance. Proof of this is the outcry created by the proposition in the report by the Commission des états généraux entitled *La situation et l'avenir de la langue française au Québec* (The Condition and Future of the French Language in Quebec) to explore the relevance of this formula at the college level or, more recently, by the proposal by the leader of the Parti Québécois, Pauline Marois, that some courses in primary and secondary schools be taught in English. Linguistic cohabitation's negative impact on the non-dominant language is deemed to be a gospel truth in Canada. One could certainly question the perception that French still occupies that position in Quebec. But many francophone elites and parents would certainly take a dim view of more anglophones, and thus of the English language, in their schools. And further, since inter-community tensions in Quebec are discreet, the need to foster rapprochement by means of schooling is not generally felt to be a priority.[16]

One may wonder, however, if this apparent unanimity risks fracturing a little in the years to come. In the study cited above, 90 percent of school principals stated that much is at stake for Quebec's future in the relations between francophones and anglophones, and more than half felt the school was not stepping in sufficiently in this regard. They strongly favoured educational activities as the means of promoting a better understanding of the other community. But a not negligible percentage of respondents leaned toward structural measures: common schooling (41 percent), twinning of schools (37 percent), and even unified school boards (20 percent). English-language school principals are particularly positive in this regard, as is confirmed by a recent report of the Quebec English School Boards Association. Francophones seem more fearful of the impact that enhanced and more frequent contacts could have, especially on the integration of newcomers.[17]

However, the criticism that community-controlled schooling encourages the propagation of stereotypical views of the other community appears to be well founded when directed at the French-language school system. Data from several studies agree on this point. A preliminary analysis of French and English second-language programs showed that both sides carefully avoid dealing with conflictual issues. But the treatment of French-language Quebec culture is clearly deeper and more exhaustive in the English sector's French second-language programs. The French sector's English second-language programs ignore almost completely the existence of an anglophone Quebec community. Apart from a few passing references to the Canadian anglophone community, an international perspective is the rule for the most part.[18]

Likewise, in the studies cited above, school principals in the two groups stated that students had more opportunities to be acquainted with the francophone community in the English schools than the other way around. Furthermore, although the majority of respondents in each sector think their institution gives a *rather fair* or *very fair* image of the other community in the classroom, they think that the English schools generally do a better job. The presentation of the francophone community in history, the social sciences, and second language classes was rated as *very fair* at 13 percent, 20 percent and 35 percent respectively, while the corresponding figures for the anglophone community in the French schools were 4 percent, 6 percent and 10 percent. A final study, the results of which will be discussed in chapter 3, also seems to suggest that history teachers in the francophone schools accord less importance to the concerns of the Quebec anglophone community in their classes than their anglophone peers do, *mutatis mutandis*, for the francophone community. In these three areas of teaching, one may wonder if the behaviour of francophones simply typifies the greater capacity that all majorities possess to ignore minorities, or if their status as a fragile majority leads them to feel, even today, threatened by the anglophone community.[19]

Still, no study sheds any light on how much of an impact these differences in the school ethos have on the mutual perceptions and attitudes of young francophones and anglophones. The only available information comes from general sociological surveys that make no link to models of schooling. The surveys show little significant differences in this regard. However, one study carried out at the college level suggests that francophone students who did not study in their own language sector hold less polarized positions toward linguistic accommodation. But this finding may simply reflect the *cohort effect*: perhaps students who made this choice already differed significantly from other francophones.[20]

BELGIUM

Educational Systems and Ethnic Relations: Origins and Evolution

The evolution of educational structures in Belgium closely followed the power balance between the two language groups and, more specifically, the linguistic politics that reflect their compromises. The Belgian case is also the most complex of the cases discussed in this book. The large number of structures, both governmental and educational, is beyond compare. Besides being divided into three communities (Dutch, French, and German) and three regions (Flanders, Wallonia, and the Brussels region), in which language and region do not correspond exactly, Belgium also has a school system founded on two pillars (secular and religious) and four levels of organizing authority (communities, provinces, municipalities, and civil society associations). Independently of the dynamic of ethnic relations, this reality leads to a fracturing of the schools. Furthermore the status of Brussels, both linguistically and educationally, is constitutional in nature. A few differences aside, the constitutional arena is practically the only place where the two communities enter into contact, and also into competition, in the area of schooling.[21]

From the creation of Belgium until 1932, Flanders and Wallonia had initially adopted two apparently different policies as regards schooling: in Wallonia, by virtue of the "nationality by birth" principle, the language of education for everyone was French, whereas in Flanders, individuals could choose their language of instruction. In actual fact, the result was similar: French was the dominant language in both school systems, which reflected the status of this language with the upper social classes and political elites of the two groups. Wallonia had a unified school system, at least as regards language (the pillars and the organizing authorities remained in place there). In Flanders, French and Dutch schools coexisted, even though there weren't two school systems. Most of the time, a socio-economic gap was added to the linguistic division, with the Dutch schools having a more under-privileged population.[22]

In 1932, on the heels of the Flemish Renaissance in the late nine-teenth century, and the growing political and economic mobility of the Dutch, the law of 14 July concerning linguistic regulations for primary and middle school instruction led to a partial redefinition of the schooling compromise. The "right of the soil," that is, the division of territory along linguistic lines, prevailed henceforth, in both Flanders and Wallonia. But many factors contributed to bilingualism remaining more pronounced in Flanders. Reform did not apply to the Catholic school system, which, at the time, was as important as the public system. At the primary level, the law permitted schooling in the other language, which had been almost exclusively for the teaching of French in Flanders. At the secondary level, even if the law was a little more restrictive, the transition classes, originally de-signed to help francophones adapt to Flanders, served to maintain a relatively permanent system of education in French.[23]

From the early 1960s, the situation began to evolve in a more rad-ical way. Language conflicts intensified. Just as the Québécois were reclaiming "a Quebec as French as Ontario is English," likewise Flemish nationalist elites sought to establish unilingualism on a terri-torial basis in Flanders, just as it was in Wallonia. In 1963, the law of 30 July concerning language regulations for schools expanded the principle of education in the language of the region to all primary and secondary schools in all systems. It also abolished transition classes.[24]

Today, the school structures in Flanders and Wallonia are relatively simple, at least insofar as language is concerned. Pupils study in Dutch or French respectively. The other language can be taught as a subject, although Wallonia, which interprets the law less rigidly, has recently initiated pilot projects in bilingual education. In theory it is possible to opt for a school of the other language if the head of the household officially declares that the language of the home is not that of the region. But to do so one has to cross language barriers since there are generally no services of this type offered in either Wallonia or Flanders. The only exception is in language-accommodating municipalities situated near linguistic borders and around Brussels, where minority students have the right to attend preschools and primary schools of their own language. These schools answer to two governments: the administrative aspects are under the direction of the community where the school is situated, while the pedagogical aspects are the responsibility of the community corresponding to the pupils' mother tongue. These schools and, to a larger extent, the whole question of linguistic accommodation, are the source of continuous conflict between the two communities. A certain number of private international or European schools are an exception to the unilingualism of the Walloon and Flemish systems.[25]

In Belgium as a whole, 55.8 percent of students attend a Dutch-language school, and 43.6 percent a French-language school. These percentages approximate the respective national population of each community, according to estimates by academics. Linguistic questions at the time of the census have in fact been forbidden since the 1960s. Students enrolled in either linguistic sector, however, find themselves in schools subject to different authorities. Thus, in 2006–07, 68.3 percent of students studying in Dutch attended a school in the free subsidized system, 16.5 percent in institutions reporting to the provinces or the municipalities and, finally, 15.3 percent in institutions directly under community control. In Belgium's French community, the tendency is more or less the same, though free subsidized confessional education is slightly less popular (50.2 percent of the total number of pupils).[26]

As far as language and schooling are concerned, the situation in Brussels, the Flemish city where the majority of residents were Dutch-speakers until the beginning of the twentieth century, always was and still is much more complex. Until 1932, the situation there was very close to what had been the case in Flanders: freedom to choose the language of schooling led to the very marked dominance of French. This allowed francophones to maintain their language while fostering the gradual growth of bilingualism among the Dutch-speakers, which was largely achieved as early as the beginning of the nineteenth century.

In 1932, as in Flanders, the freedom to choose one's language of instruction was abolished in Brussels. However, the law concerning the linguistic regulation of schooling at the primary and secondary levels continued to protect the balance between the language of schooling and the language of the home, which, in a context of galloping Dutch-speaker assimilation, was tantamount to promoting French. Transition classes were essentially aimed at allowing Dutch-speaking students to adapt to an environment where French continued to be the more prestigious language. It was an unequal dualistic school system in which students attended primary schools in their linguistic community, but where the Dutch-speakers subsequently chose to attend French schools as a strategy for social mobility. Essentially the law of 1963 on the use of language in administrative matters reaffirmed this compromise, which was unsatisfactory for Dutch-speakers and which was becoming equally so for the francophones against a background of increasing immigration.[27]

In 1979 a constitutional revision partly addressed the fears and desires of the two groups. Freedom of choice for the head of the family, a long-standing francophone demand, was reintroduced. But Dutch-language schools also received stronger support from the government, allowing them to offer a lower teacher-student ratio than the French-language schools, which made them more attractive. The francophone community was expecting that freedom of choice would result in more Dutch students in their schools. Exactly the opposite occurred: the Dutch-language schools ended up with increased numbers of francophones. This trend stemmed from two factors: first, active recruitment within the francophone community by Flemish authorities and, second, the more significant presence of immigrants in the French schools, which pushed a certain number of francophones to enrol in the more homogeneous Dutch schools.[28]

In any event, the student population of Brussels remained stronger in the French-language schools (83 percent) than in the Dutch-language schools (17 percent). But, in both cases, these percentages bear witness to a certain capacity for attraction by the other group.

People who grew up in homes where French was spoken exclusively (50 percent) or combined with an immigrant language (10 percent) represented 60 percent of the Brussels population. The population also included the 10 percent of adults who grew up in an entirely Dutch family, 10 percent who were bilingual (French and Dutch), and 20 percent who were allophones. Consequently, French-language schools attracted 25 percent more students than their population base, and the Dutch schools 5 percent more. But, as mentioned above, the composition of these gains in class size were quite different. At the French-language schools, it was the allophone students, while in the Dutch schools it was the traditionally bilingual and francophone students.[29]

On the whole, the last fifty years have seen a radical transformation in the schooling model for the two national communities, reflecting a change in the power balance. The situation has changed from an education that essentially targeted the linguistic assimilation of the less prestigious group, the Dutch-speakers, in favour of the dominant language, French, to a compromise favouring the retention of both French and Dutch in the territories where the particular language dominates. In this new linguistic balance, Brussels, like a few language-accommodating municipalities, represents the battlefield where dominance is still ambiguous. Without speaking of "winning back Brussels," as others did for Montreal, Dutch-speakers in recent times have clearly played a markedly more significant role in both the social and the educational spheres. Nevertheless, the status of the French language is barely eroded and the institutional completeness of the French community remains intact.

The Extent and Impact of Educational Segregation

Throughout Belgium, with the exception of Brussels, inter-community segregation in education remains extremely high. Barring any indication to the contrary, estimates put the French presence in Flanders at 5 percent, and the same for the Dutch presence in Wallonia. The two educational systems are very homogeneous, and a large majority of students are schooled without contact with the other group. As well, each community exercises tight control over teacher training and the recognition of university diplomas, which results in a high degree of homogeneity among their teaching personnel, even for the teaching of a second language. This practice makes it impossible, or at least extremely difficult, for the graduate of a francophone university to teach French in a Dutch school, and vice versa.

To date, the impact of this strict inter-community isolation has not been a matter of major contention, in either public debate or research. However, a few studies have shown that the level of prejudice and stereotyping is relatively high among both French- and Dutch-speaking youth, in contrast with the extremely positive relationship that both groups maintain with English language and culture. However, it is difficult to distinguish what in these attitudes is a result of segregated schooling and what can be attributed to other factors such a family socialization or media coverage. Furthermore, when the homogeneity of the two school systems is questioned, the discussion has more to do with the weakness in teaching the other language than with the promotion of contacts between students from the two communities. The prohibition on bilingual education and the various formulas for French schooling in the Flemish community, where the opposition is strongest, are especially debated.[30]

Also missing are data about the formal and informal education that predominates within the Dutch- and French-language schools. The debate over the loss of "Belgian identity" is recurrent, notably within the francophone community. But no research has explored the impact of schooling in this regard on young people. We are equally ill-informed about the difference that may exist in the subjects that are key to identity development, such as history, second language, and civic education. These should be important because, unlike the other societies we are looking at in this book, these two sectors do not share a common curriculum. School and extracurricular activities, which allow students from the two communities to get together, receive financial support from the twinning program sponsored by the Fonds Prince Philippe de la Fondation Roi Baudouin (the Prince Philip Fund of the Roi Baudoin Foundation). Since its inception the Fondation's Trèfle Program has reached 324 primary and secondary schools. The stay, which includes an entire class and lasts three to five days depending on the age of the students, has a two-fold goal: learning a language and the mutual discovery of unique cultural features in a context of respect for the other's identity. The impact of the project on either of these dimensions has yet to be formally evaluated on a large scale, although, according to the testimonies collected during the fiftieth anniversary of the program, participant satisfaction appears to be high. A recent analysis shows, however, that the program has more difficulty attracting students from vocational schools, where the teaching of the other language is much less frequent, and from schools where the immigrant presence is strong.[31]

In Brussels, formal and informal contacts between French-language and Dutch-language schools are equally limited since these institutions are under the control of their respective communities. The responsibilities of the Brussels-Capital region in educational matters are limited to school transportation and property management. But even for these secondary considerations, it was judged best to create parallel structures run by the two communities. However, as we saw above, since freedom of choice is the norm in Brussels, the students in the two systems are more heterogeneous than the teachers or the formal curriculum being taught.

In the French-language schools, which do not keep rigorous data about the mother tongue of their students, it is estimated that close to 35 percent of the students do not come from unilingual francophone families. As for the Dutch-language schools, only the secondary level has a significant Dutch-speaking population (33.7 percent). In preschool, 32.1 percent of the students have French as their mother tongue, 33.4 percent another language, 24.9 percent are traditionally bilingual, and only 9.5 percent are unilingual Dutch-speakers. At the primary level, the percentage of Dutch-speakers reaches 13.7 percent, while the share for the other groups decreases slightly (30.3 percent for French, 31.1 percent for other languages, 25 percent for the traditionally bilingual). At the secondary level, francophones and allophones return to French school: they represent only 21 percent and 20.9 percent of the student body at Dutch schools. At all levels, the non-Dutch-speakers are underrepresented in the free subsidized schools, that is, the Catholic schools, and more present in schools under the responsibility of the municipalities or the Flemish community. It is not known if this phenomenon results from the education offered at the Catholic schools or by the shift of Dutch parents toward this type of institution. But it is clear that at the pre-school and primary levels, the effect of musical chairs is at play. Francophones and wealthier immigrants are abandoning French-language schools for the Dutch-language public schools which have greater financial means and, until very recently, were less multi-ethnic. But, as a result of this movement by francophones and immigrants, Dutch-speaking parents themselves are more often choosing free subsidized schools.[32]

As we will see in the next chapter, the crossing of boundaries and the cohabitation this produces can be problematic, especially for Dutch-speaking teachers who see their traditional mandate to foster the reproduction of culture, language, and identity markers as being radically called into question. Nevertheless, although a number of Dutch- and French-speaking students attend schools together in Brussels, the impact of common schooling on mutual attitudes is a question little explored in the research. Similarly, the opposite situation of isolation that prevails in Wallonia and Flanders has not been extensively examined either.

NORTHERN IRELAND

Educational Systems and Ethnic Relations: Origins and Evolution

From the creation of Northern Ireland after the partition of 1921 until the middle of the 1980s, Northern Irish school structures accurately reflected the division within the society. Indeed, even though the Protestant-dominated Northern Irish state was tempted to impose common schooling, a segregated school system has been in place since 1923. Protestant students attended *controlled* schools, which were funded and officially public, while Catholic students attended *maintained* schools, which were controlled by the Church but subsidized to some degree by the state. The controlled schools were supposedly open to all, but their multiconfessional Protestant character was obvious to all, especially to Catholics. Even though this segregated system was often criticized, it lasted for more than sixty years without major protest.[33]

This remarkable stability, which some would see as immobility, can be traced to two factors: first, the powerful influence of the Catholic Church and, second, the strong consensus within the two communities about the desirability of separation in school and society. Even the emergence of violent conflicts in the late 1960s, which the Northern Irish diplomatically called "The Troubles," led to no major changes to the system of separate schooling. Initially, the polarization actually accentuated the prevalence of segregation, notably in the urban areas where until then Protestants and Catholics experienced a certain degree of integration.[34]

However, after more than fifteen years of civil war, some parents and educators again called into question the dominant model of community-controlled education, whose role in the maintenance of the tensions concerned them. The creation of *integrated* schools appeared to be a way of fostering social change, but other factors motivated these decisions: the difficulty of parents in mixed marriages to make a schooling choice without antagonizing one or other of their families, and the dissatisfaction of some Catholics with the autocratic climate that prevailed in schools dominated by the Church. During the 1980s, integrated education was essentially promoted in the field, but the idea received little help from the British government, which was then exercising Direct Rule. In 1989, however, the Education Reform Order made integrated schooling a legitimate alternative, granting it funding on par with the other two options. In the late 1990s, this sector, which counted some fifty schools, took in 5 percent of the student population. These integrated schools received much more media attention nationally and internationally than their demographic importance warranted. But, as they liked to say in Northern Ireland, their existence constituted for journalists the only good news they could report. This explains why this innovation seemed to play a significant role in mutual perceptions and the depolarization of the society.[35]

But it is clear that, since the 1999 Peace Accord, educational structures have not evolved in this direction. In putting to the forefront a communitarian definition of the exercise of power, the new Northern Irish Constitution reinforced efforts by the two groups to protect their own turf. The existence of Responsible Government, though its future is constantly compromised, has contributed to a polarization in the choice of schooling, which had been left mostly to experts and parents during the twenty-five years of Direct Rule. As in other contexts, financial accountability was also, for some years, at the centre of the education debate, and it gave weight to the opponents of integrated education, who denounced it as a too costly way of fostering school contacts between Protestants and Catholics. So the Department of Education of Northern Ireland (DENI) then began to promote the desegregation of a certain number of schools, called *transformation* schools, rather than to create new integrated institutions. It was an economical solution. But, according to its critics, this solution did not always respect the requirements for an equal number of students and teachers from both communities, something that was central to the spirit of the original plan. DENI also recently established a less ambitious threshold of 30 percent. Moreover, the educational plan of these new desegregated schools does not necessarily demonstrate a commitment to inter-community rapprochement, as we will see in chapter 2.[36]

The traditional sectors, controlled and maintained, today include more than 95 percent of the students of Northern Ireland, largely along denominational lines, though boundary-crossing does occur. The Catholic community benefits from strong institutional completeness, which was strengthened in the mid-1990s by the adoption of a more equitable funding formula for the two sectors. The Human Rights Advisory Commission ruled at the time that the inequality of resources between the two sectors largely explained the inferior academic performance and mobility of the students in the maintained sector.[37]

Moreover, the survival and teaching of the Irish language are now promoted simultaneously by the 1999 Peace Accord and the European Charter on Minority and Regional Languages, to which Great Britain was a signatory in 2000. Originally the preserve of the most militant Republican fringe of the Catholic community, the number of Irish speakers is growing rapidly. This includes some 7,494 students (about 2.4 percent of the total student population) spread across 35, mostly primary, schools. Attempts have been made, more or less successfully, to promote the advantages of bilingualism and of the Irish language as the common heritage of all citizens of Northern Ireland. But its clientele is essentially Catholics, who may not be practising but who still identity as such. Indeed, while a number of Catholics, notably within the Republican movement, today hold a negative view of religion as a conservative force, they feel that the rebirth of the Irish language justifies a new commitment to the institutional completeness of their community.[38]

For almost a century, the resilience of the boundaries between Catholics and Protestants has been striking; although schooling choices have multiplied over the last three decades, it is doubtful that the strong relationship between school structures and community divisions will weaken significantly in the coming years. Several recent initiatives, such as the policy on inter-community relations, *A Shared Future*, along with the report evaluating the school system, *Schools for the Future*, reiterate the government's preference for enhanced collaboration between the two sectors, especially as regards the services offered, without radically questioning the principle of parents' freedom of choice and of community control. But it remains to be seen how the population, and above all pressure groups, will react to these perspectives.[39]

The Extent of Inter-community Contacts

While parents' freedom of choice is, in theory, limited only by the state's financial capacity to open new schools, it is striking to observe how limited boundary-crossing is. According to a recent study[40], 48 percent of students attended a controlled school, 47 percent a maintained school, and 4 percent an integrated school. Maintained schools receive 94 percent of students declaring themselves Protestant, while the proportion is 92 percent for controlled schools. Among Protestant students who drop out of their own sector, 5 percent attend integrated schools and only 1 percent go to a school in the other sector. Among Catholics, 4 percent favour maintained or integrated schools. The crossing of boundaries has increased slightly since 1998–1999: 4 percent by Protestants and 7 percent by Catholics. The selection of integrated schools has also increased among Protestants, although it is stagnating among Catholics. According to some observers, this tendency stems from the fact that it is almost exclusively the former *maintained* schools that were turned into integrated schools, owing to the resistance of Catholic clergy to seeing their schools so converted.

Contrary to the situation in Quebec and Belgium, the popularity of crossing boundaries is stronger at the secondary than at the primary level. Among Protestants, boundary-crossing has risen from 4 percent to 14 percent, essentially to the benefit of integrated schools (13 percent). Catholics showed a slight increase (from 7 percent to 9 percent), again in favour of the integrated schools (7 percent). This situation is largely explicable by the recently abolished selectivity of the Northern Irish school system. In a context where admission to Grammar Schools, which alone led to the most prestigious exams, was limited, the choice of integrated schools seemed to be the lesser evil. Even though the integrated schools did not select their students, they enjoyed a better reputation among Protestant parents than did the ordinary public schools.

The probability of contact with peers from the other group varies considerably according to the type of school attended. As one would expect, integrated schools have the most balanced population: 40 percent Catholic and 50 percent Protestant. The profile of each school differs, however, depending on the concentration of the two communities in the neighbourhood or region where the schools are situated. Controlled schools consist of 86 percent Protestant students, 5 percent Catholic, and 9 percent whose religious affiliation is undeclared. In the Northern Irish context, the latter may be non-practising or belong to a religious minority. It is clear, then, at least insofar as mandatory schooling is concerned, that the great majority of young Protestants and Catholics continue to be schooled in two largely segregated systems.[41]

However, unlike in Quebec and Belgium, the issue is recognized and widely discussed. As early as 1977, a study had destroyed the myth, propagated by supporters of community control, that attendance at segregated schools did not prevent students, teachers, and administrators from maintaining relations. According to the principals interviewed, students would interact frequently only during sports activities, which, most of the time, were marked by strong competition. All other types of contact, for both students and school staff, were virtually nonexistent. Consequently, the Ministry of Education as well as the Office of the First Minister and Deputy First Minister for Northern Ireland supported rapprochement activities among the schools under the auspices of school authorities or non-governmental organizations through programs such as Interschool Link or the School Community Relations Program. According to a study conducted in 2002–03, 59 percent of schools were involved in these types of encounters, which were either one-time in nature or relied on longer-term twinning of schools. Activities happened most frequently at the primary level, where 22 percent of the students were involved. In the secondary schools, activities were reserved for the better students, apparently to preserve the school's image. These activities involved less than 5 percent of the students. For the most part contacts happened outside of the schools (field trips or leisure activities), and their superficial character was often criticized. Students did not always understand that the purpose of these activities was the improvement of inter-community relations, even when the majority (83.4 percent) declared their appreciation of them. As we will see in chapter 2, the impact of these activities on student attitudes and behaviour is unclear.[42]

Young Northern Irish are also meeting at formal rapprochement activities organized by community and recreational centres. Thus

52 percent of sixteen-year-old students stated that they had gotten together in various contexts, whereas for students aged twelve to seventeen, the figure was 43 percent. However, with growing residential segregation (80 percent) and continuing inter-community tensions that include incidents of violence, the frequency of interaction, during unplanned activities not explicitly targeting reconciliation, will likely remain limited.[43]

The Respective Impact of the Two Models

The debate over the relevance of the two models of schooling – community-controlled or integrated – was essentially about their impact on two largely incompatible social objectives: the maintenance of two groups historically in competition with one another and the transformation of their relationships. In principle, decision-makers in the world of education declared themselves in favour of integrated education. According to numerous polls, this was also the case, year after year, for 50 percent of the population. But when we compare these results with the actual behaviour of parents, a great deal of opposition clearly remains in the field, despite the social desirability of this type of schooling. Those who come from the traditional educational sectors, maintained or controlled, are essentially corporatists. They argue that, in a limited educational market like Northern Ireland, the competition coming from the integrated schools and, more recently, from the Irish-language schools limits their ability to fulfil their mandate of cultural reproduction of the community. Initially it was mainly the Catholic hierarchy who expressed concern, given the large popularity of the integrated schools among Catholics. Since this choice affected Protestants even more, representatives of the controlled schools began to voice their anxieties. Political parties avoided endorsing one model over another in their election platforms; they insisted on the importance of freedom of choice for parents. Only Sinn Fein, influenced by French republicanism, explicitly stated that common schooling would be necessary in a reunified Ireland. Nonetheless, in the actual context of Northern Ireland where the Catholic community is fragile, all parties acknowledge the role played by the Church and its schools in protecting Catholic identity. Moreover, although the inequality between Protestants and Catholics gave rise to many disputes and their eventual correction, the issue of inequality was never raised in the debate about the respective relevance of separate or common schools. In a situation where institutional pluralism is so entrenched, the problem was interpreted as justifying increased and more equitable support for maintained schools, rather than as an issue of segregation.[44]

In the 1980s, integrated education was challenged to justify its relevance. Parents, students, and even teachers in these schools often faced violent threats because of their choices. Research was aimed not at demonstrating the positive impact of common schooling on inter-community relations but on showing the absence of negative consequences for their respective identities. A meta-analysis of the conclusions of studies conducted on large and small numbers of students revealed two complementary realities. First, increased contacts between Protestant and Catholic students contributed to the importance of ethnic boundaries and their markers: having to confront the other on a daily basis, youth were more aware of their own identity and culture. Second, at the same time, there was a general decrease in stereotypes and negative attitudes about the other group and also a personalizing of contacts. As we will see in chapter 2, it is important to remember that the question of inter-community relations was central to the activities of integrated schools at this time.[45]

Given these rather positive facts, beginning in the mid-1990s, the burden of defending the model of community-controlled education fell upon its supporters. They faced a double dilemma in this regard. They had not succeeded in demonstrating that the ethos supposedly specific to their sector would have a significant impact on maintaining students' cultural identity and group loyalty. But in any case, if they were to do this too openly, they would be blamed for having contributed directly to past tensions, a charge they strongly rejected. However, in 1985, an exhaustive ethnographic study had shown that, even if the two sectors were sharing a largely similar formal curriculum, very different socialization practices contributed to maintaining and accentuating distinct identities. The implicit curriculum, such as religious and national symbols, feasts celebrated or sports played, contributed to this dynamic. Principals and teachers also retained defensive and stereotypical perceptions about the other community, although to what degree they were transmitting these to the students is unclear. Defenders of community control pointed out that the situation had evolved a great deal. Maintained and controlled schools were now encouraging education for mutual understanding through the formal curriculum, where they shared the same programs of religious culture and history. Extracurricular activities aimed at rapprochement were also cited to prove that segregated schooling did not prevent the promotion of harmonious inter-community relations.[46]

Research comparing the attitudes and behaviours of students according to their type of schooling weakens this position, but not in so conclusive a manner as to contribute much to the debate. An early study, carried out in the 1990s, showed, as one would expect, that students enrolled in integrated schools had more contacts and friendships across community boundaries, both at and outside of school. Furthermore, contrary to the findings of the 1980s, this study seems to indicate that identities would be more blurred in the new integrated schools, which, we should remember, were not always created with a clear normative plan in mind. Students accorded less importance to their community identity than they did to other personal and group characteristics (gender, lifestyle, personal taste). But it is difficult to pinpoint the specific impact of integrated schools on this tendency, given the other factors which contribute to a growing individualism among the youth of Northern Ireland.[47]

Another more recent study on attitudes and conceptions of citizenship showed that students lacking contacts with their peers in the other group were slightly less positive about mixed marriages, political compromise, and sharing common institutions. The study also showed that integrated education increases the frequency of these connections and the perception that the discussion of inter-group relations is a good thing. Hence the proponents of this model find confirmation for their point of view. However, 50 percent of the variance was not linked to school contacts but to the attitudes of parents and to religion: thus Catholics were generally more open than Protestants. Furthermore, relations outside of school played a slightly more important role than did the relations the students established in the school. Consequently, the other camp could also find arguments to support its position.[48]

CATALONIA

Educational Systems and Ethnic Relations: Origins and Evolution

In contrast with the three preceding cases, which are divided educational systems within divided societies, the boundaries between Catalan- and Spanish-speakers have always been fuzzier, both socially and educationally. A variety of factors noted in the introduction explains this state of affairs: the high socio-economic status of Catalans, the fact that the majority of Spanish-speakers had originally migrated from poor regions of Spain, and, finally, the extent of bilingualism within the Catalan elites.[49]

In the twentieth century, common schooling for the two groups has been the dominant model. As the power balance evolved, educational content, especially the language of instruction, became the subject of debate rather than educational structures. Influenced by the French model, the Catalan school system is also nonconfessional, though private schools are funded.[50]

Before 1939, most students did their schooling in Spanish, though several schools used Catalan as well. After this date, the Franco dictatorship imposed Spanish-only common schools. Coupled with numerous attacks against the public use of Catalan, this situation contributed to the creation of an entire generation of Catalan-speakers illiterate in their own language, although they continued to use it to some degree in civil society and especially in private life. During the process of democratization that followed the death of Franco, two issues were particularly debated regarding what model to favour in linguistic and educational matters. First, should Catalan-speakers, who were emerging from forty years of diglossia, that is, of using Catalan for ordinary conversations and Spanish in most other social settings, adhere to a major process of linguistic normalization and agree to send their children to Catalan-only schools? Second, what should be the educational status of most Spanish-speakers, who were mostly unilingual working-class immigrants isolated from both the Catalan majority and the former Spanish-speaking administrative elite?[51]

The complexity of these dilemmas was particularly evident during the transition period, which ended with the adoption of the 1983 Law on Linguistic Standardization, when initiatives multiplied. Spanish-language schools now had a couple of options. Some maintained their linguistic character while beginning to teach Catalan: this was a popular option in the suburbs of Barcelona, where the overwhelming majority of students were Spanish-speakers. Others, especially in the outlying regions, chose to become Catalan-language schools, with a significant amount of time allotted to teaching Spanish. From a comparative perspective, it seemed that a process of polarization of the school system was underway, perhaps leading to the institutionalization of pluralism within the schools.

Instead, in a very interesting and apparently highly consensual dynamic, the process came to an end in 1983. The Law on Linguistic Standardization explicitly opted for common schooling, giving priority to a clear normative position about the non-desirability of separating students on the basis on language. The law also reaffirmed the necessity for students to master both languages by the end of their schooling. Spanish continues to be taught, largely as a second language; and immersion programs meeting the needs of non-Catalan students are now widespread. To respect the Spanish Constitution, the Law on Linguistic Standardization recognized the right all students to be educated in the language chosen by their parents, at least at the primary level. This did not, however, include the right of particular communities to control their own schools. However, the administrative requirements permitting the exercise of this right, which the Spanish Supreme Court judged constitutional in 1994, were set out in such a restrictive manner that availing of this right is neither encouraged nor frequent.[52]

Sharing common schools has largely been the norm for twenty-five years. It was even strengthened in the 1990s by the tendency to reserve immersion programs for foreigners, although they are now directed to reception classes, as we will see in chapter 4. Increasingly, Spanish-speakers are enrolling in regular Catalan-language schools, even though the government recently announced its intention to develop, at the secondary level, a type of immersion class that would better meet their needs. And so, in 1999–2000, 96 percent of primary school students were schooled exclusively in Catalan; this includes schools where the majority of the student body is Spanish-speaking. The Catalan immersion school in which there is a significant use of Spanish during class time has practically disappeared at this level. At the secondary level, however, 45 percent of students are schooled exclusively in Catalan, 47 percent where Spanish has a significant presence, and 9 percent only or mostly in Spanish. It is still very difficult to obtain statistics; this reflects the reticence of Catalan school authorities to discuss the issue of Spanish-speakers' schooling, beyond the sole challenge of their learning Catalan.[53]

The status of the Catalan-speaking community as an emerging political and economic majority in relation to a clearly less powerful Spanish-speaking community seems to have allowed Catalan-speakers to control the educational agenda. However, the fact that Catalan authorities have accepted to do so much promotion of bilingualism within the school system points to the very real fragility of the Catalan language. Although few administrators would admit it, the choice of common schooling was probably also influenced by fear that the inverse option, institutional parallelism, would result in Catalan-language schools being a minority option. This would have been unacceptable in a society trying to correct years of linguistic oppression.[54]

The Extent and Impact of Common Schooling

The mere existence of a normative, administrative model of common schooling does not guarantee that students from different backgrounds will be educated together. In most Western societies, residential concentration linked with social class composition and parents' preference for certain schools result in schools where one type of clientele concentrates at a higher percentage than their proportion of the general population. Catalonia is no exception to this rule, although the absence of national data in this regard makes it very difficult to evaluate with precision the degree of segregation between Catalan- and Spanish-speakers. Since the latter are strongly concentrated in the old working-class suburbs of Barcelona, de facto segregation between the two groups is surely higher than official discourse admits. A recent study shows that 23 percent and 45 percent of students at the end of primary school almost never used, respectively, Spanish or Catalan in their social networks. This suggests that the normative school model by itself probably produces actual interactions and contacts in less than a quarter of the students.[55]

Yet, the relevance of adopting this model is little debated; it seems to be taken for granted, just as educational parallelism is in other societies. The institutional completeness of the Spanish-speaking community constitutes neither an issue nor a research question. One may assume that changing the model is not the desire of the main protagonists and that this situation reflects either their actual agreement with the political choices of the majority or an absence of organization and mobilization. Only one legal challenge to the Law of Linguistic Standardization has gone to the Spanish Supreme Court, which ruled that the Catalan model respected the Constitution. For the most part, the protest about the injustice being done to the Spanish-speaking minority was led by the daily newspapers in Madrid during the adoption of the 1998 law and, more recently, during the debate about the autonomous status of Catalonia. If it exists, Spanish-speaker opposition to common schooling is rather muted. However, if given the opportunity to choose, Spanish-speaking parents and students would prefer schooling in their own language, even if they value the teaching and learning of Catalan. Thus, in a survey carried out in 1995, 82 percent declared themselves in favour of the teaching of Catalan, but 70 percent are opposed to the current model – immersion in Catalan, with Spanish taught as a subject. Although recent data are not available, it is possible that this opposition was accentuated by the Law of Linguistic Standardization, which extended the predominance of Catalan up to university level.[56]

One should not conclude from the preceding that public authorities or academics are not anxious about the consequences of schooling in Catalan for Spanish-speaking students. However, this preoccupation is almost exclusively about equality of opportunity rather than the maintenance of their language and culture. From the beginning, for the Catalan left wing, the choice of common schooling was justified by the potentially perverse effects of school segregation for Spanish-speaking students, whose socio-economic and educational status was quite low. One might be slightly suspicious of the left's sincerity in this regard, given how little attention it gave thereafter to de facto segregation. But the educational success of these students has received sustained attention. The main finding from this important body of research is the absence of causal links between the Spanish-speaking community's educational gap and the current schooling model. According to a number of corroborating studies, the educational performance of Spanish-speakers in Catalan immersion equalled that of pupils who studied in Spanish, and, as one would expect, they had a better grasp of Catalan. The slight negative effect on their ability to read and write in Spanish disappeared with time as their education continued. Still these optimistic observations need to be set in context. Indeed, as we saw above, the comparison group is small. Furthermore, this is about students benefitting from an education in Spanish and not about attendance at schools controlled by their communities. Otherwise, the fact that results in Spanish on the PISA international test are equivalent (65 percent in Spain and in Catalonia), even though a large proportion of the students were Catalan-speakers and the Spanish-speakers studied mostly in Catalan, would suggest that the immersion system is generally effective.[57]

The Catalan case is also characterized by the weakness of discussions and research into the consequences of common schooling on the vitality of Catalan, the former minority-status language. This is the preoccupation that justifies the option for the community-control model in Belgium and Quebec. As to its use in society, Catalan authorities have avoided until very recently making available linguistic data that go beyond mere familiarity with the language. As we will see in chapter 4, this taboo has been lifted, and a number of studies show that the use of Catalan has not necessarily progressed at the same pace as familiarity with the language. On the other hand, there is a greater intergenerational transmission of Catalan among youth who studied in immersion, a trend evident among Spanish-speakers as well. Furthermore, among young people of all languages, the use of Catalan grew significantly, though interactions continue to be the principal determinant of the dominant language.[58]

Together these data do not allow us to evaluate rigorously the actual relationship between common schooling and the larger sociolinguistic dynamic. Common sense clearly argues in favour of a positive impact for young Spanish-speakers. But pessimists argue that educational cohabitation could erode the use of Catalan among Catalan-speaking students. A 2003 study of fifty-two representative schools in the Catalan educational system showed a net predominance (around 75 percent) in the use of Spanish during inter-group exchanges, even when Catalan-speakers had a significant presence. Indeed, only when Catalan-speakers make up more than 70 percent of the student body at a school does Catalan become the lingua franca.[59]

As to the disappearance of inter-group boundaries, and notably the identification of Spanish-speakers with Catalan society, researchers concur that the impact is moderate. Even though attitudes toward Catalan and identification with Catalonia have progressed among Spanish-speakers over the last fifteen years or so, there is still a significant gap in this regard with Catalan-speakers. It is the language spoken at home, more than factors linked to knowledge of the language or schooling, which influences identity development among students. But here again, we are unable to isolate the impact of common schooling, since we do not know if these findings would have been different had Spanish-speaking students attended schools controlled by their own community. In any event, normative adherence to the chosen model remains strong in Catalonia; in the absence of truly conclusive data one way or the other, its relevance is not in question.[60]

Relevance and Limits of Different Models of Schooling

What lessons can we draw from the preceding four case studies? Our analysis suggests that there is no straightforward answer to the rhetorical question that serves as the title of this chapter: does control of one's own institutions create cultural isolation or assure harmony? In comparative education there is an elegant way out of this dilemma: affirm that every society has developed a formula adapted to its needs and characteristics but not suited to other contexts. But the application of cultural relativism to the analysis of policies has its limits. The point of comparative analysis is not the simplistic transfer of solutions applied elsewhere. But it does raise questions about the dominant presuppositions underlying national educational choices. Furthermore, as we saw in Northern Ireland, there is often more than one formula that can lead to democratic debate.[61]

That said, taking a position on the best schooling model would demand evaluating in an abstract way the legitimacy of three respectable but often conflicting social objectives: equality of opportunity in education, the maintenance of the different groups' culture, language, and identity, and social cohesion. But, their order of priority cannot be analysed apart from the specific context where the relative intensity and urgency of the problems can be evaluated. This task is easier in situations of extreme polarization, for example: where one group is living in extreme educational and economic marginalization; when a language is on the verge of disappearing; or, finally, in the aftermath of a civil war. But in most Western societies like the ones we have been studying here, and even in the case of Northern Ireland, the conflicting social objectives are equally attractive.[62]

Furthermore, research is far from conclusive as to which strategy is best suited to fulfill these objectives. Common sense would suggest that the maintenance of languages and cultures is more secure under community-controlled education, while social cohesion and the promotion of positive inter-ethnic relations are better supported by common schools. But each of the four cases studied shows that the existing relationship is more complex.

Thus, nothing indicates that Protestant or Catholic parents who choose integrated schooling, or that francophone parents in Brussels or anglophones in Quebec who choose to cross educational boundaries, are any less concerned about the survival of their identity or culture. In some instances, attendance at common educational institutions seems to contribute to the maintenance of strong identities. In Catalonia, where common schooling is imposed, the cohabitation of language groups seems not to have had the negative consequences for the minority language that its opponents in Quebec and Belgium feared. But, conversely, one cannot prove that the institutional completeness that prevails in these two societies has had the negative impact on social cohesion that Catalans seem to dread. Institutional completeness, to a certain degree, undoubtedly contributes to the development of stereotyped perceptions of the other group, but it can also be promote stability in societies where ethnic tension could have been more violent. Similarly, the belief of Catalan authorities that equality of opportunity is better fostered by common schooling is probably well founded in part. This belief, however, is far from confirmed by the international literature, when we compare the findings on students attending not schools that are de facto segregated but schools controlled by their own community.

Another approach is to evaluate the respective relevance of national choices by the degree of liberty they guarantee the person. This, all things being equal, is the desirable result of all public policy in a democratic society. The solution allowing parents and students the most autonomy in their choice of social priorities, and the educational formulas likely to make this happen, should be privileged. In such a paradigm, the situation that prevails in Northern Ireland would be the most favourable. The government does not determine what the principal objective of education is, and a large variety of possibilities are available. Quebec and Belgium are in the middle of the continuum. In Quebec, anglophone parents may opt for any existing formula, but the goal of maintaining French language and culture is clearly imposed on parents and students from other groups. In Belgium, liberty is minimal in Flanders and Wallonia, with few exceptions. But it is at its maximum for parents of the two groups in Brussels. In Catalonia, Catalan- and Spanish-speaking parents, as well as immigrant parents, have very limited schooling options since the government has opted for a formula that tries to reconcile equality of opportunity, social cohesion, and the maintenance of the fragile majority's language and culture. Nevertheless, this order could be different, depending on one's evaluation of the fairness of giving more liberty to some or to restricting everybody equally.

But the liberal perspective, applied to educational policies and ethnic relations, is not without limits. It is the subject of numerous critiques, allowing us to see why, in certain cases, some approaches that restrict the liberty of parents or students can appear preferable, or at least just as good. The first criticism has to do with the overestimation of rational and informed choices by all categories of parents. A great deal of research shows that it is above all an educated minority from the upper classes who pursue a conscious strategy in the choice of schooling. Without falling into paternalism or preconceived notions about less educated parents, this nuance may be well founded. This is particularly important in the area of ethnic relations, where the pressure to conform coming from a society's dominant groups can be very strong. Indeed, it may be unrealistic to expect a majority of parents to show more commitment than their government to protect a threatened language or to fight inter-ethnic tensions. A passive strategy of equal support for all options can also contribute in the medium term to protecting the unequal relationships that exist in society and educational system.[63]

Likewise, the idea that sociological relationships can be reduced to the sum of individual behaviours is rather naive. There may be a very important gap between the short-term choices that parents make and their collective reaction in the long term when they are confronted by the consequences of their own past actions, notably in contexts where the survival of a language is tenuous. Various violent irredentist movements confirm this. Restricting the impact of market forces before they destroy a community can represent a wise strategy of safeguarding social cohesion for future generations.[64]

Finally, in line with another well-known criticism of the liberal perspective – that the sum of individual interests does not always lead to the common good – we may question the extent to which a large number of options can be sustained before other important educational objectives are jeopardized. From this point of view, the recent inclination of Northern Irish authorities to limit integrated schooling is an authentic democratic dilemma difficult to resolve. Can one favour the needs of certain parents who define social cohesion as their main priority at the expense of accessibility and the quality of education for all? The same logic would apply mutatis mutandis to formulas that support the maintenance of minority languages and cultures, though in this case, a distributive conception of justice appears to make more sense.

2

Crossing School Boundaries and Rapprochement: Why? Under Which Conditions?

Even in societies with significant inter-community and educational divisions, there are always parents and students who decide to cross these boundaries. As we saw in the previous chapter, examples of this are numerous. Some are happy with specific activities aiming at rapprochement or even informal relationships during leisure-time pursuits. Others look for more structured approaches built on common schooling, integrated schooling when it exists, or, in other cases, an integration into the school system of the other community, unplanned by the authorities. The reasons people make such choices vary considerably. Some are looking first and foremost for immediate linguistic or economic results. Others hope this voyage into the unknown will result in cultural enrichment, openness toward the other, even a personal transformation. As to the public authorities who support such initiatives, their expectations may be diverse, but the impact of enhanced inter-community relations always figures prominently.[1]

Yet history and social psychology teach us that the relationship between these two realities is far from unambiguous. Conflicts and civil wars do affect communities that have been traditionally integrated economically, structurally, and even culturally. The heightening of less important tensions, which were for a long time peacefully ignored, tends to occur when modernization leads to frequent contact and increased competition in spheres of influence the groups had hitherto shared. Also, even when good will prevails, knowledge of the other does not always improve inter-group relations. Many studies show that prejudices and stereotypes are reinforced following poorly planned rapprochement initiatives.[2]

Inter-group contact theory was developed in the 1950s by American social psychologists aware of this dilemma in the context of the desegregation of Blacks and Whites. The theory has since been enriched by a good many international studies carried out in experimental situations or in everyday life. This theory proposes a coherent set of contextual, affective, cognitive and identity conditions that need to be implemented so that contacts between different groups who are part of the same society will produce changes in attitudes or behaviours. It also identifies the nature and extent of the impacts one may expect, depending on the characteristics of the intervention or the situation where the relationship is occurring. In line with what it teaches us, we will examine the various experiences described in this chapter.[3]

These experiences are grouped not from a nation-based perspective but on a continuum corresponding to their degree of intensity and the extent of risk for individuals who are involved: the unplanned integration of Anglo-Quebecers or of French-speaking residents of Brussels, in the other group's school system; the voluntary integrated education supported by the authorities in Northern Ireland; and, finally, the specific activities aiming at inter-community reconciliation in Northern Ireland and Quebec. We will explore the same questions for each example:

- How do the initial characteristics and actual methods for implementing these initiatives respond to the conditions that contact theory identifies?
- What motivated people to become involved, and how did this experience affect them?
- What does local research teach us about the consequences of these initiatives for mutual relations and, more generally, about the state of inter-ethnic boundaries in society?

CONTACT THEORY

Favourable Conditions

When individuals who see themselves, or are seen, as belonging to different groups enter into contact, they bring with them past baggage of varying importance. The rigidity of the "us/them" categorization and the stereotypes that surround this, the importance of one's own group being accepted, and the degree of anxiety at meeting the

Other vary according to the marker that separates them and to the state of inter-ethnic relations in the society. Nonetheless, these phenomena are always present, in varying degrees, during naturally occurring or planned get-togethers whose objective is rapprochement. Contact theory has identified, through experimental and laboratory studies, the favourable conditions that diminish preconceptions and go beyond them. It constitutes a very interesting heuristic device for analysing the experiences of shared schooling or increased contacts between youths from competing ethnic groups. However, the state of current research does not permit us to make rigorous pronouncements on the relative importance of each of the stated conditions.[4]

A first group of conditions has to do with the immediate context that is required. All things being equal, frequent activities, of significant duration, and supported by persons or institutions in authority, show the most positive results. Emotionally, the contact should be enjoyable and not give rise to strong anxiety or to the expression of negative feelings that can lead to behaviours of avoidance or confrontation. The participants' motivation also plays a role in the transformation of attitudes and behaviours, particularly when the contact is voluntary. Still, the impact of intrinsic or extrinsic motivation is unclear. This element may in fact be crucial, depending on whether the goal of rapprochement has official support and strong social desirability.[5]

Contact should also allow for the deconstruction of stereotypes and a partial redefinition of inter-group boundaries. For this to happen, a number of cognitive and identity conditions must come together. Most agree that status equality must prevail during contact, even if this condition is rarely attained in society. Minimally, this supposes the adoption of clear norms guiding activities that, where possible, bring together persons who are likely to consider themselves equals: for example, in the American case, Blacks and Whites of similar social class. In other words, adding other obstacles to an existing equality gap must be avoided.[6]

Cognitively, contact theory also emphasizes that individuals considered typical of their group must engage in various behaviours that contradict the dominant stereotypes and contribute to their deconstruction. Still, there are two schools of thought on the desirable consequence of such a process. Some believe it is preferable that persons from the two groups be de-categorized so that they see each other as individuals, and are thereby encouraged to seek out more contacts in the long term with persons not belonging to their own group. On the contrary, others assert that individualization restricts the deconstruction of stereotyped views of the other group. They point to a well-known social-psychological process whereby the new friend (Black, Jewish, etc.) is seen to be an exception to the rule. It would thus be important that young people continue to see each other as typical of their group so as to create a long-term societal impact.[7]

In all these cases, however, there is agreement about the positive consequences of an activity which leads to a shared common identity, or *supra-identity*, for example, as happens with members of a sports team, professional association, or a charity group committed to a common goal. This does not exclude *a priori* continuing identification with primary allegiances; but this supra-identity must help individuals transcend it in the short or medium term to foster a much less rigid identity in the long term.[8]

Potential Impacts

A positive contact can be measured by identifying its positive effects on the cognitive, identity, attitudinal and behavioural dimensions of the people involved. However, research shows that this objective is difficult to attain: findings obtained are not always decisive. Indeed, many social phenomena outside the contact situation can limit its long-term impact, even if several favourable conditions were present from the outset.

The cognitive and identity dimensions clearly appear to be the most resistant to change. For this reason one should not expect significant impacts following episodic contacts or even structured experiences lacking intensity. When more favourable conditions are combined, the results are clearly less grandiose than the pure and simple disappearance of stereotypes or the redefinition of the "us/them" boundary. The first result may be a modification of the complexity or quality of the stereotype, or else the establishment of more personalized relationships with members of the other group, who are now seen much more as individuals than they were before. The second result may be more frequent references to a new supra-identity: "We are all youth, ecologists, future teachers." Or, there may be a tendency to heighten the importance of membership in one group in relation to other factors: "I am francophone (or anglophone, Catholic, Protestant, Dutch …) but also a youth, a future teacher, a member of a sexual minority." When the intervention is well done, or if the state of inter-ethnic relations in the past was not very polarized, a partial symbiosis of two group identities may occur: "We have many things in common and my identity (Quebecer, Northern Irish, Belgian ...) is built on certain elements from their culture."[9]

Subsequent affective and behavioural impacts appear to be more frequent following increased contacts. Various studies have noted attitudinal changes in: the appreciation of members of the other group; the understanding of their concerns; the aptitude for compromise; and the desire to have more contact with them in the future. People's actual behaviour, however, may prove to be a more reliable indicator than simple declarations, especially if the latter are made shortly after the experience. The changes observed in this regard include: the actual number of inter-ethnic relations during and after the contact; the decrease in situations of conflict and the increase in mutual help; and, finally, the gradual tendency to foster cooperation and choices favourable to both groups over competition. Ideally, the positive consequences from an affective and behavioural point of view are maximized when all the favourable conditions identified above are present. However, they can still result from activities that do not satisfy the situational conditions of frequency, significant duration, or support by authorities, and certain affective or cognitive conditions.[10]

SCHOOL INTEGRATION UNPLANNED BY AUTHORITIES

Two movements illustrating this first example are described in the last chapter: that of Quebec anglophones, entitled to an English-language education, who opt for French-language schools and that of the francophones of Brussels who, in an educational free market, decide to enrol in Dutch-language schools.[11] Although marginal in terms of the overall school population in both societies, the number of students affected by such an experience is nonetheless significant: 6,000 in Quebec and 8,500 in Brussels. Studies of these crossover experiences and their consequences have been qualitative in nature and focused on specific schools.

The Model

Several characteristics of the situation created by this type of boundary-crossing deserve to be emphasized. First is the asymmetry for those involved. It is a unique case compared to other approaches based on reciprocity. Parents of one group voluntarily initiate contact. Their children, especially in the primary grades, follow along more or less passively. The teachers, as well as the parents and children of the other group, are in reactive mode – negative, positive, or mixed – in the face of this rapprochement that they did not initiate. It is thus about three dynamics out of sync with contact theory.

One structural condition is clearly absent for all groups: explicit support by authorities. The students, no matter their origin, and the teachers benefit from frequent and intense contact, which is not the case for the parents from the two groups. If contact were to have cognitive and identity impacts, it would be expected among the students and teachers, since the school setting is likely to maximize exposure to a variety of behaviours favourable to the deconstruction of stereotypes and to the individualization of relationships. Nevertheless, the connection between real life and unplanned school integration limits our ability to draw conclusions about the affective, cognitive, and identity conditions, which are more easily identified in situations where the unfolding of activities is foreseeable. Thus, for the parents who initiated the contact and their children, the nature (pleasant or unpleasant) of the experience, and the degree of anxiety this can create, will depend on how they are received by the host school, especially in terms of language support or accommodation. For teachers, the perception that students from another language will unduly increase their workload or stop them from achieving their goals is crucial. As well, the teachers will very probably treat the students as individuals, and the parents as representatives of their ethnic group. Finally, for the children and parents of the host school, the degree to which favourable affective conditions are achieved will vary depending on whether they perceive the presence of the other group as a threat or as a linguistic advantage.

Thus, predicting a priori the expression of significant attitudinal and affective impacts is risky. As to identity, the situation for the children is probably the most favourable, because of the existence of equality norms and of the possibility that supra-identities will be created by sharing in the daily school routine. But the degree to which these favourable conditions allow for a recategorization of the whole group is difficult to predict, especially since research studies focus on primary schools. For teachers and the parents of the two groups, equality of status will prevail, provided they belong to the same social class, but not in the school where an asymmetric relation between teachers and parents is a given fact of life. Six years of co-habitation will probably foster the emergence of a supra-identity, in particular among parents who are able to share in common struggles or plans, but we cannot predict its long-term resilience and impact.

The Experience

What do the experiences of unplanned crossings of school boundaries in Quebec and Belgium over the last few years teach us? Although the research data from the two societies are not strictly comparable, they do point to the existence of some shared characteristics in the area of ethnic relations. First of all, it is the traditionally dominant but dwindling group that attends the schools of the fragile majority and not the other way round. The fragile majority seldom crosses over, even in Brussels, where school choices are not regulated as they are in Montreal. Relationship dynamics in such settings are thus very specific and quite unlike the American situation, where contact theory was elaborated. Boundary-crossing also occurs where inter-group tensions are not publicly acknowledged, even if everyone agrees they persist under the surface. Persons who initiate contact, and those who live it, articulate their motivations, fears, and expectations in largely instrumental and especially linguistic terms, even if this dimension is not always problematic. They have difficulty describing the phenomenon that is really bothering them, specifically, the shifting of boundaries occasioned by contact. Finally, following a voyage into the unknown at the primary level, the large majority of parents and students "go home" for secondary school. Thus, whether or not the favourable conditions for rapprochement were achieved, we know little about the long-term impact of these experiences of integrated schooling. By adolescence, students will have become familiar with segregated schooling, but their parents will have had little opportunity to meet each other on a regular basis.[12]

QUEBEC   In Quebec, only one large-scale study explored the experience of crossing school boundaries.[13] Parents of grade 6 students and their teachers at a French-language primary school in the Montreal West Island were interviewed. Over 50 percent of the students were young anglophones who were entitled to attend an English school. The study shows, first, that the anglophone parents' motivations were more complex than one would have imagined. The mastery of French by their children, in a context they hope to be more efficient than traditional immersion, was most certainly central. But economic considerations were not the only reason for sending their children there. The parents were worried about the large exodus of young anglophones to other Canadian provinces; they hoped that the positive experiences that their children would have in a French school, or even a certain cultural hybridization allowing them to pass from one group to the other, would contribute to their decision to remain in Quebec. The fact that these parents consider the mastery of French a more important objective, at least at the primary level, than attendance in their own school system would suggest a significant development in their views about identity: the recognition of Quebec's French character and, consequently, their own minority status. Although respondents admitted that the transformation in linguistic relations was a shock they experienced with some difficulty, they absolutely want their children to avoid this difficulty. For some parents, speaking the language of the majority stems from an ethical conviction. For others, accepting things as they are is better than remaining apart.

Contrary to what contact theory postulates, these parents have accepted to accentuate their own and their children's minority status for the time being by enrolling their them in a majority institution and to increase the level of potential anxiety to which they are exposing themselves. In effect, they consider that the potential linguistic, cultural, cognitive, and even social rewards are greater than the risks incurred. However, they were aiming at identity impact: neither the deconstruction of stereotypes about francophones, which parents did not seem to think existed, nor the establishment of a shared identity blending young francophones or anglophones (although some respondents did not rule this out). At the level of affect, or emotion, the impact was as expected: the feeling of familiarity and ease of interaction with the other, as well as easier crossing of boundaries – boundaries, however, that continued to exist. When the anglophone parents retrospectively evaluated the experience, they observed that the outcome is mixed, particularly as regards their children's mastery of French. They attribute this mostly to their opting for a former *anglo-friendly* Protestant school, a choice they made precisely to minimize the degree of anxiety that they and their children would experience in a completely francophone milieu. They also note that, even if their children seem to have acquired a hybrid identity, most choose to return to an English school. The parents do not necessarily interpret this as the failure of their initial plan but rather as a natural desire to maximize their children's school performance and creativity.

As for francophone parents, although less directly concerned by the experience, they often stated that they chose the school because of its unusual character and of the possibilities for language contact for their children. For them the presence of anglophones is a positive contribution since they want the same things for their children: a better command of English, feelings of being at ease with anglophones, and an ability to cross boundaries. We must bear in mind that parents who would feel threatened probably chose the other neighbourhood school, the former *franco-French* Catholic school. In addition, both francophone and anglophone parents who are members of the Board of Governors have adopted various measures to promote the status of French at the school, which demonstrates their awareness of the delicate balance to respect in this regard.

Teachers react to the presence of anglophones with much more scepticism. More than the other groups, they stress the limited results achieved, which they blame on the school's largely bilingual climate and the anglophone nature of the neighbourhood. Some teachers have adopted a defensive attitude by complaining about their increased workload. In general, however, this is not the main preoccupation, doubtless because the families are well off in both economic and educational terms. When it comes to identity, however, the teachers' criticism becomes harsher. Anglophone parents, they charge, use the school for instrumental purposes but show little interest, even hostility, at the introduction of curriculum content based on francophone culture.

Indeed, the anglophone parents interviewed seem unaware of cultural differences, insisting on the similar social-class status of francophones and anglophones in the West Island. As well, the boundary between culture and politics is not perceived in the same way by the two groups. Some parents were hesitant about their children learning the songs of Gilles Vigneault, a singer closely identified with the nationalist cause, although for teachers he is first and foremost a pivotal monument to Quebec culture. Nor do French teachers and English parents relate to the language question in the same way.

Parents feel the question is resolved, and they seem unaware of the degree to which teachers perceive the status of French, in the school and in society, as fragile. The contentious history between the two groups is seldom mentioned by anglophone parents, who analyse their relationships with francophones, and even their own failure to learn French in the past, from an essentially individualistic perspective. This underscores, sometimes explicitly but mostly implicitly, the teachers' less positive assessment.

The differences of perspective, the unspoken comments, and the lack of understanding are not insurmountable obstacles to positive impacts from unplanned school integration. One can argue that adults' preoccupations do not influence, either directly or mainly, their children's relationships. As well, these phenomena do not totally eliminate the process of individualization and the deconstruction of stereotypes among the adults themselves. But it does point out one glaring weakness of a common schooling that does not incorporate to the goal of transforming ethnic relations: the absence of places to debate lasting contentious issues, even in societies where inter-ethnic tension is not substantial.[14]

BELGIUM   In Belgium, the data on francophones moving into Dutch-language schools in Brussels come from various sources. A recent study showed that, as in the Quebec case, parents' motives are primarily instrumental. Indeed, in a context where access to immersion schools is much more limited, the choice of a Dutch-language school is mostly to ensure that children will learn a language whose prestige and power continues to grow. However, other factors tied to a strategy of social and educational mobility also play a role: the Dutch-language schools of Brussels often have a better reputation than their francophone counterparts because of better funding and, until recently, fewer immigrant students.[15]

Concerning the impact of the phenomenon, several studies identify the not insignificant organizational and pedagogical implications of the school population's new linguistic heterogeneity. Thus, it is often difficult for teachers to communicate with parents to ensure educational continuity when certain students pass from one language sector into the other. In addition, many teachers coming from Flanders had a poor grasp of the situation in Brussels and were not prepared to step into a multilingual and multicultural context. The program, too, despite several recent improvements, was not well adapted to the challenges of de facto immersion schools that are now Dutch-language schools.[16]

Other evidence illustrates the feeling of threatened identity some Dutch teachers and parents seem to be experiencing at the rapid transformation of their traditionally homogeneous institutions. This fear, largely reflected in the press, has resulted in the adoption of a protectionist registration policy that, since 2003–04, gives Dutch-speaking parents priority in enrolling their children at the preschool and primary levels in Brussels' Dutch-language schools.[17]

However, the most important study examined the effects of inter-community contact on attitudes about the language, community, and culture of the other group by comparing francophone and Dutch-speaking students schooled together in Brussels with control groups of students schooled without inter-community contact in Flanders and Wallonia. Several elements of this study merit analysis in the light of contact theory. First of all, even if inter-community contact has a positive impact on the attitudes of students in these two groups, it is particularly more marked on the francophones. Researchers explain this tendency by the fact that, when franco-phones cross the boundary into a Dutch-language school of Brussels, they experience a situation of contact more intensive and structured than do their Dutch-speaking peers. As well, they enter into contact with native speakers of higher status, teachers and administrators, which confers a high value to Dutch. The study also shows that, in spite of the fears reiterated by some teachers, more francophones than Dutch-speakers say they use the language of the other community with their friends or during extracurricular activities (66 percent and 20 percent, respectively). As in Northern Ireland, researchers were also interested in studying the connection between the progression of favourable attitudes toward the other language and/or the other community and the relationship with one's mother tongue and own community. As expected, the studies confirmed that these two variables are independent: enhanced contact does not engender less positive attitudes about one's own group.[18]

As to unplanned school integration in Brussels, from an essentially linguistic perspective, we have little data as to its impact on group identities and political attitudes. Nonetheless, researchers have identi-fied the particular profile of traditionally bilingual francophone or Dutch-speaking students in this regard: their hybrid identity especial-ly predisposes them to play a mediator role between the two groups.

INTEGRATED EDUCATION

The Model

Integrated education, as it was set up in Northern Ireland, seems to be the example that comes closest to the ideal model defined by contact theory. Involving frequent and intense relations (common schooling) and receiving recognition from the authorities, it responds to the favourable contextual conditions for rapprochement. These conditions are true for both the students and the teachers who belong to the two groups. For parents, as in the case of unplanned integration, their contacts are more episodic, but not negligible. Furthermore, as opposed to common schooling imposed by the state, the preferred model is voluntary, which maximizes the probability that the other affective conditions, that is, pleasant contact and low levels of anxiety, are met. The extent to which these conditions are achieved, however, varies among the students, especially those in the primary grades, who, we may assume, are there because of their parents, and among the teachers, who may have chosen a position in an integrated school because it was the only employment available (37 percent of teachers of integrated secondary schools, according to a 2003 study).[19]

As to identity and cognitive conditions, status parity between the two groups is an undeniable asset. Clearly put forth normatively by proponents of integrated schooling, this parity affects both the curriculum and the balance between the two groups who make up the teacher corps and the student body. This, however, is not always respected in new de facto desegregated schools. Nonetheless, even in these schools, students and teachers are exposed to a variety of behaviours by the other group likely to deconstruct stereotypes. In addition, through professional, pedagogical, and extracurricular activities, they have many opportunities to develop supra-identities of one kind or another. For as long as integrated schooling was a militant movement, these opportunities may have existed for highly committed parents.

Given these positive characteristics, integrated education should have important affective and behavioural impacts on the students, and even on the other actors involved (parents, teachers, administrators, etc.). One could expect, for example, that participants appreciate members of the other group more, feel more at ease, and intend to continue having contact with them on other occasions. We should also note that inter-ethnic friendships and cooperation in other areas are more frequent. As to cognitive and identity impacts, modifications to the quality of the stereotypes, as well as a certain decategorization and individualization of relationships among peers sharing similar experiences, are probable. Still, based on these initial conditions and general characteristics of implantation, it is difficult to predict to what extent these effects will have a bigger impact on the perception of the other group as a whole and on the emergence of a common identity.

The Experience

Numerous studies done in Northern Ireland over the last twenty years show that parents who opt for integrated schooling do so from a variety of motivations. Although a strong majority see the occasions for inter-group contact offered by such schooling in positive light, researchers are not unanimous about the percentage of parents for whom this is the main motivation. Indeed, other factors are often mentioned. For example, some Catholic parents appreciate the participatory character of integrated schools in contrast with the autocratic climate that reigns in schools run by the Catholic Church. Couples in mixed marriages see integrated schooling as a solution that permits them to avoid taking positions on one side or the other when dealing with their respective families. Finally, as we saw in the first chapter, some families opt for an integrated school at the secondary level as a social mobility strategy.[20]

For teaching personnel the situation is even more complex. There is clearly a group of principals and teachers who are principally motivated by their desire to improve inter-ethnic relations or, in the past, to help decrease the violence. Nevertheless, especially in the new de facto desegregated schools, other interests, such as student thievery and the general employment situation may also play a part. As to the motivations of youth, a 2003 survey of four hundred secondary students attending integrated schools found that 58 percent were personally involved in the choice of their schooling (30 percent on their own and 28 percent in collaboration with their parents). The main reason given was the presence of brothers, sisters, parents, or friends in the school (41 percent), while 24 percent mentioned its integrated nature. The number of students forced to enrol by their parents was minimal.[21]

Integrated education also seems to attract persons whose identities are less polarized than those of the general population. Principals of integrated schools have a strong tendency to declare themselves Northern Irish instead of Irish or British, and among teachers there is generally a near absence of republican or loyalist political affiliations, which however represent the majority of votes cast during previous elections. This moderation in terms of declared identity does not imply that those involved in integrated schooling necessarily exhibit more positive attitudes or behaviours in community relations than does the majority of the Northern Ireland population. A study of five hundred former integrated-school students shows that 80 percent of them had no (26 percent) or very little (59 percent) contact with members of the other group before attending an integrated school.[22]

School integration, as observed or reported by students and parents, seems to have been experienced in a positive manner. Older research, of course, identifies moments of tension, in particular when violent events involving extreme polarization had serious repercussions for the educational climate. This was the case during assassination attempts that caused death on one side or another, or during the hunger strike by Bobby Sands and other republicans in 1982. These situations were managed by very open approaches in which the expression of emotions was encouraged, in a context of respect for the inclusive nature of the school and the debates that took place there. These crucial moments do not seem to have left a negative mark on the former students, who were probably better supported emotionally than the students who attended segregated schools.[23]

In general, integrated schooling has been a pleasant experience for young people, creating neither great anxiety nor negative emotion. Students are particularly proud of their acquired ability to learn from the other group and to get along without major conflict. They also appreciate the egalitarian and friendly climate that predominates in their school. And so, 93 percent of the respondents interviewed in the study noted above say that attending an integrated school had a significant, positive impact in their life, and more than 70 percent consider this approach as the one to promote, though they insist that its elective character be preserved. As to the parents, in several studies, they declared themselves very satisfied with the degree of parental participation allowed by integrated schooling, with its pedagogical vitality and the diversity of experiences to which it exposes their children. Some studies do report conflicts with administration or teaching personnel, more often for reasons having nothing to do with inter-ethnic relations. But in a few isolated instances frictions did arise over the display of community symbols in the school, such as flags or emblems, or over the balance of the two cultures, for example, during sports activities.[24]

Everyday life for administrators and teachers is more complex, especially in recently desegregated schools. Even though few of them express any anxiety or negative feelings, two major challenges emerge from recent research. The first has to with the degree to which education management requires a specific approach in integrated schools. Schools have responded in three ways. The first group of schools is passive: for them, student integration creates educational integration on its own and no particular intervention is required. The second group is more reactive. If questions of an inter-community nature pique the interest of students, or if problems of coexistence emerge between parents and teachers or among students, this group responds with ad hoc curricular, extracurricular, or professional approaches. Finally, a third group of schools subscribes to a more proactive approach. They have developed explicit policies on inter-group relations, especially concerning the question of flags, emblems, and the curricular treatment of contentious subjects, for example, in history. In some instances they employ a coordinator of integrated education whose mandate is to promote rapprochement and equal treatment of students in both groups, an important issue in the former maintained schools, where Catholics often represented only 30 percent of the student body. In all these instances, however, principals, teachers, and parents agreed that everyone must respect the balance between standard school concerns, such as scholastic success and other educational goals, and the active promotion of integration.[25]

In relation to the often diffuse character of integrated ethos, the most recent research asks questions about avoidance strategies toward the tensions, and even disparities, in some schools. In certain instances these avoidance strategies are consciously chosen by teaching staff who feel ill-equipped to deal with contentious issues at the school or in the classroom, or who are resolutely opposed because they believe that focusing on similarities will have a more positive impact on inter-ethnic relations in the short- and medium-term. In other instances the weak treatment of the division between Protestants and Catholics, which continues to survive in the larger society, has to do with the very nature of integrated education and the individualization of relations that intensive common schooling creates. Students are weary of old battles, and they show little interest in educational activities explicitly targeting reconciliation. In some schools, the marginal but not insignificant presence of new immigrants, often the object of fairly strong prejudice, accentuates this state of affairs.[26]

The Impact

Research on integrated schooling's impact presents no big surprises as regards the predictions of contact theory. The affective and behavioural consequences are the most visible, especially among students who had few or no relations with the other group before the experience. A vast majority (96 percent) of former students think that integrated schooling helped them to feel more at ease and more secure in mixed or multicultural environments. They also state that they acquired a greater respect for diversity, a better understanding of the other group's concerns, and an increased capacity for compromise. Several behavioural indicators support this positive assessment. Thus, after attending an integrated school, the percentage of inter-ethnic friendships among former students went from 41 percent to 67 percent and, among those living as couples, 58 percent had a partner from the other community. These data are largely confirmed by experimental studies carried out in the 1990s among students attending integrated schools, which we summarized in the previous chapter.[27]

Cognitive and identity impacts are more difficult to evaluate. Former students particularly appreciated hearing members of the other group talk about their reality and about how the differences within their own community were often more significant than the differences between Protestants and Catholics. Numerous common activities also contributed to the development of various shared identities, which appear to have lasted. The majority of respondents do not report a change to their principal identity but rather an extension of the markers attached to it: hence they become an *integrated* Catholic or an *integrated* Protestant. Nonetheless, the percentage of former students who refuse to be classed as belonging to one group or the other is high (25 percent) and clearly higher than the percentage for the Northern Ireland population as a whole (17 percent). This diversity characterizes political choices as well. Some declare that their opinions were reinforced after attending an integrated school, but that they are now based on rational arguments. Others say they have adopted more moderate positions.

Attending a school where the definition of integration is passive, reactive, or proactive probably influences the students' choice of identity strategies, be they individualization, the positive categorization of the other, or the sharing of a common identity. Up to now, however, researchers have not delved deeply into this issue. Nor is there any consensus about the more general impact this generation of youth will have when it reaches adulthood. More critical observers point to their limited demographic weight. They also point out that the individualism and moderation characteristic of the students, teachers, curriculum, and practices within the integrated sector limit this generation's capacity to truly contribute to a transformation of the antagonistic ethnic divisions that persist in Northern Ireland. To the contrary, others believe that the more important presence, even if it is not dominant, of citizens with mixed identities will contribute positively in the medium term to a greater depolarization of inter-community relations. But both camps agree that this is an ongoing challenge with which integrated schools must grapple.[28]

SPECIFIC MEASURES AIMING AT INTER-COMMUNITY RAPPROCHEMENT

In the absence of common schooling, most multicultural societies implement activities permitting young people from groups segregated at the institutional level to get to know one another better and to develop positive attitudes. These activities are numerous and affect both majority groups and immigrant communities, but they have seldom been studied in depth and even more rarely been the object of rigorous evaluation. After presenting a summary of these types of activities in two societies and, where appropriate, of their impact, we will turn our attention to the Creating Collaborative Space (Créer un espace de collaboration) project, which brought together students from two Quebec universities, one English and one French, and to the Speak Your Piece program for young Northern Irish Catholics and Protestants at the secondary and post-secondary levels. These two programs are aimed explicitly at inter-community rapprochement, and they broach the issues most likely to create tension between the two groups. These programs are well documented and have been the subject of comparative analyses and discussions between the Northern Irish and Quebec teams who initiated them. In addition, their respective impact has been analysed largely through the lens of contact theory, which maximizes comparability with the experiences described above.[29]

The Model

Specific activities targeting rapprochement among young people differ according to whether one compares them to integrated education or to unplanned school integration.

Compared with integrated education, specific, or ad hoc, activities are a little bit the poor cousin. They satisfy less often the contextual conditions that contact theory stresses: the contacts created by this type of intervention are less frequent and less intense and, although they may be supported by the authorities, their status is lower than common schooling. On the affective level, well-defined projects assure that students from the two groups are on equal footing and should also be a pleasant experience for the young people involved, at least when their participation is voluntary. But this is not always the case, when, for example, the activities are a mandatory part of their schooling, or for the youngest pupils, when they take place during their regular school routine. Since ad hoc activities bring together students who do not know each other very well and who will have fewer occasions to develop regular contacts, they run the risk of creating more anxiety than do daily shared experiences within an integrated school. The limits to the approach at the identity and cognitive levels are in the same vein. They do indeed expose participants to the differing behaviours of the other group members, but the lack of frequency and intensity of these get-togethers probably results in weak decategorization and individualization and a sharing of supraidentities that is at best temporary.

Nonetheless, certain of these weaknesses could reveal strengths in addressing the critiques directed at integrated schooling. Mandatory one-time rapprochement activities are more likely to bring together persons whose previous attitudes and behaviours were polarized. The display of greater anxiety or more negative emotions, if it is well managed, could also aid in approaching contentious issues with more frankness, although, as we saw above, the sharing of daily life often leads to greater caution, even to more censorship. Since individualization is less pronounced, structured contacts are perhaps more likely to lead to a recategorization of the whole group or, at least, to a modification of the quality of the stereotype in this regard, provided that the frequency and intensity of the contact are sufficient.

Compared to unplanned school integration, the evaluation of one-off approaches is more mixed. At first glance, it seems evident that unplanned integrated schooling favours a stronger intensity of relationship than do simple one-time contacts. In addition, cognitively and in terms of identity, children educated with their peers from the other group throughout primary school are clearly more apt to modify their stereotypes of each other, to stop categorizing one other, and to develop supra-identities that transcend inter-communal divisions. But since in this case rapprochement is not explicitly supported by the authorities, one-time activities with this goal in mind could have a more immediate impact on the students' image of each other's community as well as on their political attitudes than would common schooling that did not discuss or debate such issues.

THE EXPERIENCE AND ITS IMPACT

Quebec

Doubtless because of the relatively non-conflictual nature of relations between francophones and anglophones, programs specifically targeting rapprochement among young Quebecers from the two communities are limited. Twinning programs at the national (Canadian) level have been in place for more than thirty years; so, too, have other initiatives in Quebec that foster contacts between the multi-ethnic schools of Montreal and the homogeneous schools in the rest of the province. Links have also been established with indigenous schools. But it was only in 2007 that Quebec's Ministry of Education launched the Quebec Linguistic Exchange Program (Programme d'échanges linguistiques intra-Québec, or PELIQ-AN for short) to help run and evaluate three twinning models in six primary schools on the island of Montreal.[30]

Nevertheless, as we saw above, contacts outside of the school are not negligible, especially in Montreal, where the students often go to the same recreation centres or are members of the same sports teams. A recent study, carried out in four French-language secondary schools in Montreal, showed that more than 73 percent of the students had engaged in recreational or sports activities in which they had contact with students speaking the other language. The fact that the sample is strongly concentrated in the West Island of Montreal (three of the four schools) is likely to bias the results a little, since the contacts in this area are fostered by the equal size of the two communities. However, even at schools in the East End, a massively francophone area, 47.5 percent of the students had participated in such activities. In addition, this phenomenon is neither episodic nor sporadic since most of the students stated they do spend, and have spent, quite a bit or a lot of time with anglophones, sometimes over several years.[31]

The students favourably evaluated the climate during their time together, both for the level of interaction and inter-group collaboration and for the equal status of the languages. The activities recorded thus seem for the most part to meet the favourable conditions identified by contact theory. Likewise, students who did not participate in activities that brought together peers from the two groups generally mentioned a lack of time or interest (75 percent) rather than a preference for doing things only within their own language group (28.8 percent). A large majority of them believe that such activities could improve relations between the two groups and wish that they could be introduced into their school.

The impact of these contacts on a group of variables was also identified by a comparison between participants and non-participants. As one would expect, this impact essentially affects the affective and behavioural dimensions. Students in contact have more esteem for the other group and identify with it more. They also said they wanted more contact in the future. At the cognitive level, there is a slight effect on the personalizing of relationships with members of the other group, but no significant evidence of decategorizing or re-categorizing. Nevertheless, the tendency to categorize is weak, as much among the participants as the non-participants. This would seem to indicate that young francophones and anglophones in Montreal do not conceive of their respective identities as strongly antithetical. Nor have the contacts generated major changes in the evaluation of the state of relations between Quebec's linguistic groups or in the capacity of students for compromise and negotiation. In this regard, the sample is characterized by a median positioning in which the dominant evaluations are either slightly unfavourable or slightly favourable. These data seem to suggest that young Montrealers live their relationships with the other group in a way typical of Quebec as a whole: non-polarization and harmony on the interpersonal level coupled with isolation on the social and, especially, the political level. Participation in mixed activities, which have a favourable impact on the other dimensions, does not fundamentally change this reality.

As we will see later, these findings are very similar to those for Northern Ireland. They suggest at the very least that contact that does not have the goal of challenging group relations and political attitudes will have little effect on these dimensions. This is why other members of the team wanted to get involved in action research, inspired by the Irish program Speak Your Piece, which would explore and question the boundary between francophones and anglophones in Quebec. This was set up as a twinning project that, for one year, brought together fifteen students in teacher training at two Montreal universities, one English and one French, who were mostly preparing to teach history, geography, and citizenship education at the secondary level. This project, carried out in 2003–04, had two objectives: to explore students' linguistic and cultural identity and their perceptions of the state of inter-communal relationships in Quebec and, based on their findings, to develop innovative classroom programs to deal with these issues. The project was subjected to a qualitative analysis based on systematic observations during the research process, two group evaluation meetings, and in-depth interviews with participants.[32]

These future teachers developed five educational projects. Three focused on the development of teaching materials likely to be used in French or English second-language classes, or history and citizenship education, as well as during more informal activities. However, two projects were not completed because of time constraints and an underestimation by some participants of the level of involvement required. In this regard it should be noted that the voluntary character of the initiative, which determined several of the positive attitudes identified below, created limitations. The activities were not part of the training program, nor were they credited. Twinning thus did not respond to the preliminary conditions identified in the literature, specifically, a strong endorsement by people in authority, even though it was organized by two professors. Two projects addressed socio-political questions directly: coverage by the French and English media of issues related to relations between the two communities; and the different historical visions and versions of the Patriot Rebellion of 1837–38 in the two school systems. Two others focused more on culture: one on the role of empathy in understanding culture shock experienced during inter-group contact, and the other on the relationship of young francophone and anglophone street children to hip-hop music, which is largely in English.

Finally, a last project, historical in nature, brought together all the participants and allowed them to reflect collectively on how they had benefitted from this twinning experience. This included a trip to Grosse Île to focus on relations between anglophones and francophones in the nineteenth century and on the role that third-party groups have played since the arrival of the Irish in the dynamics of inter-community relations in Quebec. Indeed, a site such as Grosse Île calls into question the traditional definition of francophones as Catholic and anglophones as Protestant. It also helps future history teachers to grasp concretely the concepts of divergent memories and historical consciousness discussed in chapter 3. The visit resulted in a bilingual video that is used regularly in various courses at both universities to sensitize students to the role of the school in the promotion of relations between francophones and anglophones and to make them aware of the long history of the immigrant presence within this dynamic.[33]

The first objective – exploring cultural and linguistic identities and inter-group relations – is of more interest to us here. The study showed that these were more complex among participants from the anglophone university, in which many francophones and immigrants are enrolled, than among participants from the francophone university. The former had more contacts with the two communities, and their perception of their identity development showed a multiplicity of allegiances. The latter identified more unambiguously with Quebec and generally interacted less frequently with anglophones. No participant manifested any strong rigidity about identity, probably because of the voluntary nature of their involvement in the project.

After nearly a year of sustained contact, the participants from the two groups reported a certain number of changes, especially affective and behavioural. A significant minority had at first expressed fear of becoming involved in the experience, which dealt especially with the status of their language and the tensions that could be generated by an open discussion of mutual perceptions. In retrospect, all confirmed that respect, dialogue, and a spirit of openness prevailed. In addition, although most already had positive attitudes toward the other group, contact helped them to be even more open and to develop empathy for their concerns. Everyone expressed the desire to get involved in similar projects or projects targeting other communities and to include this dimension in their future teaching, whether or not they ended up working in a school where the other language group is present. Generally speaking, they felt that they will be more sensitive to signs of intolerance or of ethnic tension in their classes and will know how to handle the situation.

The cognitive and identity impacts, however, were more limited, in part because, as in the preceding study, many of the participants already had less stereotyped perceptions of the other group. All the same, a few stated that they will in future be more vigilant of the danger of categorizing persons and of the media's role in constructing stereotypes. The students' identity, without being radically redefined, did evolve and, above all, become clearer. Indeed, twinning proved to be one of the rare occasions in their education where they had the opportunity to explore this question. On the one hand, students whose identity was already mixed felt that it would henceforth be more coherent. On the other, francophones, whose identity was almost exclusively *franco-québécois*, are now more open and recognize a component in this identity that is linked to their knowledge of the English language and to their relations with the other language group.

The project thus appears to confirm that the exploration of a certain number of contentious issues does not compromise the quality of relations between young people of different groups, provided it is undertaken with due respect for the favourable conditions identified by contact theory. This exploration even enables them to broaden the definition of their own identity and to develop empathy for the other group's perspectives and preoccupations. However, several attempts to institutionalize this type of twinning in the participating universities have failed. The project thus remains a one-time initiative that has not yet been repeated.

Northern Ireland

As we saw in the preceding chapter, Northern Ireland has for the last twenty years systematically supported various programs promoting reconciliation activities between Protestant and Catholic youth. These programs are now under the responsibility of the school boards, known in Northern Ireland as Education Library Boards, but funded by the central government. Two studies allowed for the evaluation of the conditions of implementation and, to a certain degree, of its impact, based on the perceptions of the principals, teachers, and students involved.[34]

For the most part, contacts would take place outside the school setting and consist of field trips or recreational activities bringing the two groups together, which explains why nearly half the budget is allotted for transportation and access to the various sites. The choice of neutral meeting places seemed necessary to some, especially in situations of residential polarization, when a visit by one group to the school of the other could create anxiety for parents or students. However, this choice means that the activities were often limited and superficial. According to the evaluators, most activities rarely went beyond the initial stage of getting acquainted and developing personal connections with the other group. Those in charge of the program now think that students should pass through two additional stages as the contact becomes more firm: the development of cooperation and the recognition of similarities on the one hand, and the discussion of differences and contentious issues on the other. As to this second point, evaluation results revealed marked resistance on the part of teachers.[35]

A survey of the students confirms this perception: 65.4 percent describe the activities in which they had been engaged as allowing them to get a sense of the past, 46 percent to become acquainted with new friends, 44.6 percent to learn new games, but only 38 percent report a better understanding of the views and opinions of the students from the other group. In this regard, intensive programs where the students are required to live together in the same place for several days, sometimes for a week, proved to be more positive. However, because of the demanding nature of these programs, they were less frequent. On the whole, though the teachers' involvement was well received, they lacked training and failed to make the necessary connections between the increasingly institutionalized rapprochement activities and the pedagogical practices pertaining to inter-community relations that they could use in their classes. The study relative to the students confirms this. Indeed, while 83.4 percent stated that they appreciated the activities in which they had participated, many of them did not realize that the goal of the contacts was to improve inter-group relations, a situation that is perhaps understandable at the primary school level but that raises many questions at the secondary level.

Unlike in Quebec, assessment of the effects of contact activities has not been rigorous. Nonetheless, the perceptions of the students during evaluation interviews are instructive in this regard. The impact seems to have been mostly affective, though some behavioural modifications can be detected: 78.9 percent of the students appreciated meeting students from the other school; of these, 59.6 percent reported that this contact changed their attitudes about them, mostly in a positive way. Also, 83.4 percent would like to participate again in a twinning program. Nonetheless, a substantial percentage of the students (41.6 percent) expressed dissatisfaction with the limited opportunities to interact informally with students from the other group and to get to know them better. Secondary students lamented the lack of opportunity to discuss certain issues more deeply and to have a debriefing about the exchange activity itself. In line with the conclusions of older studies, these data suggest that the program's impact on the mutual perceptions of groups in conflict in Northern Ireland and on the political perceptions of future citizens is somewhat marginal. In response to these weaknesses, the Ministry of Education recently put together a guide to support schools in the development of better inter-community relations. This guide acknowledges the centrality of Protestant-Catholic conflict, while taking into account the challenges facing ethnic minorities. However, it is difficult to predict that this document will counteract the inertia in certain schools that are accustomed to benefitting from budgets for ad hoc rapprochement activities, without necessarily having to articulate a clear vision of the ins and outs of such initiatives.[36]

In tandem with these large-scale but mainly untargeted activities, the 1990s also saw the birth of the Speak Your Piece project; the title of its publication, *Exploring Controversial Issues,* clearly defines the preferred approach: peer-to-peer political education. This project, which ran from 1995 to 1999, relied on a series of videos developed by Channel 4 of the BBC called *Off the Walls.* The videos openly presented discussions on four themes: identity, culture, religion, and politics and the future. The treatment of each theme followed the same approach: a dramatization that showed four young characters reflecting the complexity of identities and political positions in Northern Ireland and among their friends; an exploration of similar issues created by the Israeli-Palestinian conflict in Jerusalem; and a studio debate in which some thirty young people, representative of a variety of communities and political positions, interacted. The videos were distributed widely to more than five hundred schools or community action groups working with youth. But, strictly speaking, Speak Your Piece was actually a structured approach of support, designed by a team at the University of Ulster, for forty teachers and community workers testing the program with their respective clients. There was a systematic follow-up of its implementation with thirty youth chosen from among the participants. Testing the approach with future teachers from the same university was also part of the evaluation, which was recently completed.[37]

The work with the participants, assigned to six composite groups, made it possible to propose a philosophy based on three principles to guide action with the youth: permit a frank and inclusive dialogue, supply alternative solutions to violence and avoidance as responses to violence, and facilitate the development of the necessary skills for participating in the democratic process. As the authors of the report point out, these broad principles needed to be updated with more concrete courses of action. The implementation of the project over more than two years allowed for the identification of a five-pronged approach: encourage youth to share their life histories; expose them to a wide variety of alternative opinions and multiple perspectives on particular issues; help them to clarify and resolve their internal personal conflicts; nudge the group toward results considered equitable by all the participants; and encourage the development of creative thinking to deal with controversial issues. In other respects, although the literature identifies a number of ethically acceptable stances concerning the degree to which one's own positions should be made known, the specific context of Northern Ireland led participants to delegitimize completely the stance of "neutral facilitator." It is thus anticipated that teachers and community workers adopt the same questioning approach as the youth.

Throughout the project, action-research was the preferred perspective, alternating observation of the youth sessions, interviews with facilitators, a follow-up of the participants' evaluations, and a sharing session fostering more intensive reflection. The final report of the project did not include a systematic, statistical evaluation of the long-term effects on the attitudes and behaviour of the youth; instead it presented a series of indicators about the implementation elements, which the participants judged to be positive or problematic, and about perceptions of immediate changes brought about by the experience.

As to the first point – implementation – the following elements can be retained. For the teachers and facilitators, to participate in the Speak Your Piece project was to become involved in an adventure that demanded great flexibility and a capacity for redefining actions. Indeed, depending on the composition of the group, the reception differed and the strategy had to be adjusted. On the whole, the work was done by homogeneous groups, at first glance making things easier, but it may have limited the expression of different points of view. Conversely, managing the less frequent mixed sessions demanded strong skills at handling tensions and emotions. In this regard the teachers and facilitators stated that the support they received during the two years was essential, but that not all their peers had the ability or the interest to debate controversial questions with young people. The fact that the project fostered a political education resulted in teachers of history and citizenship education being especially committed to it. The audiovisual support was greatly appreciated, particularly the part with the characters, which most considered to be an excellent conversation starter, even though some felt the characters were too stereotypical. Likewise appreciated was the comparative perspective; choosing a society (Jerusalem) where the challenges of inter-community relations are even more problematic than in Northern Ireland helped them to step back and be more objective.

The fact that the teachers and facilitators had volunteered for the project certainly played an important role in their overall positive evaluation. They stated often that they had journeyed as far as the young people, if not farther, since they more often experienced the conflict when it was at its peak. However, the teachers-in-training who participated in the project reacted more negatively. They were, in effect, simultaneously subjects and objects of the interventions and had not chosen freely to be involved in them. Several felt threatened, at time in their community convictions, but more often in their conscious decision to put the conflict aside in order to move on to something else. We must recall that the University of Ulster is the only place in Northern Ireland where teacher education brings together students from the two communities. Some feared that revisiting these old demons would compromise their friendships, which were more important to them at this stage of their personal development than dealing with controversial subjects in the classroom. These findings are not at odds with those reported in the Quebec project, in which youth were volunteers.[38]

The young interviewees reported experiencing insecurity less often than did teachers and facilitators. Still, a minority, more significant among the youth than among the teachers and facilitators, questioned the relevance of the project. In this situation there were two extremes. Certain youth who had strong identities, and who lived the conflict on a daily basis, did not appreciate having their certitudes upset. Others, who adopted a more individualistic and liberal perspective toward group allegiance and who, for the most part, lived in middle-class neighbourhoods where relations were peaceful, stated that they were affected very little by the issues raised. Still a majority of the youth felt the project had a positive impact. For some, it allowed them to reflect on complex issues and to develop their critical thinking skills. For others, especially those with strong identities, their participation led them to question their presuppositions and especially to become aware of the need for collaboration and a sharing of perspectives in the search for a solution in Northern Ireland.

In any event, the Northern Irish experience of ad hoc activities targeting inter-community rapprochement seems to be consistent with contact theory. Concerning favourable conditions, the experience confirms, among other things, the relevance of voluntary activities that do not create strong anxiety and the importance of being exposed to the varied behaviours of individuals considered typical of their group. As to effects, this type of activity had more impact on the affective and behavioural dimensions than on the cognitive and identity dimensions. Still, approaches like Speak Your Piece, which deal directly with the political dimension, seem to influence the civic attitudes of youth about accepting the compromises necessary for inter-group harmony.

Also, contrary to the Quebec example, because the two Northern Irish initiatives affect a large number of participants and have a high visibility in the media, they foster support for the transformation of inter-community relations in the wider society. Indeed, various data show that the people in charge of developing policies and programs are increasingly sensitive to the importance of including inter-community relations in other school programs, as we will see in the chapter 3. In addition, without being able to identify rigorously the specific impact of the many specific or structured activities in this regard over the past thirty years, several observers detect an improvement in the level of civic debate in Northern Ireland, specifically on the topic of inter-community divisions.[39]

Teaching History: Can Memories, Knowledge, and Citizenship Competencies Be Reconciled?

Of all social systems of identification or stratification, ethnicity is the one most clearly tied to a belief in a real or imagined common origin. Other processes of communalization, such as those linked to gender or social class, rely partially on historical accounts about past oppression and present or expected liberation. But in neither of these are continuity and solidarity over time such crucial aspects, especially in modern societies. Indeed, while most markers of traditional ethnic belonging, such as language, culture, religion, and lifestyle have been radically redefined, the belief in a common historical trajectory becomes central to maintaining inter-group boundaries, and consequently distinct identities.[1]

This centrality of historical continuity in communalization is particularly evident with respect to nations, where it is directly supported by a large state and political apparatus. But smaller groups also create historical accounts or narratives that strengthen their cohesion, although their identity is based more on traditional markers due to their strong internal similarity. These narratives, sustained by so-called "ethnic" institutions and organizations, sometimes complement national accounts, for example, in the case of immigrant minorities that promote their specific contribution to the large multicultural family. However, these narratives often conflict with the majority narrative, especially in the case of minorities who have endured slavery, conquest, or colonialism.[2]

The degree to which coexistence supposes state recognition of forgotten memories is today an intensely debated subject in various multicultural societies. Some see the reparation of past wrongs as a fundamental democratic requirement for establishing more egalitarian relationships among citizens. Others, to the contrary, fear a process of "victim competition" that reinforces ethnic boundaries and results in historical narratives full of negativity. Without going into this debate here, one can say at the very least that forgetting clearly plays as important a role as remembering when it comes to ethnic relations. However, the conditions that make forgetting possible and legitimate are rarely defined in the same way by dominant and dominated groups.[3]

The relationship between the discipline of history and the memories upon which communalization is based is not straightforward. At first sight, history, while acknowledging partial and partisan narratives, tries to distance itself from them, in part by applying to the examination of facts and their interpretation a critical, scientific approach that historians call the historical method. The historical method can contribute to inter-community rapprochement by introducing citizens to the complexity of inter-group relations, to the multiplicity of social backgrounds, and to the limits of identity narratives based exclusively on conflict. Yet, historians, too, are social beings, rooted in a community and specific social groups. Historians thus share the historical memories of some groups more than others, which can lead them to be biased, by act and, above all, by omission. Thus chapters in the history of women, workers, and ethnic groups were neglected over the years in the Western world. Today it is recognized, without falling into cognitive relativism, that the presence of historians of diverse social backgrounds has contributed to making the discipline more rigorous and more inclusive. However, historians have no control over the utilisation of the knowledge they have created, especially the fact selection made by persons or groups wanting to reinforce their own identity narrative.[4]

The link between memory and knowledge, which is much closer than historians want to admit, is particularly evident in classroom history, although today it has largely gone beyond the stage of the one-sided account intended to assure allegiance to a unitary national state. As to the formal curriculum, first, the selection of what constitutes legitimate and required school knowledge supposes a choice where value judgments and unequal power relations play a certain role. The resulting program, far from reflecting the sole actual state of knowledge, instead constitutes a compromise. It takes into account the prevailing depictions of the nation and ethnic relationships in society, the pedagogical requirements connected to the characteristics of the students and the management of the class, and, to some degree, the logic of the market, especially as regards textbooks. Other considerations include: the international, national, regional, or local slant of the programs; the decision on whether or not to include certain events or activity proposals in competency-based programs; and, the space reserved for multiple interpretations or controversial subjects. The actual curriculum's delivery by the teachers and its reception by the students again accentuate the composite aspect of teaching history. The selection and interpretation of program components in terms of specific memories is quite widespread and less controlled.[5]

Also, for the last ten years or so, in response to phenomena real or imagined – such as the disaffection of youth with regard to politics and the increase in violence and alienation – there has been a strong return to civic education, rebaptized with the flavour of the month as "citizenship education," and to its close association with the teaching of history. The expectation is that this will help students develop the various competencies that foster community life and social cohesion, such as tolerance and respect for diversity, critical thinking about social phenomena, and commitment to the struggle for equality and inclusion. This expectation is not always favourably received by historians. Some fear that it will unduly shift the balance by turning the teaching of history into an instrument of politics or by subordinating it to present social objectives, however noble these may be. Others argue, however, that history does not have to misrepresent itself in order to contribute to citizenship education. Its contribution would lie in the objective examination of social facts that the historical method makes possible.[6]

How is this double challenge of teaching history – the reconciliation of memories and knowledge, on one hand; the preparation for "shared citizenship," on the other – experienced in fragile majority societies? In this chapter, the four societies under study are divided into two groups. The first is composed of Northern Ireland and Belgium, where the two narratives are very similar and are voiced by groups enjoying more or less equally the status of a sociological majority. The second group includes Catalonia and Quebec, where an historical local majority's identity narrative is contested from within and from the outside by the dominant national narrative. We are interested in two issues: the development of the formal curriculum and the debates this engenders, and the implementation of the actual curriculum by the teachers and its reception by the students. This second issue, however, is only dealt with in societies where it was subjected to analyses that are relevant to our study. Particular attention is paid to the majority Other in the discussions and practices connected to the teaching of history and citizenship education, though the evolution of the depiction of the minority Other is touched upon when relevant.

Finally, using comparative analysis, we will try to identify a few conditions that foster the reconciliation of divergent memories, knowledge, and requirements of shared citizenship in the teaching of history in societies with fragile identities.

NORTHERN IRELAND

The Formal Curriculum and the Debates It Created

Among the four societies, Northern Ireland distinguishes itself by the fairly equal status of the two competing groups and by their cohabitation in a small space. The process of defining educational programs thus supposes collaboration, not always easy but real, between Protestants and Catholics, and all the more so since 1989, when they started sharing a common curriculum. Northern Ireland is also the only place where inter-group relations gave rise to long-standing violent conflict. This makes it impossible to ignore their respective preoccupations and to pass over contentious issues in silence. As well, the need for a citizenship education that promotes community life is strongly felt. These characteristic features are largely reflected in the curricular choices pertaining to the teaching of history and citizenship education and in the rather limited debate to which they gave rise.[7]

In primary schools, neither history nor citizenship education is taught; rather, one finds mixed approaches that focus on knowledge of the immediate environment and the quality of interpersonal relationships. Thus we will focus here on secondary schools. History is taught for an hour and forty-five minutes to two hours per week during the first cycle; it is optional during the second cycle. The first question that arises, as it does in all divided societies, has to do with the point of reference. Before the 1989 reform, the Protestant sector was essentially teaching the history of Great Britain, and the Catholic sector that of Ireland. As part of the History School Project in

England, which insisted on more recognition of the diversity of identity narratives and the promotion of more active approaches, the double integration of Northern Ireland with Great Britain and Ireland was recognized, while situating its history in a European and global context. It was hoped, especially by adding the European dimension, that the promotion of the two groups' common supra-identity would contribute to mutual understanding. For the most part, the new 2003 curriculum maintained this focus on an Irish history at the centre of larger and larger concentric circles. The first program was developed during Direct Rule by Great Britain and the second under the authority of Northern Ireland's new Responsible Government. The program's continuation, along with the absence of debate, testified to the consensus that seemed to have established itself on this question. The only discordant voices came from England, where the New Right was disturbed throughout the 1990s by the loss of British identity, including English identity, created when the responsibility for developing their own history curricula was transferred to Scotland, Wales, and Northern Ireland.[8]

The second issue, clearly more complex, has to do with the balance of the two groups' perspectives, especially on the controversial issues that mark almost all of Northern Ireland's history: the British conquest and the settlement of the Loyalists in the seventeenth century; the conflictual relations between Ireland and Great Britain in the nineteenth century; the partition of 1922; and the 1968–98 civil war, diplomatically referred to in Northern Ireland as "The Troubles." From the reform of 1989, and even more when elaborating the new program in 2003, two complementary strategies were implemented. The first, which was expected, insisted upon using the historical method to examine facts, interpretations, and students' preconceived notions. Student would be expected to develop the necessary skills to do historical research themselves, approach the subject in a critical manner, and assess the different arguments or points of view. The second, more specific to Northern Ireland, stressed that the teaching of history show extreme sensitivity to inter-group balance and make a positive contribution to inter-community relations. Thus, the program made provision for the study of motivations, roles, and impacts of key persons or groups, from a pre-determined list reflecting the experience of the two groups. In addition, the leeway for teachers wanting to deepen their understanding of certain periods or specific challenges was defined. As well, the fact that the Northern

Irish curriculum is based on a cross-disciplinary perspective resulted in closely associating the teaching of history with education for mutual understanding and also with two mega-objectives structuring the entire program of studies: the individual development of the students and their future contribution to society. The teaching of history should, among other things, help students to understand how history influenced their personal identity, their culture, and their way of life or how history was selectively interpreted in order to create stereotyped perceptions and to justify viewpoints and actions. In addition, they will explore the actual causes and consequences of Ireland's partition and critically evaluate the media's influence in the depiction of important historical events.[9]

A last challenge, unresolved to this day, concerns the teaching of recent history, especially the civil war, whose victims or their families are still part of the students' immediate environment. The extreme caution shown by the authorities in this regard suggests that, as already noted in other contexts, hot historical issues need to pass through a cooling-down period before they can be studied in school. On one hand, teaching about the civil war is reserved for "Key Stage 4," which groups students from fourteen to seventeen years of age, and where the History program is optional. On the other hand, although the 1989 program originally anticipated an entire section devoted to the study of conflict, it has been watered down since 1996 in response to the anxieties of teachers and certain parents, and the choice of whether or not to deal with the civil war rests with the teacher. This compromise has lasted despite two rewrites of the program. Time and again this situation has been denounced by specialists in the teaching of history and by persons involved in fostering inter-community rapprochement. However, some aspects of the civil war are addressed by the Citizenship Education program, which is mandatory throughout secondary school, and separate, in Northern Ireland, from the History program.[10]

The stated objective of the Citizenship Education program is to develop the capacity of young people to participate in a positive and efficacious way in society, to influence the democratic process, and to make informed and responsible decisions as lifelong local and global citizens. However, as is the case in many divided societies, the concept of citizenship is not defined, nor, above all, is the geopolitical unit in question specified. Given the terms of the 1998 Peace Accord, which recognizes the coexistence of two citizenships, it is worth bearing in mind that the young people are all expected to participate in the society and institutions of Northern Ireland, but also to varying degrees in those of the Irish Republic and of Great Britain. Four central themes are stressed: diversity and inclusion, equality and social justice, democracy and active participation, and human rights and social responsibility. To deal with the issue that interests us, we note first the sophisticated treatment of the concepts of identity, achieving human rights, and inequality. Also, under the theme of diversity and inclusion, the students will have the opportunity to explore the religious and political factors that influence individual and group identities, to understand how individuals and groups express this identity, including through the political process, and finally to explore how and why sectarian or racist conflict can emerge in a community. Likewise, under the theme of human rights and social responsibility, they will have to examine cases, both local and international, where human rights have been seriously compromised and also learn how different rights need to be balanced in a democratic society. Finally under the theme of equality and social justice, young people will have to explore inequalities based on socio-economic conditions or generated by ethnic or religious group membership.[11]

The teacher's guide also addresses many issues that are directly linked to inter-community relations. It suggests involving the students in analysing the degree of diversity in their school, by looking at both the makeup of the student body and the institutional ethos, in order to become aware of whether they are getting their education in a homogeneous, segregated institution or, if this is not the case, to evaluate to what degree the various identities are equally respected. As well, students are encouraged to reflect critically on religious and political symbols, such as murals, flags, and musical instruments, and on the legitimacy of limiting their expression, taking into account both democratic parameters and the necessity of exercising a certain moderation in the expression of their identity with symbols that may hurt the other group.[12]

If this program seems somewhat audacious, several cautionary notes and ambiguities suggest that ministerial authorities and planners know they are venturing onto slippery ground. For example, the Key Stage 4 program specifies that the various issues for debate should not always be studied in detail and that the choices teachers make should be influenced by the realities of the community that the school services as well as by the future the students envisage. One may wonder how to interpret this Sybilline phrase, but pushed to the extreme it may involve adjusting activities depending on whether or not the students want to stay in Northern Ireland.[13]

However, just like the History program, the local and global Citizenship Education program has not created much controversy. One may assume that, by its non-specification of the national state to which this citizenship refers, the inclusion of the subject of inter-community relations in a larger perspective about diversity, and the leeway it leaves the teachers on whether or not to address these issues, the program is sufficiently flexible to respond to the needs, interests, and fears of everyone. Still, these same aspects are criticized by certain scholars and organizations active in inter-community rapprochement that fear the program will have little impact on segregation and the avoidance strategies that are now gradually replacing past conflicts. As we will see in the following section, several evaluations tend in part to support their view. In the long run, the Northern Irish experience does indeed raise the following question: In divided societies, is citizenship education that turns a national identity into an abstraction possible and desirable, or does it only represent a stopgap measure until one of the two groups imposes its definition of the nation?[14]

The Actual Curriculum

Northern Irish research on the effective implementation of the history and citizenship education curricula and on their reception by the students has been very rich over the past fifteen years, in contrast with the few studies carried out in the other societies we are studying. This may be attributable to the great challenge that the teaching of these subjects represents for the future of ethnic relations.

As to the perspectives and practices of the history teachers, three studies, using simple interviews and/or in-depth observation in the classroom, noted several points. First, although all the teachers approached history in a generally balanced way by avoiding overtly partisan perspectives, large differences were evident in pedagogical approaches and readiness to debate controversial questions. Five broad positions were identified: affirmation of their own group's perspective, objection to the other group's perspective, promotion of a neutral civic identity and a common history, pointing out other identities so as to limit the prominence of group identities, and re-definition of respective identity narratives so that students from the two communities recognize them as legitimate rather than as mu-tually opposed. However, there is no agreement about the dominant model. An initial study reports that most teachers share the last two perspectives and strongly doubt the possibility of putting forward a common history. A second study, in contrast, shows that the major-ity of teachers see the history course as an oasis of peace and are hardly interested in debating past wounds. Although they do not truly believe in it, most teachers will opt for the civic culture and common history perspective. According to a third study, two princi-pal factors explain the differences in approach favoured by the teachers: their normative position as to the intrinsic or extrinsic value of teaching history, on the one hand, and the types of students they are teaching, on the other. Indeed, it is in the elite schools, which bring together middle-class students, where teachers most often con-nect the teaching of history with the present and use approaches based on this perspective, while in ordinary schools, situated in work-ing-class neighbourhoods, where group identities are more sharply defined, traditionalism prevails.[15]

Another finding concerns the pessimistic judgment of teachers about their impact on youth. Indeed, a strong majority believes that, though history can help improve ethnic relations, their teaching has little influence on the students' preconceptions, acquired from their families and from society. As we will see further on, the students are much more positive in this regard. We thus find ourselves with a chicken-and-egg dilemma. Teachers are not fully exploiting the po-tential of history for exploring and critically analysing conflict be-cause they doubt they can have a real effect on their students. In turn, this wait-and-see attitude is contributing to students main-taining their preconceived notions.[16]

Two more recent surveys looked at the implementation of the local-global Citizenship Education program. The first focused on what history teachers thought about the introduction of this new discipline. Of the 221 secondary school teachers who responded to the questionnaire, more than two-thirds felt the two disciplines were complementary and intended to collaborate in common pedagogical activities with the citizenship education teacher. The one-third of teachers who were opposed, above and beyond the organizational challenge, were against it on principle. Of particular concern was the danger of turning history into an instrument to promote social goals, such as positive ethnic relations, and the incompatibility of a normative vision, such a citizenship, with the historical method, which is essentially critical.[17]

Research looking specifically at the implementation of local-global citizenship education tends to support the observations on the teaching of history. Thus, in a systematic follow-up on the introduction of the reform in twenty-five secondary schools from 2003 to 2007, researchers from the University of Ulster noted quite different interpretations of the very nature of this program, not only between the schools in the different sectors, but even within the schools themselves. These differences had to do, in part, with the balance between the local dimension and, for the teachers, the less threatening global dimension, and the respective weight given to knowledge relative to attitudes and competencies. The study also concluded that training was very important. Indeed, if the first cohort of teachers in the experimental program were recruited from among volunteers, then beginning in 2007, citizenship education, which is now extended to all schools in Northern Ireland, will be taught by persons who are not necessarily interested in civic relations.[18]

Despite reservations about the effective implementation of these two programs, the reception by the students seems generally positive. A first study based on a sample of 1,737 students from Catholic and Protestant schools showed that young Northern Irish appreciate the history courses they get at school, more than young British students, and that these courses have a strong influence on their identity and political development, which contrasts with the teachers' rather pessimistic opinion.[19]

A second study explored the connections between the teaching of history and the identity-construction of students aged eleven to fourteen years, who had been followed for three years, and how the students reconciled the different historical accounts they received at the school and in the community. An original methodology was used: groups of students who were representative of the school sectors and types of neighbourhoods, conflictual and non-conflictual, had to classify images of monuments, symbols, and historic, political, and cultural artefacts, indicating which ones they identified with. The research showed, first, that if community membership has some impact on the symbols that the students consider important, it is far from being the main influence when they conceptualize their relationship to history. Indeed, only one-third of the choices were connected to Protestant Unionist or Catholic nationalist history. The others were family history, local heritage or world history. However, identification with the identity narrative of one's community increases with schooling. The older students seem to have learned to use selectively the historical content presented in class to justify, and sometimes make more complex, their community allegiance. The students thus showed an active relationship with the history taught at school, navigating between two extreme poles characterized by the authors as *appropriation* and *resistance*. Likewise, the students appreciated the teachers' commitment to presenting multiple perspectives, which allowed them to develop alternative accounts to the politicized stories to which they are exposed outside of school. The authors point out that, since the students will in any case make connections between the history taught at school and the community's version, teachers ought to mediate the process to ensure that it is less selective and more critical.[20]

The study also showed that the relationship to history varies strongly according to the gender of the students, the type of school they attend, and the degree of conflict that prevailed in their area. Boys showed more interest in military or partisan political history, while girls preferred social or regional history. Protestant students preferred the more distant past while students in the Catholic schools showed more interest in the last thirty years. In addition, when students lived in areas where there was little inter-community conflict, the two groups saw the civil war as a central element of their common Northern Irish identity, while in areas marked by conflict, partisan perspectives tended to predominate. It is thus proposed that the teaching of history be more varied in terms of themes and periods studied and that more connections be made between the past and the present. Teachers are encouraged not to confuse the common curriculum with uniform instruction and to adjust their teaching depending on students' preconceived notions and interests.

The impact of the new Citizenship Education program on the students' knowledge, attitudes, and abilities was also explored in the evaluation mentioned above. It showed that the teaching of history, first and foremost, influenced the students' relationship to other cultures and human rights and their commitment to democratic values and social inclusion. It had little impact on their political participation, their community identities, or their perception of the Protestant-Catholic conflict, although the percentage of students declaring themselves to be world citizens did increase with years of education. These findings are largely explained by the focus of the teaching, at least, as perceived by the students. Indeed, the students reported they had heard about racism, environmental protection, and community involvement, but very little about religious sectarianism or conflict resolution. The authors concluded that the program seems to have a positive influence on the attitudes and behaviour of the students in their immediate environment, but that its long-term impact on ethnic relations and democratic participation has yet to be demonstrated. Once again, important differences were noted between the sexes, with girls systematically reporting a lower level of confidence in their ability to be inclusive and less commitment in this regard.[21]

BELGIUM

As we saw above, French-speakers and Dutch-speakers are largely segregated territorially and administratively, with the exception of Brussels, where daily but not institutional coexistence is the norm. In addition, the issue of inter-community relationships, although debated politically and in the media, is strategically avoided by both the population and researchers. Not surprisingly, therefore, when it comes to identity, some academics have characterized the prevailing situation in Belgium as the "federalization of memory." Flemish identity is still today influenced by a feeling of past victimization, especially in terms of language, though the actual status of the community probably no longer justifies this central fear. Among francophones, essentially long attached to the national state, the Walloon identity is more recent and largely reactive. Becoming a minority due to the political and economic developments of the last thirty years is seen as an injustice and is taking on increasing importance.[22]

However, there have been few initiatives to compare the opposed narratives, let alone reconcile them. While there is interest in rapprochement, present stereotypes rather than past memory are much more the subject of interventions, as is witnessed by the Trèfle Program described in chapter 1 and the various media-led initiatives after the hoax announcing the dissolution of Belgium.[23]

The role of teaching history in maintaining distinct narratives, fostering inter-community rapprochement, and strengthening feelings of common Belgian membership is not a subject of major debate or controversy. Studies comparing programs and practices on this issue in the two communities are noticeable by their absence, although some academics have done comparisons between Wallonia and France on the one hand, and Flanders and the Netherlands on the other. Several observers of the educational and political scene think that this state of affairs reflects to some degree the taboo that inter-community relations represent but also the strict segregation of universities along language lines. Even the historical works of the Roi Baudouin Foundation, whose mandate and interests are clearly national in scope, do not tackle this issue directly. Indeed, we see the adoption of a broad perspective based on human rights and participation and, in the matter of inter-community relations, much more interest in the exclusion of immigrant populations than in the relations between the two linguistic communities.[24]

Examining the two history curricula confirms the schizophrenia that reigns in this area in Belgium. The curricula, we must not forget, are developed in an absolutely autonomous way by the Dutch-speaking and French-speaking communities, the federal state having no jurisdiction in educational matters.

In the French community, at the primary level and the first cycle of the secondary, the teaching of history is part of a program of multi-disciplinary initiation that also includes geography and socio-economics. It is essentially structured around the acquisition of basic competencies and leaves a great deal of leeway to the various community, religious, and municipal pillars regarding the delivery of services. The content is based on the immediate experience of the students and thus gives some attention to what might be called "Belgian realities." However, these realities are perceived through the ambiguous concept of "our regions." An attentive reading of the document permits one to interpret this as referring to Wallonia and the Brussels-Capital region. Belgium, or the federal state, is only mentioned on a few occasions, for example, under the theme of independence. As to Flanders, it merits not a single mention.[25]

In the second and third cycles of the secondary level, history is a specific discipline that was subject to a legislative decree in 1999. The decree only established the terminal competencies and knowledge required, leaving to the various school authorities the freedom to tailor the content, spell out their learning objectives, and implement the methods and means necessary. The Decree confirms two reorientations, most interesting for our study, taken in 1972 and 1994 respectively. On the one hand the aim is to stop teaching Belgian history in isolation and to integrate it within general history, leaving the teacher a great deal of leeway, and, on the other, to replace the history of Belgium with the history of "our regions," the ambiguity of which we have already seen above. Unlike the other societies we are studying, there is no support for an approach going in concentric circles from the specific to the general. Priority is given to a Western history that focuses on broader global perspectives and on regional realities. Great stress is also placed on the historical method and its contribution to the intellectual formation of youth. The role of the teaching history in citizenship education, which is not the subject of a particular program, is recognized. Nevertheless, it is a citizenship that is to be exercised in the world of tomorrow, without specifying in which political community this is supposed to happen.[26]

Throughout the program, Belgium is only mentioned in the twentieth century, while Flanders is totally absent. A key moment (Belgium in Europe and in the world: supra-nationality, federalism, and regional identity) and a conceptual tool (analyse, characterize, compare, evaluate a nationalist, federalist, or universalist opinion or system) could make it possible for teachers to discuss the question of inter-community relations. However, one may wonder if the association of another conceptual tool under this key moment (identify the democratic or non-democratic character of a political system or tendency) could encourage the expression of prior traditional prejudices about Flemish nationalism, if it were to be discussed. In any event, in the document it elaborated to specify the terminal competencies and knowledge required in a genuine History program including learning activities, the Federation of Catholic Secondary Schools, which takes in nearly 60 percent of the students from the French community, did not take this possibility into account. The topic of Belgium in Europe and in the world between 1945 and 1989 is now reduced to that of Europe in the world. Likewise, among the examples of learning activities, lessons on the major stages in Brussels's history from the tenth to the eighteenth centuries, with highly detailed content, make no mention of the linguistic composition of the city during this period. This omission is astonishing, to say the least. Indeed, we are familiar with the central role that the increasing francization of Brussels plays in the Flemish identity narrative and, more broadly, in that of other fragile linguistic communities. Testimony to this is the coining of the expression *bruxellisation* (literally, "brussellization") to designate a metropolis's or a historic capital's loss of dominance.[27]

The Flemish program subscribes even more, if this is possible, to the perspective that competencies are central and content is completely secondary. In primary school, history is not taught as a specific subject but, through the cross-cutting theme of social competencies, there are a few statements that connect history, citizenship education, or geography. The most relevant for our purposes are those that focus on: the consciousness that Flanders is one of the communities of the federal state of Belgium and the need for students to familiarize themselves with the symbols of the Flemish community, such as its national holiday, its flag, and even its national anthem. As to this second objective, there is no equivalent for Belgium. And Wallonia is mentioned nowhere at either the primary or the secondary level.[28]

Although the teaching of history is part of a specific program, its introduction notes that the historical realities and societies to be studied may be freely chosen and that only the competencies targeted are mandatory. Among the thirty or so concepts covered during the four years of secondary school is one dedicated to linguistic groups, but nothing indicates that it ought to be addressed in the specific context of Belgium or Flanders. In a few places, there is content referring to the national reality or to ethnic relations, but these are very broadly formulated. For example: during the first cycle of secondary education, students eleven to thirteen years of age are expected to become familiar with the history and culture of Flanders; during the second cycle, students thirteen to fifteen years of age should learn to indicate in what periods their region had an impact beyond its borders; and finally, during the third cycle, students fifteen to seventeen years of age should learn to analyse the divisions in the evolution of Belgian society since 1830. This last competency, however, is associated with a more generic competency: analysing the fundamental conflicts and decisions that can challenge societies. However, given the lack of research on the actual curriculum relative to the teaching of history in Flemish classrooms, and especially its connection to inter-group relations, it is difficult to know precisely what type of educational strategies and activities such objectives give rise to.[29]

Contrary to the French community, the Flemish community has defined, since the late 1990s, the competencies to be mastered in citizenship education.[30] The most recent program describes a series of competencies linked, according to the age of the student, to:

participation in the immediate community; understanding human rights; and decision-making in democratic societies or participation in political organizations. This program makes only one reference to Belgium when discussing such organizations. In the rest of the document, it is clear that the political community, or reference group, is Flanders. Flanders is defined as a multicultural society where pluralism should be a permanent feature and where students should be educated so as to respond to this challenge. But a reading of the document reveals that it is referring exclusively to diversity created by immigrants and refugees. No competency relates explicitly to coexistence with francophones, to linguistic conflict, or to the division of the federal state.

QUEBEC

The Formal Curriculum and the Debates It Created

Unlike in the two previous examples, in Quebec, the ambiguity of dominance has already been partially removed in both society and the school system. Indeed, with its heavy demographic weight, the francophone group has largely recovered its status as a sociological majority following a radical transformation in ethnic relations over the past thirty years. It has a predominant influence on the social production of memory and on the educational agenda. Still, this dominance is far from absolute. On the one hand, Quebec is the site of numerous competing national narratives possessing varying degrees of compatibility with the narratives of the majority group. These narratives include those of the Native Peoples, immigrant minorities, and, in the case that most interests us, the anglophone minority. The need to integrate these perspectives into the teaching of history is all the more essential since, as we saw above, francophones and anglophones share a common curriculum. On the other hand, given that support for sovereignty remains high, the degree to which citizens identify exclusively, first, or equally with Canada or with Quebec varies. This reality necessarily poses the question of what focus the History program should adopt.[31]

Traditionally, this second issue has received the most attention, in both public debate and research. As far back as the mid-1960s, a study for the Royal Commission on Bilingualism and Biculturalism had exposed major differences in the History programs and textbooks

of French and English Canada. Three aspects were especially highlighted: the time devoted to different periods, among others to New
France; the interpretation of controversial historical events, such as
the Conquest of 1760 or the Patriot Rebellion of 1837; and the role
attributed to the teaching of history. In this regard, the report noted
the epic, sometimes messianic, tone used in the French-language
textbooks, where history was clearly put into the service of national
survival. Considering the much greater autonomy enjoyed by the
anglo-Quebec community in educational matters, we can assume
that these differences also existed between Quebec's two linguistic
school sectors.[32]

Beginning in the 1970s, with the modernization of Quebec, the
programs of all Canadian provinces became more alike. As in the
other contexts, the teaching of history in Quebec was increasingly
dissociated from a single grand narrative by emphasizing, on the one
hand, the historical method and, on the other, multiple perspectives.
Thus the province's 1982 Quebec and Canada History program, a
course offered only in the fourth year of secondary school, that is,
the second-to-last year of mandatory schooling, has a two-pronged
emphasis: the development of an understanding of the connection
between the present and the past; and the promotion of active methods where the students learn to interpret history from a variety of
documents. Even then the program expressed certain concerns about
citizenship education in a pluralistic context, especially understanding the diversity of social groups, the existence of interdependence
and conflicts, and openness to the diversity of values. The program
was supposed to have resolved, at least so it was thought until the
controversies over the new program of 2006, the question of the
society of identification. The goal was to understand the evolution of
Quebec society within the context of Canada, North America, and
the Western world, using a concentric circles approach fairly similar
to that of Northern Ireland.[33]

However, it is clear that the teaching of history still retains an important identity function, since it aims to strengthen the sense of
belonging to Quebec. But, contrary to the messianic discourse of the
past, the historical relationship is critical and pluralistic in nature.
Thus, the teaching of history is about contributing to the construction of an inclusive civic nation, as much in the French-language
sector, which is becoming multicultural since the adoption of Bill
101 in 1977, as in the English sector.[34]

Two principal criticisms of the program's content have been limited to circles of experts. The Professional Associations of English History Teachers faulted it for being too focused on Quebec in relation to Canada, a characteristic they were partially circumventing, though not totally because of the requirements of the provincial exams. On the other hand, the report by the Lacoursière Commission stressed that the program was not sufficiently adapted to the changing reality of the province, especially regarding the attention paid to First Nations and ethno-cultural groups in Quebec history and to non-Western societies in world history.[35]

The new program, developed as part of a reform that stretched from 1999 to 2007, was influenced by these criticisms, but even more so by three major pedagogical currents at the international, national, and local levels: the competency-based approach, project-based instruction, and the re-emergence of citizenship education as a specific discipline. Concerning this last point, Quebec opted to create a general area of training that could engage all disciplines, educational and extracurricular activities, and a field of knowledge associated, in primary school, with social studies and, in secondary school, with history. The teaching of history was also greatly increased and, above all, integrated more consistently into the overall educational process.[36]

At the primary level – where previously there was an integrated approach, largely influenced by the social sciences, to learning about one's own milieu, community, and country – the area called "social studies" now incorporates geography, history, and citizenship education. The first cycle is essentially an initiation into how space, time, and society are depicted, while the second cycle aims at more varied competencies, such as understanding the organization of a society or territory and interpreting change. An integration of the national and global dimensions is achieved by a focus on local realities, which always includes a reference to other societies or times. The competency-based approach and the use of sweeping time periods mean that the events that some nationalists consider significant do not appear as a unified narrative; rather, they appear when they are required by the logic of the program. Thus, the Conquest is invoked to illustrate the changes that occurred in Canadian society between 1745 and 1820, as are the Napoleonic wars, parliamentarianism, and the lumber trade. This characteristic, a major problem of the History program at the secondary level, was not challenged at the primary level, probably because people had become accustomed to the prevailing approach based solidly on the social sciences.[37]

As well, despite the program's title, the goals, competencies, and content specifically associated with citizenship education occupy a limited space. Under the broad area of "community life and citizenship," there is proposed a rather disparate listing of some twenty concepts dealing with knowledge, attitudes, and behaviours, grouped under three headings: valorization of the rules governing life in society and democratic institutions; involvement, cooperation, and solidarity; and, finally, contributing to the culture of peace. However, their articulation and disciplinary translation are rather limited. With no definition of the meaning of citizenship to be found in any of the documents for the secondary or primary levels, the ambiguity only increases.[38]

At the secondary level, where the reform has been gradually introduced since 2003, history and citizenship education profit from two-and-a-half hours per week in the first cycle and two hours per week in the second cycle. The program is built around three competencies: examining social reality in an historical perspective; interpreting social reality with the help of the historical method; and increasing one's citizenship awareness with the help of history, this third competency being rendered somewhat more affirmative at the second cycle, since the program speaks of strengthening the exercise of one's citizenship. Maintained and even strengthened is the option for an historical education based on complexity and critical detachment. Hence, one finds expressions such as "relativizing one's interpretation of social reality, especially by taking into account prior representations" or "establishing the facts of social reality by identifying the interests of actors and observers and by examining different points of view."[39]

The first-cycle program deals with world history. It stretches from the dawn of humanity to the twentieth century and adopts a Western perspective throughout on themes such as the emergence of ancient civilization, Christianity, Renaissance, and the expansion of the industrial world. This somewhat ethnocentric perspective is attenuated by systematic recourse, as in the primary level, to comparison with non-Western societies. The second cycle clearly stresses the history of Quebec, from the first indigenous occupants up to contemporary issues, that is, up to 1980. In the first year of this cycle, the third year of secondary schooling, teaching is done from a traditional, chronological perspective, while in the fourth year students study diachronically the development of four major issues: population, the economy, culture, and power. This second-cycle program became the subject of heated debate in spring 2006. It resulted in some fifty articles or open letters in Quebec's mainstream media.[40]

In a preliminary version, which unfortunately, at least for the ministry(!), was made public by the media, the program consisted of six broad themes: the worldview of the first inhabitants; the emergence of Canadian society, which included the history of New France; parliamentarianism and the development of liberal ideas, which dealt with the period from 1760 to 1867; industrialization, concurrent with the formation of the Canadian federation; modernization, based essentially on Quebec society; and, finally, public space, which is the occasion to study contemporary Quebec. Different people and events that could have been covered in a more thorough manner but, given the status of the document, were not.[41]

Opponents essentially attacked on two fronts: first, on the limits of the program itself and, second, on its hidden aims. In the first instance, they denounced the absence of key events from the identity narrative of francophone Quebecers, such as the Acadian deportation, the Patriot Rebellion, the conscription crisis of 1917, and the unilateral repatriation of the Constitution in 1982. They also argued that the determination of historical periods and the concepts studied effectively presented a version of history where conflictual events were passed over in silence or overlooked. Hence the Conquest appears as one of the elements of "the development of liberal ideas in the British colony," (!) while the neo-nationalism in the 1960s and 1970s and the referendum crises were buried in the mega-concepts of modernization and public space. Critics also made a somewhat questionable connection between these limitations and two pedagogical options in the new program: its more inclusive character, which acknowledges a variety of perspectives, and its association with citizenship education. Little more was needed to prompt some critics to declare this a federalist plot to make the political status quo acceptable to future generations.[42]

Obviously, this accusation was refuted by ministry authorities and supporters of the program, who noted that it was initiated by a sovereignist government and developed by historians, educational specialists, and teachers of all political stripes. But when the open letters are read, it is clear that to a strictly political issue was added the concern that the central narrative of the francophone group, and thus its identity, had been called into question, even deconstructed, both by the inclusion of other perspectives and by the critical function of the historical method.[43]

In any event, public authorities had to take the controversy into account in the final version of the program. In addition to one time-line and one detailed description of events to deal with, realities and concepts were redefined in a more nationalist way. Thus the emergence of "Canadian society" became that of "New France"; the Conquest and the change of Empire are the subject of a specific theme; and the focus is now put on protest and struggle in regards to the experience of parliamentarianism in the British colony. In an even more striking way, the social reality that was framing parliamentarianism – democracy – was replaced by "nation," although it specifies that the angle of entry remains that of the influence of liberal ideas on this concept.[44]

Despite the fears expressed by opponents, the place of other groups is rather limited, except for the First Nations, whose presence is significant. The anglophone minority is mentioned under the themes of the Conquest and struggles in the British colony, but, with the exception of the Irish, it deals with the members of the economic elite who are in conflict with the French-Canadian elite. The contributions of anglophones in times past, such as by James McGill or John Molson, are identified as cultural milestones, but are not mentioned during the modern period. It is rather during the study of the diachronic themes of population, culture, or power that the students have the opportunity to discuss relations between francophones and anglophones, provided the teachers give priority to this vantage point rather than that of immigrant groups. Among the proposed realities, concepts, and cultural milestones are the settlement of the Eastern Townships, Coburn's paintings, the Centaur Theatre, and Hugh MacLennan's novel *Two Solitudes*. The least one can say is that, if there is a conspiracy, it is not to make the identity narrative of Anglo-Quebecers key to the construction of the new Quebec nation.

Citizenship education is much more explicit than in the primary program, not only because it is the subject of one of the three components but also because the topic of citizenship, which must be dealt with under all social realities and concepts studied, is specified. Thus students will have the opportunity to reflect upon differences, interests, and coexistence under the "change of Empire" theme and the debate around the conceptions of nation when they study protests and struggles in the British colony. Similarly, under the theme of "population and settlement," they will look at the connections between the variety of identities, prudently described as "social," and belonging to Quebec society, and between individual and community interests when they study authority and power. In a pluralistic society like Quebec, these options update the competence of "strengthening the exercise of citizenship with the help of history" where the reconciliation of diverse identities and common belonging is identified as a priority challenge.

Nevertheless, one may wonder if these approaches are spelled out clearly enough to permit a balanced discussion of the relations between francophones and anglophones, especially when one considers the great ambiguity that characterizes, one, the statements about coexistence and citizenship and, two, the most relevant crosscutting competencies in this regard. In addition to the aforementioned non-definition of the concepts "citizenship" and "citizenship education," two limitations especially need to be flagged. First of all, nowhere is there a discussion of the different nature of group identities or of the relationship to Quebec of national minorities such as anglophones, the First Nations with their distinct legal status, or groups of immigrant origin. More, ambiguity and contradictions abound when it comes to defining a civic culture that would be distinct from the *majority* French Canadian culture.[45]

The evolution of the teaching of history and citizenship education in Quebec reveals a paradoxical situation. An attempt was made to dilute the more conflictual aspects of history in order to promote shared citizenship, though, on the whole, the program is still dominated by the identity narrative of the majority group and seems unlikely to lead students to discuss in depth the historic cleavages that divide their society. This situation has succeeded at the same time in upsetting the more nationalistic elements and in not radically changing things. Still, it is probable that, if teachers are willing, they can use the program to develop in their students the competencies that will contribute in the long term to inter-community rapprochement, such as comprehension of the complexity of historical facts, critical detachment in relations to one's own presuppositions, or sensitivity to multiple perspectives.

The Actual Curriculum

Compared to Northern Ireland, there has been little study of the actual implementation of the history and citizenship curricula or the connections between this education and inter-community relations in Quebec. This lacuna is surprising given the importance of French-English relations in the history of Quebec and Canada and the growth of historical consciousness among teachers and students in North America.

An initial study of limited scope, carried out in 2004, explores how nineteen francophone and anglophone teachers approach the question of the Other when they teach the history of Quebec and of Canada. They were asked about the role they attribute to history, the importance of teaching it to students, the content that should be take priority in this regard, the methods they use, and the treatment of several controversial issues, such as the Conquest, the Rebellion of 1837, the October Crisis, or Bill 101. First, the study shows that in neither the French-language nor the English-language sector is there a crude instrumental use of history as a means of promoting the collective memory of one's own group. The teachers share an approach based on the development of critical thinking, the use of the historical method, and exposure to a variety of perspectives. However, francophones teaching in French and anglophones teaching in English have radically different ideas about the purpose of teaching history.[46]

The former see their courses as training for the future citizens of a francophone Quebec, which they nevertheless recognize as pluralistic, and make very few references to Canada. When their students are multicultural, the teachers want them to share the historical memory of francophones, something they believe is necessary to ensure authentic integration. The latter consider that the teaching of history should prepare their students to live in Quebec and see themselves as ambassadors of francophone culture for the often unresponsive young anglophones. Indeed, since they have remained in Quebec after more than thirty years of questioning the linguistic power imbalance, they probably developped some sensitivity to the québécois cause. But they see Quebec as an integral part of Canada.

The two groups also differ in the importance they give to the issue of relationships between French and English Quebecers. Francophones hardly ever mention this challenge, the anglophone presence being systematically approached as outside of Quebec and treated in the context of political conflict. Some teachers continue to hold stereo-typed views, even resentment of the anglophone minority's historical dominance. For anglophones, on the other hand, the issue of rap-prochement between French and English Quebecers is central. But they deplore important omissions from the curriculum, notably about the *new* anglophone community, as well as a certain tendency to focus on conflictual relationships.

A second study, carried out between 1998 and 2001, looked at how young Quebecers of French Canadian origin assimilated the historical memory of their group. The author noted the persistence of a *melancholy narrative* among the four hundred youth aged fif-teen to twenty-five years enrolled at the secondary, CEGEP, and uni-versity levels, even though they belong to a generation born after the Quiet Revolution and the major changes that Quebec experienced in sociolinguistic dynamics. The students were asked to summarize the history of Quebec in two pages. A thematic content analysis of the summary followed. Essentially the narrative discourse of the youth divided Quebec history, characterized as a never-ending battle for survival, into three great periods: before 1763, a relatively idyllic New France; from the Conquest to the Quiet Revolution, a succes-sion of conflicts with anglophones marked by the clear dominance of the latter; and post-1960, a promising and positive renewal of social development and identity that was compromised by two ref-erendum defeats. These perceptions are strongly at odds with recent advances in historical research, especially of the period from 1763 to 1960, which portray a far more vibrant and less depressing Quebec, and with the formal curriculum to which the youth have been ex-posed. A central question emerges: why are the students developing a narrative based on victimization?[47]

The authors think, and it would seem that the preceding study sup-ports this, that some teachers, especially those in the secondary schools and the CEGEPs, share this narrative, which reinforces the one the students get from their families and the media. However, for the great majority of teachers, the problem lies with their use of peda-gogical approaches that do not call into questions the students' pre-conceived notions. Indeed, as we saw in the case of Northern Ireland, simply examining facts and interpretations critically is not enough to deconstruct identity narratives strongly impregnated in the collective unconsciousness. The students, just like the teachers and ordinary citizens, are perfectly capable of living with two histories – the account taught in the classroom for assessment purposes, and the other heard in their community, which they consider as authentic. According to the authors, if the teaching of history is to contribute to the modification of ethnic boundaries, teachers and students need to become more conscious of these memory narratives by introducing them as educational material.

CATALONIA

As we saw above, among the four societies under study, Catalonia is distinguished by relationships showing little polarization between Catalan- and Spanish-speakers and by the absence of educational segregation, at least at the legal and organizational levels. In addition, widespread bilingualism, which is actively promoted by the state, results in a certain fluidity across inter-group boundaries.

Catalonia is by no means free of various identity narratives, now more acknowledged, reflecting the experiences of groups who have contributed to its long-standing diversity, such as the Roma and the Spanish-speaking immigrants from the interior, or characterizing its current pluralism, such as the immigrant communities. Nevertheless, the central conflict of memory is related to the history of Spain. It opposes, or at least opposed until the fall of the Franco regime, a dominant Spanish national narrative that was uniform and conservative, to a Catalan narrative, which was delegitimized in the public and educational spheres and based on linguistic and cultural resistance, as well as on the memory of past conflicts and democratic struggle. The Spanish narrative, largely teleological, postulates the existence of Spanish territorial continuity from antiquity to the modern era, the Reconquista (literally, the Reconquest) representing the key element in this regard. Furthermore, the Spanish narrative considers regional pluralism not as a national trait but as a problem, even the cause of the anarchy that Spain experienced from 1931 to 1936, which justifies the promotion of a strong, unified central state. Nor is the Catalan narrative always exempt from these failings, among other things by the sometimes too close connection that it establishes between the institutions of the Middle Ages and those of today. But by the double nature of its discourse, which was both minority and leftist, it was bound to develop a much more complex and critical perspective. This is evident in the significant participation of Catalan historians in the movement contesting history as an identity narrative, initiated internationally in the early 1960s.[48]

Four periods can be identified in the teaching of history and citizenship education since the fall of the Franco regime; however, only during the last period, specifically since 2006, did Catalonia actually share responsibility for defining the curriculum. Indeed, until that date, the Spanish government was setting the curriculum, though the Constitution foresaw that the autonomous states could adapt up to 35 percent of it. To answer the question of whether fragile majorities can effectively reconcile memory, knowledge, and citizenship competencies, we must examine the new Catalan curriculum, which has just recently been made public. However, the other periods are not without interest, since they sometimes gave rise to controversies reminiscent of the debates described above.

From the fall of the Franco regime until the adoption in 1990 of the Organic Act on the General Organization of the Education System (Ley Orgánica General del Sistema Educativo, better known by its acronym LOGSE), the teaching of history, like other disciplines, represented a field of educational experimentation and innovation in Spain as a whole. Indeed, a highly uniform and centralized system was gradually opening up to a decentralization of responsibilities, as much for the schools and the teaching staff as for the regional communities. In Catalonia, the new history curriculum was largely influenced by the program of the Rosa Sensat social science working group launched in the late 1960s in the non-formal sector. It began to deal with the generally more problematic aspects omitted from contemporary history, including the working class and the worker movement, the Second Republic and the civil war, and the Franco dictatorship and the role of the opposition. A much more active pedagogy and composite approaches associating chronology and diachronic study of common themes were introduced.

The law of 1990 maintained many of these changes and institutionalized them. At both the primary and secondary levels, history was to be taught in a group of disciplines that also included geography and the social sciences and whose common curriculum was organized around four broad themes: society and territory, the historical process and change, the contemporary world, and moral life and ethical reflection. Under the second theme, covered principally by history, a series of chronological modules, from prehistory to today, was associated with two thematic modules: the first on historical methods, and the second on social and cultural diversity. Within these blocs the students would learn to examine critically the relationships among the various regions of Spain. In theory these themes were sufficiently vast and flexible that program developers and teachers could adapt their curricular projects to their specific situations. The Spanish Right harshly criticized this program. Its opposition intensified in 1996 when it came to power (however, as part of a minority government, which prevented it from radically modifying the curriculum).[49]

Moreover, an extremely heated media debate followed the publication of a report by the Royal Academy of History, which presented an extremely negative assessment of the teaching of history. Two major weaknesses were denounced: the small place given to the history of the past in comparison to the contemporary period and the vague, partial view that students were acquiring of the Spanish historical process – essentially of the construction of the unitary national state. Three culprits were identified in this regard: "sociologism," "pedagogism," and political circumstances. In the first instance, the authors were targeting multidisciplinary approaches and the utilization of history to clarify present realities. In the second, they denounced the pedagogical obsession that had the effect of relegating knowledge to second place behind competencies and methods. But it was the third accusation that created the most debate and particularly interests us here. The members of the Academy had, in fact, accused the autonomous regions of turning history into an instrument to promote peripheral nationalisms and particular identities. Paradoxically, the Academy seemed to believe that a return to focusing on the construction of the Spanish national state in the curriculum, as long as this was not heavy handed, respected the neutrality requirements of the discipline.[50]

These accusations, but especially the one that related more directly to the competition of memories, elicited two types of responses. On the one hand, some defended the legitimacy of the Catalan and Basque curricula by demonstrating that they were not particularly militant vehicles of regional identities. One study showed that the content of history textbooks most often used in these regions focused principally on the Spanish state and Western Europe, while regional realities accounted, on average, for about 10 percent of the content. Catalonia distinguished itself, however, by slightly more references to itself than to Spain (15 percent and 12 percent, respectively); these equally limited percentages indicate the importance of European and international themes. The authors of the study also demonstrated that the values in the Basque and Catalan programs

were the same as in the common Spanish curriculum, namely, respect for diversity, the blending of cultures, and tolerance. On the
other hand, some deplored that the debate over the teaching of history was based on the legitimacy of using history as an instrument
to promote divergent memories and that little attention was paid to
the role of the historical method in the intellectual, social, and civic
development of the students. Given the near absence of studies on
the historical consciousness of the students, especially as concerns
the crucial question of nationalism and inter-group relations, the
arguments on each side remained largely prescriptive.[51]

In any event, as soon as there was a majority government in
Parliament, Spain adopted in 2002 a new history curriculum. This
decree gave history and geography the central role that had been
taken away by the LOGSE. It severely restricted the autonomy of educational specialists and set up an extremely structured approach to
the content and to the chronological order in which it should be approached. Multiple perspectives were no longer encouraged: the program presents an objective and linear image of the past that the
students are supposed to appropriate in an essentially instrumental
way. However, the program does retain a certain respect for the pluralism of the Spanish regions by permitting the various autonomous
communities to add elements they consider essential. The Generalitat
(the Catalan government) used this limited flexibility to develop a
program that maintained the proposed structure while promoting the
Catalan identity narrative. This program promulgated that history
and geography should form future citizens of the Catalan nation, obviously an integral part of the Spanish state, but having its own specific identity. The common program introduced additions and changes
to all the periods, including the historical development of the Catalan
nation in the Middle Ages, the Catalan political movement from the
nineteenth century on, and finally the Republican Generalitat in the
twentieth century. Some reproached the Catalan government for entering into competition with the Spanish government. It left out, according to the critics, several components that once characterized the
Catalan approach to teaching history, including the importance of
class differences, internal conflicts, and socio-economic history and a
pedagogical dynamism that typically integrated the disciplines and
used the historical method to analyse thematic situations.[52]

However, the 2007 program, adopted in a much more autonomous manner by the Catalan state, seems to show that the return to

traditional perspectives was more a strategic response to Madrid's
bullying than a sharing of conservative nation-building perspectives.
Starting in 2005, the Generalitat launched an important consultation with the intent of developing a national consensus on educational matters. Five major areas gave rise to reflection documents
setting forth basic principles and propositions. The teaching of history comes under the social and cultural area, while citizenship education, which becomes a mandatory subject, is part of personal
development. The area of languages and communication, which favours a multilingual and multicultural perspective, also includes several objectives related to inter-community rapprochement.[53]

The reflection document on history teaching rejects straightaway
the temptation to teach an encyclopaedic history and encourages the
development of competencies and the understanding of current
issues. In choosing the content, teachers will have to take into account the students' grasp of the major stages of world history, a
satisfactory knowledge of Catalan's general development, and a
deepening knowledge of the processes and problems upon which the
students should reflect and apply the historical method. Citizenship
education is situated in a rather original way within the process of
learning to live in the contexts of widespread uncertainty in the area
of identity and ethics and of developing strategies that facilitate the
building up of shared allegiance.[54]

The programs at the primary and secondary levels largely reflect
these orientations, although the government has strengthened certain elements connected to identification with Catalonia. At the primary level, for 2 hours per week, the teaching of history is integrated
with the teaching of general knowledge about the natural, social,
and cultural environment. To both years of the upper cycles, another
35 hours of human rights and citizenship education have been added. During the four years of secondary school, students will receive
on average 105 hours of social sciences, geography, and history, and
35 hours of human rights and citizenship education. The two programs seek to reconcile, to varying degrees depending on the students' ages, an equivalent commitment to three objectives: knowledge
of Catalonia's history, geography, and specific traditions; establishment in and identification with this society, openness to social, cultural, and group diversity; and the struggle against discrimination
and inequality between persons and groups. The history curriculum
is thus largely an instrument to promote social objectives, but it still

emphasizes the historical method and critical analysis of the phenomena studied.[55]

The nation-building aspect, which emerges more in the History program but which is not absent from the Citizenship Education program, is somewhat mitigated by the adoption of a territorial definition emphasizing the multiple contributions that have fashioned Catalan identity. At the primary level, it is not always clear if "Catalonia's specific traditions" refers to ethnic elements linked to the Catalan-speaking group or, to the contrary, if it could also include elements from a merging culture. At the secondary level, the inclusive aspect is more explicit. Thus, the Citizenship Education program distinguishes territorial identity from cultural identity and tries to get students to interpret and integrate the familial, national, and political plurality that surrounds them. At the end of the cycle, they will be aware of the existence of the various levels of citizenship: local, autonomic (a neologism designating the Catalan level), Spanish, European, and global. Likewise, the connections between teaching and identity formation are conceived in the light of plurality, complexity. and liberty, and the stress is on the importance of preserving the diverse memories of past actors while looking for new elements of social cohesion.

More precisely, during the four years of secondary school, students study both a chronological history, divided into four periods, and diachronic themes, by respecting in both instances the principle of concentric circles from Catalonia, expanding to Spain, Europe, and the world. However, an analysis of the content shows that the world and Catalonia occupy the larger part of the program, with references to Spain and Europe being much less systematic. In addition, plurality is defined in a general manner, without explicit mention of long-established groups or, most specifically, of Spanish-speakers. The different interpretations that a teacher may have to deal with classroom while analysing, for example, the relationship between Catalonia and Spain in various historical periods are not mentioned.

There is, however, an implicit recognition of relationships between Spanish- and Catalan-speakers in the Language and Communication program. Since the teaching of Catalan and Spanish is mandatory for the two groups, the program includes a number of components promoting rapprochement at both the primary and secondary levels. Thus, students in primary school will study the similarities between Catalan and Spanish, learn to appreciate the linguistic diversity of their specific context and of Spain, and develop a critical attitude toward linguistic stereotypes. Students in secondary schools, in addition to these same competencies, will become aware of the equality of the languages, speak in a nondiscriminatory manner in this regard, and develop empathy for the communication difficulties of persons who speak languages other than Catalan. They will also understand that to learn new languages is to open oneself to a better understanding of the world, and while being conscious of belonging to a linguistic community they will develop a sense of confidence toward the variety of languages that they will not hesitate to use in various contexts.

It is too early to know the know the reaction to this ambitious curriculum, clearly subscribing to a civic perspective, which could give rise to opposition from both the most nationalistic elements of the Catalan population and the social science and language specialists. The latter would deplore that their respective disciplines are subservient to the goals of identity and social transformation. However, as it is somewhat akin to a potluck – vast and ambiguous – there is probably something in it for everyone. Some will be able to interpret it in a traditional manner by focusing on the identity narrative based first and foremost on the Catalan nation-building group. Others will adopt a solidly consensual and inclusive discourse. A minority will use it to enable repressed memory and a critical perspective to surface. The respective importance of these three groups will be determined by the intensity and adequacy of the training that current and future teachers of history and citizenship education will receive. Indeed, various studies have shown that current teachers essentially learned history by memorizing content and that, while largely favourable to more dynamic approaches, they feel very poorly equipped to deal with them. It will also be necessary to observe Madrid's reaction. The fears of the opponents of Catalonia's new autonomous status will be challenged and strengthened at the same time. Indeed, the new program puts forward a civic definition of territorial identity uncommon in fragile majorities, but that only makes it more threatening in the eyes of persons for whom there can be only one process of nation-building on Spanish soil.[56]

THE LESSONS OF COMPARATIVE ANALYSIS

As we have just seen, the challenge of reconciling conflictual memories, respect for knowledge, and development of citizenship competencies in the teaching of history is very acute in divided societies. As it is difficult clearly to identify a dominant group, the cacophony of identity narratives is strident. Even the definition of what constitutes national history is difficult, since there often is no consensus among the groups about their primary allegiance. Persons belonging to fragile majorities, whether they are educational specialists, teachers, or students, also strongly resist any steps that would erode the memory that serves as a base of their unique way of life. Moreover, in societies where conflict is longstanding, it is often easier for one or other of the groups to integrate the immigrant community into their narrative than to question their respective relationships.

To respond to these tensions, one may be tempted, more than elsewhere, to turn the teaching of history into an instrument to promote the development of shared citizenship. Citizenship education focused on the future can represent one way out of the empty space created by the absence of a common narrative about the past. However, some groups, without mentioning the historical discipline itself, do not recognize their story from this pacifying retrospective vantage point, which in their eyes unduly smoothes over contentious issues. Despite these common challenges, the variability of responses illustrates the need for a clear vision of the role that the teaching of history can play in the intellectual development of students and inter-community rapprochement.

The two societies where the two groups enjoy an equivalent status have diametrically opposed approaches. In Northern Ireland, the teaching of history aims to confront and go beyond opposed memories to create a new, more social type of citizenship. This goal enjoys relative consensus, and although antagonistic narratives persist in the society, significant progress among the students is evident. In Belgium, on the other hand, there is consensus around the promotion, in segregated school systems, of contradictory narratives that ignore each other and of a citizenship that overlooks the political community where it is embodied. Here avoidance is preferred to confrontation. But it is worth bearing in mind, given recent constitutional developments in this country, that the potential contribution of the teaching of history to inter-community rapprochement is dramatically underutilized.

In the two societies where a national minority constitutes a regional majority enjoying relatively dominant status, the experiences are similar. Quebec and Catalonia share a common attachment to promoting their specific memory by the teaching of history and a recent commitment to redefining it in an inclusive and pluralistic way.

However, initiatives to concretize this openness to diversity gave rise to a major controversy in Quebec, which points to greater polarization in ethnic relations and identities, while similar initiatives in Catalonia seemed to enjoy a broad consensus.

Moreover, in all instances where evaluative or exploratory studies were carried out on the actual curriculum, they concluded that the teaching of history had a positive impact on students' attitudes, despite the unequal progress and limitations created by larger social dynamics. Provided there was no hesitation to question preconceived notions and to address contentious issues, and so long as dynamic pedagogical methods were promoted, this schooling can be a fundamental critical exercise for students of diverse origins to confront their vision of the past. Without necessarily casting it radically into question, students can have access to a more complex level of analysis of events and a better understanding of each other's perspectives. The dynamic relationship that develops between the historical method, on one hand, and the respective narratives, on the other, can serve as a basis for the student to develop an authentic historical consciousness.

But for this to happen two prior conditions are indispensible. First, political authorities must commit to staying the course on the goals sought and not yield to the vagaries of public opinion, which can sometimes react emotionally to what it perceives as the erosion of its traditional identity. Second, teachers must receive the kind of training that will equip them fully to fulfill the complex educational and social mandates with which they are now entrusted.

PART TWO

Diversity Stemming from Immigration: Relations with the Minority Other

4

Linguistic Integration and Equality of Opportunity: Complementarity or Tension

Whether or not they have already experienced a complex dynamic of ethnic relations, all societies that receive immigrants face common challenges. On the one hand, there is the challenge of assuring the integration of newcomers linguistically, socially, and economically and, on the other, the challenge of supporting the necessary transformation of the host society. These two highly polysemic concepts – the integration of one and the adaptation of the other – have given rise to numerous and recurring debates for the last thirty years or so. These debates have as much to do with the *how far*, that is, the definition of what is desirable, as with the *how* of making this happen. Thus, the degree to which integration demands the simple knowledge of the host language, its mastery, its dominant use, and its adoption as the mother tongue has been the subject of numerous controversies, where normative systems of what it means to be a citizen are often more in question than are the research data. Nor is there academic or public consensus about the relationship of linguistic integration with the maintenance or disappearance of heritage languages. Likewise, though it is generally agreed that integration is measured by equal participation in the society and its institutions, some put the bar higher by insisting on social interaction. They will thus denounce the naturally occurring concentration or segregation of immigrant populations, whether or not it is linked to inequality.[1]

In any event, the expectations and demands will be different for the first and second generations, since there is a broad consensus on the temporal dimension of the integration process. As well, peoples' pre-migratory characteristics, especially their social class, influence the pace at which different outcomes can be achieved. We must bear this dimension in mind when we make comparisons between societies that have a more or less planned and selective system of recruiting or admitting immigrants.

Given the intensive, all-encompassing character of schooling, the school plays a central role in instructing, qualifying, and socializing future generations, even if its monopoly in this area has somewhat eroded in recent years. It is thus an institution that is particularly affected by the challenge of integration and of adaptation to pluralism, a subject we will look at in chapter 5. Indeed, it is understandable that certain obstacles to full participation may persist in the first generation, but the democratic ideal demands that, through their schooling, the children of immigrants will acquire all the tools necessary for an egalitarian integration into the new society.[2]

However, the best strategies for reaching these goals are hardly the subject of consensus. Thus, several countries with a dominant linguistic majority, such as the United States, English Canada, or Great Britain, are divided as to the best model for newcomers to learn the host language. Are special classes better than direct integration into regular classes? And what place should heritage languages occupy? Likewise, the widely noted gap between the school performance and career of native-born students and immigrant students is interpreted very differently, and this has an impact on the measures selected. Some attribute this to the linguistic and cultural gap that families and students experience due to their non-mastery of the host language or because of their social class. They therefore insist on the addition of compensatory measures. Others contend that the schools function with an ethnocentric bias that shows up in different educational expectations for minority students or in the failure of the curriculum to take their language, history, and culture into account. They argue for a more radical approach to multilingual, anti-racist education.[3]

Is there something distinctive about fragile majority societies in matters pertaining to linguistic integration and equality of opportunity at the school for newcomers? At first glance, it would seem so. On the one hand, when language is playing a central role in the identity of a group that has experienced becoming a sociological minority, the behaviours and performance of newcomers will be particularly scrutinized. The situation could be marked by anxiety if language relations are such that the immigrant populations tend to adopt the traditionally dominant language. Likewise, the relation with multilingualism, especially in the curriculum, could be more complex. The experience of linguistic oppression can nevertheless work in the other direction, that is, by fostering a greater empathy toward immigrant languages. On the other hand, fragile majorities themselves often have a history of socio-economic and educational disadvantage. The awareness of their majority status and the emergence of new inequalities, both in society and in the school, may be slower to develop than in the more clearly dominant groups. But here, too, the memory of past victimization may lead to greater sensitivity to these phenomena.[4]

In any event, the links between these two essential objectives in the schooling of newcomers – linguistic integration and equality of opportunity – will be complex. When policies clearly favour the once dominated language, students and their parents may call into question the relevance of learning a language they perceive as less favourable to their social mobility. Inversely, when society instead opts to promote balanced bilingualism, which equates to trilingualism for the young immigrants, some may be afraid that this requirement will have a negative impact on school performance and progress.[5]

This chapter will focus on three societies in which the linguistic marker is central to the definition of inter-group boundaries: Quebec, Catalonia, and Flanders. These societies distinguish themselves by the importance of immigration, the centrality of the language question in debates about the schooling of newcomers, the expertise developed in matters of linguistic integration and equality of opportunity in the school, and the scope of the evaluative research on these issues. The three case studies follow a largely similar framework, depending on the availability of data. First we will present the characteristics of the immigration policies and migratory patterns likely to have an influence on the linguistic and educational performance of the youth. Second, we will examine how important a role the linguistic question played, or still plays, in social and educational debates, while also describing the development of policies and programs in this regard. We will also review the linguistic integration of immigrant youth, in school and in the wider society, from the perspective of both language mastery and its use. Third, we tackle the question of immigrant students' success in school and of the linguistic, social, and educational factors that influence this. The approaches implemented to deal with these problems are also discussed.

Finally, based on these comparative analyses, we offer a response to the two questions that structure this chapter. First, are the objectives of linguistic integration and equality of opportunity for immigrant students enrolled in schools controlled by fragile majorities complementary or in recurrent tension? Second, when it comes to linguistic dynamics, does the way in which these two challenges are experienced point to unique features in such societies or to something they share with simpler societies?

QUEBEC

Immigration Policy and Its Impact on the School

Since the late 1960s, Quebec, more than any other Canadian province, has wanted to assume a major role in the area of immigration, a shared jurisdiction of the federal government and the provinces. The reasons for this interest are much the same as those that account for the development of language policy, chief among these being the degree of immigrant assimilation into the anglophone community and its consequences for the demolinguistic balance in Montreal. Evident from the beginning was also a nation-building agenda in competition with that of the Canadian government, something that would become more apparent as time went on. Thus, through a series of agreements culminating in the Canada-Quebec Accord on immigration, Quebec gradually gained control of selected immigration (which today accounts for 60 percent of the total) and of exclusive responsibility for the linguistic and economic integration of newcomers.[6]

Quebec's action on immigration is characterized by three elements. First, faced with the perceived economic consequences of a demographic shortfall and an aging population, a gradual increase in the immigration level, eventually to reach 25 percent of total immigration to Canada, was targeted. Currently the Quebec government is far from this percentage, having received only 18.3 percent of the immigrants to Canada in 2008. Still, from 2005 to 2010 with an annual average of 45,000 immigrants for a population of 7 million, Quebec has experienced a high rate of immigration when compared to other long-time immigrant-receiving such as the United States and New Zealand.

Immigrant selection is defined as the trade off of various goals: recruitment of francophone immigrants, the contribution of immigration to economic development, support of family reunification, and commitment to increased international solidarity. This complexity leads to very diversified migratory patterns in terms of both linguistic

competency and national origin. On the one hand, knowledge of
French is not an eliminatory criterion on the selection grid, although
the proportion of persons speaking French is currently above 60 percent. On the other hand, close to 80 percent of immigrants now
come from outside of North America and Europe. The five most
important countries (Algeria, France, Morocco, China, Colombia)
account for only 36 percent of the entrants, which explains the
heterogeneity one finds in most multi-ethnic classrooms. Immigrants
to Quebec are also quite diversified in terms of socio-economic
status, a marked difference from the situation that characterizes the
other societies we are studying. The distribution of the immigrant
population according to indicators such as projected employment or
level of education is largely similar to that of the host population,
although there is a slight bipolarization at the two extremes.[7] Finally,
like the Canadian policy, the Quebec policy aims at permanent
settlement. Citizenship is thus acquired very rapidly (three years),
which contributes to the important political weight that minorities
possess, both in society and in the school.

Under the cumulative effect of waves of immigration, there are
now 131,492 pupils in the educational system whose mother tongue
is neither English, nor French, nor an indigenous language, that is,
12.5 percent of the total student population. As for students who
were born abroad, or who had at least one parent born abroad, a
study carried out in 2006 estimated their number to be 206,125, or
19.1 percent of the total student population. These immigrant-origin
students may have either French or English as a mother tongue (or
another language). In Montreal, given the immigrant concentration
and the francophone residents' exodus to the suburbs and private
schools, allophones represent 36.5 percent of the school clientele,
and immigrant students, 51 percent. Thus more than one-third of
the schools consist mostly of immigrant-origin students, and just less
than one in ten have a proportion that exceeds 75 percent. However,
given the much diversified socio-economic profile of the immigrants,
there is no systematic correlation between multi-ethnic schools and
poverty in the metropolitan area of Montreal.[8]

Linguistic Integration

THE DEBATE   The linguistic situation prior to the adoption of Bill
101 cannot be described as diglossic: French was never confined to
the private sphere and the schooling of francophones in French was

always guaranteed up to university. Rather, it was the dominance of English in Montreal as the language of work, commerce, services, and advertising that posed the problem. Some thought this situation violated the rights of francophones to live in French and sent the wrong message to newcomers about the respective importance of the two languages in Quebec. As we saw above, newcomers tended overwhelmingly to opt for English-language schools. The choice of schooling was thus at the heart of the language debate in the 1970s between partisans of mandatory French-language schooling and supporters of free choice. The latter group included almost the entire anglophone community, for obvious reasons, and large portions of the immigrant communities themselves, who feared the loss of the socio-economic status they were just beginning to acquire.[9]

The issue was cut short by the adoption of the Charter of the French Language, which aimed at making the French language the normal and everyday language of work, instruction, communication, commerce, and business. The Charter's more innovative aspects concerned, first, the rights of francophones to work and to receive services in French and, second, the linguistic integration of immigrants. As to this second objective, Bill 101 made enrolment in French-language schools mandatory for francophone and allophone students while safeguarding the historical right of the anglophone community and of immigrant communities anglicized in the past to attend English-language schools. Although other institutions also play a role in the linguistic integration of adult immigrants, the social pressure to address the school situation was enormous, since it was the only public institution specifically targeted by the legislature.[10]

The place of language in the debate on immigrant school-integration tended to wane after 1977. There were three broad periods in this regard. Up to the late 1980s, the concern had to do with immigrants' active or passive resistance to enrolling in French-language schools or learning French. The media and nationalist groups focused their attention on the presence of some 1,500 illegal students of Italian, Portuguese, and Greek background in English-language schools. The situation resolved itself with time and a few amnesty measures. Numerous government pronouncements and university studies on francization appeared: some claimed that the status of French in the new multi-ethnic schools was akin to that of Latin in the classical colleges! Nevertheless, supported by provincial exam results (to which we will return later), a consensus gradually formed about the knowledge and mastery of French. As well, recent migratory patterns had changed the composition of the school population, which was now dominated by more Francophile groups such as Haitians, Vietnamese, and Latin Americans. Opposition to attending French schools had gradually disappeared, or at least was not openly expressed.[11]

In the early 1990s, the debate switched to the issue of the linguistic practices of young immigrants and their relationship with French. Three issues were key: the impact of ethnic concentration on the linguistic climate of the schools; the choice of the language of schooling at the college level, which does not come under Bill 101; and the degree to which the practices generally favourable to French in the schools will have a long-term impact on linguistic use. Although many studies and the report of the Commission des États généraux on the state and future of the French language in Quebec presented rather positive findings in this regard, the controversy remained lively until the late 1990s. This period saw the entry of relatively large numbers of young anglophone and anglophile immigrants from South Asia and Hong Kong into the school system. As well, many nationalist voices, while recognizing the real impact of French schooling on language knowledge and linguistic practice, continued to give priority to more demanding indicators, such as the language of private life or opting for French-language schooling at the college level. They contend that these dimensions, where the results are less clear, are better indicators of newcomers' future behaviours.[12]

In the 2000s, under the combined effect of an unprecedented wave of North African francophone immigration and the international situation following the events of 11 September 2001, the language debate ran out of steam, notably at the school level. It was the cultural and especially religious questions that preoccupied the media and public opinion, as we shall see in the next chapter. Although studies of linguistic integration in the schools and the wider society became fewer in number, this does not at all mean that anxiety about this issue has disappeared, especially at the grassroots. Proof of this is evident in the concerns expressed by various citizens during the Bouchard-Taylor Commission into the practices of accommodation connected to cultural differences and in the unexpected return of the language question to the Quebec political scene in autumn 2007 with the plan put forth by the Parti Québécois of a citizenship in which knowledge of French would be a central component.[13]

PROGRAMS AND INTERVENTIONS   Contrary to the dominant English-Canadian model of direct insertion in regular classes with linguistic support, Quebec opted for a closed reception class model. From the creation of the first reception classes in 1969, it was thought that immigrants required a systematic, structured approach for learning French, not simple exposure to the language in the regular class, which is often sufficient when the language is clearly dominant. The teaching of French in reception classes, which benefits from a smaller teacher-student ratio, is well developed and includes a sensitizing to the reality and the cultural codes of the host society. In regions where the number of students is not sufficient, allophone students attend regular classes but benefit from extra language support. In 2006, some fourteen thousand students, over 88 percent of whom live in Montreal, attended reception classes or received extra language support.[14]

Also, until very recently, no role was recognized for heritage languages in French-learning initiatives for newcomers. However, since 1977, Quebec has been offering a Heritage Language program, known by its French acronym PELO, to allophone students already mastering French. At the outset, the desire was to send to older established communities the message that multilingualism complemented the promotion of French. This education, which involves seven thousand students in fourteen languages, is relatively little developed due to resistance from certain teachers and from the most committed parents, who choose instead to send their children to well-funded, private trilingual schools. In addition, the program suffers from a lack of focus. While the literature insists on the connections between learning a heritage language and mastering the host language, PELO is not offered to newcomer students. As well, PELO targets primary students while the problems of mastering French are more evident at the secondary level.[15]

Following the publication of the 1998 School Integration and Intercultural Education Policy, reception programs and interventions began to evolve. This became necessary when a systematic tendency was noted to extend the time spent in the reception class, initially planned for ten months, which led to worries about the social integration of newcomer students. Also, research was showing that the young students could benefit from simpler approaches, while many underschooled secondary students needed specific services going beyond simple language learning. Without questioning the reception class model, various innovative models were explored in recent years in order to better integrate newcomers in the regular class. It could be partial immersion in linguistically less demanding subjects, team teaching shared by reception-class and heritage-language teachers, or insertion in regular classes with linguistic support. Experiments to enhance students' linguistic heritage in the regular class were also tried, influenced by the European language awareness movement for early language education. But these were far from duplicating the development that we have seen in other contexts, like in Catalonia. Indeed, despite the 1998 education reform's endorsement of subject integration, the links among the reception class, the heritage language class, and the regular class are far from systematic, and the respective place and status of the languages are subject to numerous regulations.[16]

As to promoting the use of French, the Ministry of Education each year supports more than three hundred activities in school settings. These give priority to communication in French, the consumption of cultural products in French, twinning with francophones, or family/school/community rapprochement. Several school authorities have also included this dimension in their intercultural education policy. This is particularly the case in the Montreal and Marguerite-Bourgeoys School Boards, which together take in a large proportion of Quebec's immigrant student population.[17]

THE RESULTS   The results of more than thirty years of interventions in linguistic integration in the school are generally positive. One indisputable impact is the French schooling of a large majority of newcomers (92 percent in 2007–08), who are now subject to Bill 101, and of a growing percentage of allophone students (73 percent), some of whom have the right to enrol in English schools but whose parents are opting instead for a French-language education.[18]

As to the mastery of French, at least as measured by ministry exams at the provincial level, it seems to be satisfactory. Thus, according to a study of cohorts that started secondary school between 1994 and 1996, the success rate for immigrant-origin students is 85.1 percent while the rate for all students in Quebec is 89.6 percent. The average scores are similar: 73.4 percent for immigrant-origin students and 76.2 percent for all Quebec students. However, two limitations to these results should be noted. First, the exam is taken at the end of secondary school, but immigrant-origin students' attendance rate at

the exam is already ten points lower than the general school population. More, the exam measures only partially the complex mastery of
the language at the academic level, as is demonstrated by other research on the language competencies of students or the perceptions
of teachers, which reveal various shortcomings. These deficiencies do
not appear to call into question the educational progress of most
students, nor their daily interactions with francophones, but they
could have an impact on access to the professions where mastery of
the language is essential. Besides, the comparison of the two groups
does not support the rather popular hypothesis that mastery of
French is hampered if the language of the immigrant is very different
from French. So-called linguistic distance has no negative impact on
Chinese students, who are high in the rankings, while Spanish- and
Creole-speakers are clearly struggling.[19]

As to language use in the schools, the effect of francization on
school enrolment is well established. This is demonstrated by a study
done in twenty multi-ethnic Montreal primary and secondary
schools in 1999, when the sociolinguistic context was distinctly less
favourable than it is today. In primary schools, the data emerging
from systematic observation of informal exchanges among the students showed the French proportion ranged from 67.5 percent and
99.7 percent and even exceeded 90 percent in six schools. In secondary schools, although the linguistic situation is more complex,
French was also in first place with ratios varying from 53.1 percent
to 98.4 percent. When one excludes the immigrant languages, the
data on the relative strength of French in relation to English also
confirms the francization trend. At the primary level, use of French
varies from 70 percent to 100 percent and exceeds 90 percent in
eight schools. At the secondary level, the respective percentages are
59.9 percent to 99.3 percent, exceeding 80 percent in ten schools.
On the whole, French-language use among students is clearly higher
than the level of francization that would have been expected had
they been adopting the linguistic behaviour of their parents' age
group reported in the census. As one might expect, this added value
is more pronounced in schools frequented by anglophone and anglophile students than in schools where the linguistic composition was
already favourable to French.[20]

Interviews with the students also demonstrated that the most successful approaches to promoting French lie in complementarity with,
and not in opposition to, the competencies that students already

possess in other languages. Indeed, if there is consensus about the value of French and the importance of its use, the normative positions favouring multilingualism predominate among both allophones and francophones.

Today there is more interest in the language practices of youth outside of school and on the impact of their education on their future linguistic orientations. A recent doctoral study of more than 1,600 fourth- and fifth-year secondary school students showed that their language use outside the classroom was quite varied. In social life, the three languages are about equal, although English is less important than French or the immigrant language. The young people's attitudes about these languages, however, differed considerably. They accorded paramount importance to the mastery of French for living and working in Quebec. Knowing English is considered essential for living and working elsewhere. As to their own language, it is valued in the short term because it permits them to communicate with others from their own group and, in the long term, when it is an international language, for its possible contribution to their social and economic mobility.[21]

The choice of the language of instruction at the college level has also been studied very attentively, since some see in this an important indication about the future use of French by the youth. The data in this regard show an uneven evolution. In the late 1980s, the period that coincided with the admission of the first cohort of allophone students schooled entirely in French, over 80 percent opted for a French-language CEGEP. During the following decade, this percentage decreased systematically to 53.3 percent in 2001. Since them there has been a regular increase, with the choice of a French-language CEGEP reaching 63 percent by 2007. Still, there is no consensus on how to explain the relative popularity of English-language CEGEPs among immigrant-origin students. While some are worried and see this as a basic tendency, others point out that the choice is first and foremost strategic. Having acquired a strong grasp of French, young allophones attend CEGEPs to attain the competence in English that a French-language school, particularly inefficient in this regard, would not help them to do.[22]

As to the long-term impact of schooling, a study by the Conseil de la langue française (French Language Council) carried out with 1,655 Montreal allophones aged eighteen to sixty found that 65 percent of those who had attended a French-language school were using

French most often in their public life, while the percentage was only 36.5 percent for those schooled in English. In addition, these positive results did not include young immigrants whose mother tongue was French, a group of growing importance among new immigrants. The authors show that the consequences of schooling in French are more important than other factors linked either to the situation in the country of origin or to settlement in the host country, such as prior knowledge of French or the fact of living in a French-speaking neighbourhood. In the 2001 census, the data on the language most often spoken at home by young, foreign-born allophones aged fifteen to twenty-five years also confirm that the attractiveness of French, at times together with other languages, is more pronounced in this age group than among their elders. Thus, while 24.3 percent of the foreign-born population as a whole adopted French, 18.4 percent English, and 59 percent continued to speak their own language, among youth the percentages were 30.3 percent, 12.3 percent, and 60.1 percent respectively. But the retention of their own languages and the still significant use of English allows for a pessimistic reading by persons for whom multilingualism is synonymous with anglicization in the long term.[23]

Equality of Opportunity and Academic Success among Immigrant Students

The issue of equality of opportunity and educational success has for a long time been the poor cousin in the debate about the school integration of immigrant youth in Quebec. Certainly, one finds normative statements in various government documents, including the *Policy Statement on Educational Integration and Intercultural Education*. This policy makes the promotion of equality of opportunity one of its three action principles. However, reflection on this issue has been rather limited for some time. Two factors influenced this state of affairs: first, the almost total dominance of the educational agenda by the francophone community and, second, the limitations of the data collected by the Ministry of Education and the resulting optimistic reading of it. Indeed, the linguistic marker received priority: allophones, who had settled some time ago, were being compared to francophones or anglophones, without knowing much about the situation of more recent immigrant students. The dominant perception, reiterated in official documents and by political, professional, and community authorities, was of equal or greater success, accompanied by particular problems among certain target groups.[24]

Beyond language training, action to support the educational success of immigrant-origin students consisted essentially of ad hoc efforts, such as literacy pilot projects or rapprochement activities between the school and immigrant families. More, given the absence of systematic links between poverty and immigration, support programs for the academic success in disadvantaged communities were very slow at taking into account the specific needs of immigrant students.[25]

Starting in the 2000s, however, this issue began to take up much more space in public debate. Indeed, much more precise data were now putting into perspective the hitherto dominant optimistic assessment. In addition, schools and communities were becoming more aware of the fact that a significant proportion of the immigrant population, even selected immigrants, was experiencing downward social mobility.

A recent study shows that, in comparison to the total school population, foreign-born students or those whose parents were foreign-born enter secondary school with more delay and continue to fall behind, even if they started at an opportune time. They also obtain secondary diplomas less often after five years (45.5 percent versus 57.8 percent) or even seven years of schooling (57.4 percent versus 69 percent). These students are also less likely to write ministry exams and, as we saw above, have slightly lower success rates and averages in French. But their results are similar in history and physical education, and slightly higher in English. However, they seem to be quite resilient, since they get into college at a fairly equal rate (52.8 percent versus 54.8 percent), even if they obtain secondary diplomas less often. Among the factors influencing academic success, five are particularly significant: sex, which is slightly less a factor for immigrant students; whether one is first or second generation; the entry level into the school system; academic delay; and socio-economic status. The gap between better-off and disadvantaged students, however, is less important than in the overall student population, which tends to suggest that poverty is less disabling academically in immigrant populations. Poverty is more temporary and can be accompanied by a high valuing of education, whereas in more settled populations, poverty tends to be institutionalized. As to intergroup differences, the study documented the particularly blatant situation experienced by students from Black communities. For them, the deficit in secondary-school graduation is 17 points and, among the subgroups particularly disadvantaged, specifically, Caribbean immigrants whose mother tongue is English or Creole, only four students in ten obtain a secondary diploma.[26]

The new portrait emerging is thus one of pathways marked by significant gaps during secondary schooling, which do not seem to inhibit the capacity of *survivors* to progress through the system. These data are largely confirmed by that of the Program for International Student Assessment (PISA), though less interesting because they deal only with student competencies and not their final outcomes. Indeed, Canada ranks up there among the countries where the difference between native-born and foreign-born populations is the least pronounced, both in mathematics and the language of education. However, in Quebec's French sector the gap is much wider than in the English sector of the other Canadian provinces. Thus, in reading, the gap rises to 66 points while in Ontario it is only 27 points. This could be linked to schooling in French or to the simultaneous learning of two languages by young immigrants.[27]

After the publication of the report and its widespread distribution in the schools and communities concerned, several actions were initiated as part of a follow-up committee piloted by the Ministry of Education, giving special attention to the Black community. In addition, within the organizations responsible for the intervention strategy in disadvantaged areas, an analysis of the specific needs of disadvantaged multi-ethnic communities and the development of interventions adapted to their reality is underway. Schools and universities are also reflecting on how to integrate anti-racist education perspectives with programs and actions connected to both intercultural and citizenship education. However, as we shall see in chapter 5, the current context is characterized by a major controversy over reasonable accommodation, and this risks slowing down somewhat the process of consciousness-raising. Indeed today, it is cultural integration and not equality of opportunity that is arousing almost exclusive interest in media and, to a large degree, government circles.[28]

CATALONIA

Immigration Policy and Its Impact on the School

Strictly speaking, it is difficult to talk about immigration *policy* in Catalonia, or even in Spain, which exercises essential prerogatives in this regard. Indeed, the European model predominates: essentially, immigration is endured and not planned, and the presence of illegal immigrants is significant. In virtue of the Spanish Constitution, the regulation of immigration is the exclusive responsibility of the central government, which has traditionally exercised it by the management of its borders. However, since 2000, like other European countries, Spain is engaged in the active recruitment of immigrants to meet its economic needs. These activities especially target Latin Americans, which is not without impact on the Catalan sociolinguistic dynamic. Immigration has increased noticeably. The immigrant population, which represented but 1.6 percent of the Spanish population in 1988, now stands at 12.2 percent, or some 4,526,522 persons.[29]

These immigrants mainly settle in three areas: Catalonia, Madrid, and Andalusia receive 21.8 percent, 17.8 percent, and 12.3 percent respectively of new immigrants. While Catalonia exercises no control over immigration levels or the geographic origin of the immigrants, it has experienced a major demographic change over the last ten years. In 1996 there were less than 100,000 foreign-born residents in Catalonia. In 2008, that number had grown to 1,103,790, or 14.9 percent of the total population. However, Catalonia does not experience the same concentration of immigrants in a single metropolitan area as did Quebec or Flanders. The four big Catalan cities, Barcelona (13.8 percent), Girona (20.4 percent), Lleida (16.3 percent), and Tarragona (17.7 percent), received approximately equal percentages. The sociolinguistic composition of the immigrants has also changed a great deal. North Africans represented nearly 15 percent of the immigrants received in 2007. In addition, the presence of Latin Americans continues to rise: they now make up some 40 percent of newcomers.[30]

In matters of integration, responsibilities are shared. In the 1979 Statute of Autonomy, immigration is not mentioned. However, in this respect the Generalitat exercised its sector-specific responsibilities for education, culture, and health. The Catalan government would also be responsible for implementing the guidelines adopted by Madrid on the management of illegal immigrants or the protection of their rights. Catalonia has been welcoming newcomers since 1992, with the creation of the Secretariat for Immigration and the implementation of various interdepartmental plans. However, it was especially in the 2000s that a struggle ensued to increase the Catalan state's responsibility for immigrant selection and integration. The New Statute of Autonomy, promulgated in 2006, gave Catalonia exclusive jurisdiction for the reception, socio-economic integration, and participation of immigrants, a competence shared in matters pertaining to work permits and a right to participate in decisions of the Spanish state to determine immigration levels. Despite this progress, many Catalan spokespersons, some influenced by the Quebec experience, judged the concessions by the Spanish state to be insufficient, especially as concerns the selection and control of immigration.[31]

In the school system, students of foreign nationality, who represented less than 1 percent of school enrolment in 1991, now number more than 10 percent. In addition, even though Catalonia, like France, does not collect statistics on students of immigrant-origin who hold Spanish citizenship, certain data show their presence to be significant. Indeed, in 2007, children whose mother was born abroad made up 21.4 percent of new births. From 1998 to 2005, the proportion of Spanish-speaking students from Central and South America went from 21 percent to 44.6 percent of enrolment, while North Africans saw their proportion drop from 43 percent to 27.1 percent. In the schools of Barcelona, where the use of Spanish is already more important than in the rest of Catalonia, foreign students account for 25.3 percent of the total, with a heavy concentration of Latin Americans (61 percent). The largely non-planned character of the immigration policy, on the whole, also results in foreign-born students who are poorer and less educated that native-born students. This is partly because of their parents' years of schooling and the type of jobs they have. Nonetheless, there is an inter-group difference here, too. Immigrants coming from Latin America and from the European Union, in particular, are better off, while North Africans and Africans experience very large gaps in relation to the host population.[32]

Linguistic Integration

THE DEBATE   Until recently, immigration's impact on the sociolinguistic situation was not a major issue in public debate, the public administration, or research. Foreign immigration was limited, especially in comparison with the significant presence of so-call *internal* migrants, that is, migrants from other parts of Spain. As we saw in chapter 1, they were the main focus of the public policy on language training from the beginning of the 1980s. But it is worth noting that the resistance, even avoidance, demonstrated by Catalan authorities to gathering data about language use was equally at play here. In a context where the government refused to acknowledge the existence of two distinct groups, Catalan- and Spanish-speakers, documenting the linguistic choices of third groups could be seen as leading to an undesired crystallization of inter-group boundaries.[33]

The immigration debate had long been limited to socio-economic issues, especially when the immigrants were coming from developing countries. The dominant discourse, with the exception of the right-wing People's Party, has been that of international solidarity and fighting exclusion. The necessity of newcomers learning Catalan was also brought to the fore. But various studies show that it was an objective that certain decision-makers and stakeholders were ready to set aside, if it appeared that such a requirement could be an obstacle for particularly vulnerable people. Nor had the Catalan government developed a discourse on the permanent character of the foreign presence in its territory and, in the long term, on their role in nation-building. Their linguistic use, though unfavourable to Catalan, could thus appear to be unthreatening.[34]

Nevertheless, a major turning point in recent years was the 2003 replacement of the centrist Convergència i Unió Party, in power for over twenty-five years, by a leftist coalition in which a pro-independence party, l'Esquerra Republicana, assumed the portfolios of education, immigration, and social welfare. The Citizenship and Immigration Plan of 2005 proposed a pluralistic and egalitarian society in which Catalan would represent the central vehicle for civic participation, which meant facilitating immigrants' learning and use of the language. At the same time the new Language Policy Plan gave increased importance to promoting the use of Catalan in the wider society. It was acknowledged that the results attained in language knowledge were not enough to contribute to its being a true language of communication in public life and that more evaluation studies about this were needed. The taboo surrounding the debate on linguistic use seemed to have lifted. In addition, the policy noted that promoting the use of Catalan in the immigrant population would henceforth be a major goal.[35]

These new orientations were very favourably received by the media and the public. They did not, however, generate a fundamental debate on the relationship between the maintenance of Catalan and recent immigration. By acting swiftly, the government has probably avoided any slip-up that such a debate might have generated. A certain number of issues were still debated in university and government circles, among them, the need for more control over where the immigrants came from given the recent massive arrival of Spanish-speakers or the importance of combating the concentration of the immigrant population in parts of Barcelona where Spanish, not Catalan, is the common language. In addition, in educational circles, some are beginning to question, albeit very timidly and in muted voice, the coexistence model of Catalan and Spanish in the schools, at a time when immigration is growing.[36]

However, the Catalan debate on language and immigration remains largely circumscribed by two important normative principles that have characterised language policy since its inception: first, the fact that Spanish is part and parcel of Catalan identity and, second, the complementarity of the languages, both traditional and new, which makes multilingualism highly valued. As well, since the government is only at the early stages of action as regards newcomers, and there is no evaluation data, the spirit of the moment is one of optimism.[37]

PROGRAMS AND INTERVENTIONS   Until the late 1990s, support for the linguistic and academic integration of immigrant students went through two principal avenues. First, students could be in Catalan immersion classes, which were originally created for Spanish-speakers from Spain. Then, as part of the Compensatory Education program, which mainly targeted Roma students, they benefitted from various measures to aid their learning, such as access to textbooks and educational materials adapted to their needs, or to support them in regular classes. These ad hoc arrangements, however, did not constitute a coherent whole with clear objectives. As the presence of the immigrant population increased, it is hardly surprising that these arrangements were challenged.[38]

Linguists and educational psychologists have pointed out that traditional immersion, adapted to the reality of children whose language enjoys an elevated status, does not have the same positive outcomes for disadvantaged immigrant students. The largely congruent data on the weak grasp of Catalan by newcomer students, which we will discuss below, means they are right. This is why as far back as the 1990s, certain reception classes were reserved for students of so-called "delayed incorporation," that is to say, students integrating into the school system during the course of schooling. The teaching of Catalan as a second language is carried out here in a systematic way. For students enrolled in Catalan schools as early as the primary level, the model of the more open reception class is the preferred option. These students attend the class a few hours per week, but in certain cases the reception teacher will instead offer language support within the regular class.[39]

The program of compensatory education has also been strongly criticized. It is increasingly evident that such a program cannot be the principal mode of support for the linguistic and academic integration of immigrant-origin students. The Catalan Ministry of Education confirmed this in its Action Plan for Language and Social Cohesion in the School, adopted on 2003, which turned the issue into a field for specific action.[40]

According to the document's authors, the three pillars of social cohesion are: the mastery of Catalan in a society still defined as multilingual; intercultural education; and the fight against marginalization. Linguistically, the action plan gives priority to the increase in the use of Catalan in the schools, support for learning it and using it in the family, and the creation of better adapted educational materials. All schools are henceforth required to develop a language plan that stresses sharing the Catalan language but also accords great importance to valorizing linguistic diversity and combating linguistic bias. Schools are also expected, with the help of reception class personnel, to develop a reception and integration plan for each individual newcomer that takes into account the newcomer's individual, language, social, and academic characteristics. The value of their language is to be stressed during the initial evaluation of the student with the family, but the importance of school staff addressing the students principally in Catalan is made very clear.

The Action Plan reiterates the importance of a rapid integration of the student into the regular class, especially at the primary level. At the secondary level, closed reception classes are permitted to continue, but the wish is to counter eventual segregating effects of these classes by permitting a dual registration, which favours partial integration in various subjects. In 2007–08, 24,467 immigrant-origin students – 13,636 in primary schools and 10,831 in secondary schools – benefitted from the services of 1,162 reception classes spread throughout Catalonia, while some 2,880 secondary students who were lagging far behind academically attended 360 closed special-needs classes. As well, the government recently announced important investments to train more reception-class teachers.[41]

Also, since 2003, Catalonia has implemented, again timidly, a program for teaching heritage languages involving Arabic, Romanian, Dutch, Chinese, and Amazigh (the indigenous language of North Africa), which today includes 1,845 students, mostly studying Arabic. But, it is principally by its promotion of multilingualism within regular classes, through language-awareness education, that the Catalan approach sets itself apart from the two other societies under study. As we saw in chapter 3, the new curriculum approaches the teaching of language from the perspective of complementarity, not only between Catalan and Spanish but also with the immigrant student's mother tongue. The latter's use is valued, and various activities are conducted, according to the ages of the students, to develop their metalinguistic capabilities by making them aware, for example, of lexical or syntactical elements common to the various languages or of the ways Catalan and Spanish borrowed words from other languages.[42]

The implementation of all these measures has been the subject of only a few evaluations. However, one study discovered a large variability in the reception plans for newcomers into the schools in terms of the degree of involvement, the amount of resources committed, and the approaches adopted. In addition, a recent report on the linguistic situation, despite a generally positive review, identifies a number of problems concerning language policies in the schools and the pedagogical changes connected to the new immersion approach. In the first instance, there is resistance from a few school principals who consider the promotion of Catalan as too ambitious a social goal that should not be part of their responsibilities. In the second instance, certain teachers still hesitate to take into account the linguistic diversity of the students in learning activities or evaluation.[43]

THE RESULTS   The record on the linguistic integration of newcomer students is difficult to assess. On the one hand, increased immigration and efforts to deal with it are recent and the evaluative research is still limited. On the other, the results should be analysed in light of Catalan language policies and its educational component. In the other two contexts under study, it is a question of integrating the newcomers into two distinct communities who show a strong attachment to their language and strong institutional completeness. In Catalonia, the newcomers are welcomed into common schools, nominally Catalan for the most part, but which are legally required to ensure that their students master two languages equally.

Despite this caveat, schooling in the Catalan language is an undeniable achievement. As we saw above, more than 95 percent of primary schools operate mostly in Catalan, while at the secondary level one school in two does. Spanish, although present in the rest of the schools, rarely plays the dominant role (5 percent). However, the fact of attending a Catalan-language school does not mean that the newcomer students necessarily have daily contact with native speakers. Indeed, in a recent study, even at the primary level, 38 percent of students said they had used Spanish during class activities, generally in schools where the student body is strongly Spanish-speaking. This is a common occurrence in Barcelona, where, from 1996 to 2003, the proportion of persons whose mother tongue is Catalan decreased from 44 percent to 39 percent, while the percentage of Spanish-speakers (44 percent) remained constant. This suggests a situation in which newcomers could play a key role in the linguistic balance.[44]

Still, schooling in Catalan clearly had a positive impact on immigrant students' knowledge and mastery of that language, although a number of limitations remain in this regard. An older study looking at the total foreign-born population showed that in 1996 the understanding of Catalan was generally high, varying from 90 percent among Latin American immigrants to 65 percent among African and Middle Eastern immigrants. It was, however, among children aged two to fourteen year that the knowledge of Catalan, which ranged from 60 percent and 80 percent depending on the group, was the most pronounced, thus confirming the schooling's positive impact. The ability to speak and read Catalan was somewhat mixed: the figure of 60 percent for Latin American immigrants dropped to a little over 30 percent for African and Middle Eastern immigrants. The ability to write in Catalan was weak among all groups. However, among students receiving their education in Catalan, nearly 60 percent were more competent orally in Catalan than in Spanish (30 percent). The added value of schooling on the ability to write is even more marked: the gap here is nearly 50 percentage points.[45]

However, particularly as regards the mastery of school language, an evaluation carried out among all students receiving reception services at the primary level suggests that knowledge of the Catalan language, according to the authors' terms, was only just acceptable. They are reaching the basic level set by the common European benchmark for oral and written comprehension but show weaknesses in speaking and, above all, in writing, which is likely to impede them from benefitting fully from educational activities and from being evaluated at their real skill level.[46]

The results for language use, at school and in the wider society, follow the logic of the glass being half full or half empty. They also reflect the ambiguous status of Catalan as the language of public interaction. Indeed, though the use of Catalan has progressed strongly in the public administration and in the workplace, where it respectively accounts for 97 percent and 59 percent of usage, Spanish continues to be the dominant language of inter-group exchanges in civil society. Studies carried out with samples of immigrant adults and children show that they consider Catalan to be a language useful but not indispensible to their integration process. It should be noted that there are important regional variations in this regard and that support for the Catalan language as an object of identification is higher than its use.[47]

Three recent studies by the Institute for Catalan Studies and the Sociolinguistic Centre of the University of Barcelona explored the situation in the schools. Without attempting to present a generalized portrait of the situation, the studies illustrate the importance of three factors: schooling in the Catalan language; the sociolinguistic composition of the student body; and the students' pre-migratory characteristics, including knowledge of Spanish.

Concerning the first factor, a doctoral study showed that the use of Catalan, alone or with other languages, is almost nonexistent among Japanese-speaking students of Barcelona who attend an ethno-specific school, while among their peers, educated in a public school with a large Catalan student body, 70 percent use Catalan at home and 90 percent with their friends.[48]

Two other studies look at the foreign students enrolled in the sixth year of primary school in two regions where the percentage of students whose mother tongue is Catalan is 31 percent and 83 percent respectively. This allowed researchers to identify the impact of the school sociolinguistic composition. In both cases, allophones used Catalan more than Spanish: 65.4 percent and 93 percent respectively in their class exchanges, and around 95 percent with their teachers. However, the findings were radically different when it came to the language of informal contacts. When Catalan is in a minority position in the school, Spanish alone or with other languages is the rule in more than 60 percent of the exchanges. Conversely, when Catalan is the dominant language, it prevails (more than one exchange in two), followed by Spanish among Latin American students (35.9 percent) and the language of origin (25 percent) among students who speak other languages. Among these latter students, less than 10 percent of their exchanges are in Spanish.[49]

These studies illustrate the fact that speaking Spanish before arriving in Catalonia limits the use of Catalan among Spanish-speakers, since their language already enjoys the status of a common language within Catalan society. In addition, according to another study, North African students show a stronger attachment to Catalan than to Spanish, while the inverse is true for Latin American students.[50]

It is still too early to predict what the consequences of the Catalan schooling of young allophones will be on the long-term linguistic balance. Indeed, the impact of the language policy on the practices of Catalan-speaking families is still subject to debate, even though it is clear that schooling in Catalan has had a positive effect. In 2003, for the first time in fifty years, the percentage of Catalonia's inhabitants who transmitted Catalan as the only or principal language to their children (52.7 percent) was clearly higher than the percentage of people having Catalan as their mother tongue (40.4 percent). This trend suggests that a certain number of speakers of other languages made a linguistic crossover. This is the case for Spanish-speakers, among others, who have experienced a loss of nearly 12 percent. However, these developments are still too tenuous to allow us to conclude that Catalan is reaching the status it enjoyed before the 1930s or that it bodes especially positively for the linguistic behaviour of young immigrants.[51]

Equality of Opportunity and Academic Success among Immigrant Students

Although Catalan research on this issue is little developed, there is a broad consensus on the fact that immigrant students are experiencing significant academic problems. In addition to the data on the mastery of Catalan by students in reception classes reported above, other studies dealing with more limited samples of foreign students, from the first or second generation, have suggested that they receive poorer grades in language and mathematics (a variance of 26 percent to 11 percent depending on the subject). Their rate of secondary-school graduation is clearly less: one foreign student in two receives a diploma while two-thirds of native-born Catalans do. This disadvantage was also noted in the PISA international study, where the average gap between the two groups varied by 76 points in reading comprehension and 61 points in mathematical problem-solving. In addition, a comparison done in 2003 only on mathematics ranked Catalonia fifth among countries or societies where the variance between the native and immigrant populations was highest. Only Germany, Sweden, Switzerland, and especially Belgium have more significant variances. Spain was ranked in the middle (at number 11 with 39 points of variance), which seems to confirm, as in the case of Quebec, a unique Catalan feature not necessarily sought after.[52]

The subsequent academic path of immigrant students is also problematic, as their percentage decrease through post-mandatory schooling testifies. In 2003–04, although they represented 8 percent of secondary school students, which corresponds with their percentage of the population at the time, they accounted for only 3.4 percent of bachelor-level students. Identifying the students most at risk in terms of success seems quite clear as well. Thus, according to a recent study, the rate of access to general post-secondary education for the cohort that entered secondary school in 1995, which was 66 percent for the whole of Catalonia, varied significantly depending on the group. Indeed, while it was 86.1 percent and 78.8 percent for the Chinese and Argentines, it only reached 38.1 percent and 47.8 percent for Arabs and Africans.[53]

Various explanations of why this is happening can be offered. The first is that of differences in social class and cultural capital between the native-born and the immigrant populations, and also between the subgroups themselves. The data seem to confirm this in part. Recently, however, some have questioned the importance accorded to this factor in the Catalan education debate. They point out that the immigrants' socio-economic and educational profile is far from being as negative as their academic outcomes. In fact, among persons selected or in process of regularization, the profile is higher than that of Spanish citizens. In addition, the more noticeable deficit in immigrants' results in Catalonia than in the whole of Spain suggests an attentive examination of the central role of language. In this regard, we would identify in particular the difficulty for disadvantaged immigrant families of adequately preparing their children for mandatory schooling and supporting them in it, in a context where the school language often differs not only from the family's own language but also from the dominant language of the neighbourhood they live in. Still, other analysts accord more importance to systemic factors. Indeed, despite a certain intercultural shift since 2003, adaptation to cultural diversity is still marginal in Catalan schools. The factors most often invoked in this regard are the concentration of underprivileged students in certain schools, which effectively discourages many teachers and contributes to the less positive images and expectations some of them have of immigrant students.[54]

FLANDERS

Immigration Policy and Its Impacts on the School

In Belgium, as in Catalonia, and perhaps even more so, the action of the different levels of the government in immigration matters cannot be characterized as *policy*. The federal state exercises the essential responsibilities concerning the selection and admission of newcomers by means of diverse programs linked to the issuing of visas or granting of refugee status. However, until now, its role has been rather reactive, and it has not articulated a clear vision of the objectives being pursued. Until 1974, like other European countries, Belgium was intensely involved in the recruitment of migrant workers. Once immigration was officially halted, efforts were then directed at the regularization of the foreigners who had not returned to their country of origin, the reunification of the family, and, especially, the control of the border and illegal immigration. In addition, though the Belgian government recently expressed interest in again launching a selective immigration of highly qualified workers, it has not moved resolutely in this direction, in part because of the resistance to immigration in certain parts of the country.[55]

This ambiguity also extends to the statistics on migration, which, in the opinion of many observers, are incomplete. Indeed, the data based on entries and visas do not take into account the important presence of illegal immigrants. In addition, in a context of high mobility, including immigration of European origin, the data on departures, and thus on the real migratory balance, are generally inadequate. It is estimated that over the past forty years, the entries of legal immigrants have never been less than 35,000 annually and that, since the 1990s, they have oscillated between 60,000 to more than 90,000. However, the migratory balance is clearly lower. The importance of departures is explained, in part, by the contribution of European immigration (60 percent of entries), especially from Belgium's four neighbouring countries: France, the Netherlands, the United Kingdom, and Germany. Indeed, the migration of nationals from North Africa and Turkey, and more generally, from Africa and Asia is much more permanent. As to illegal immigration, although no precise data are available, it should be noted that during the 2005 regularization campaign, 55,000 persons acquired the right of permanent residence.[56]

As a result of these limited but constant migrations, Belgium in 2007 was home to 971,448 foreigners, or about 9 percent of its population. However, this number does not include foreign-born persons who had acquired Belgian citizenship. Naturalizations have been accelerated since 2000 (following a certain liberalization). The distribution of this population is quite unequal. Foreign-born persons made up 16.6 percent of Brussels population, while it is estimated that Belgians with an immigrant background made up 10 percent. As to Wallonia and Flanders, their foreign-born population was 9.3 percent and 5.8 percent respectively.[57]

Several studies have shown that, on the whole, the foreign population is much more disadvantaged socio-economically than the Belgian population. Hence, 59 percent of persons of Turkish origin and 55.5 percent of persons of Moroccan origin live below the poverty line (as compared to 12.6 percent for total population is 12.6 percent). This negative immigrant profile affects Flanders in particular, since European immigrants concentrate in Brussels, while immigration to Wallonia is more established and thus better integrated. Until very recently, integration policies, which are essentially the responsibility of two communities and three regions, were based on social preoccupations such as access to work and the struggle against exclusion. However, in 2004, the Flemish government created the Ministry of Civic Integration and implemented the *Inburgering* (Integration) policy, where the linguistic and cultural preoccupations were paramount, even if their economic integration was stressed.[58]

In the school system, the proportion of foreign students in Flanders has remained constant for the past few years, hovering around 6 percent. However, the phenomenon is more prevalent in certain schools for two reasons: first, to date the data fail to take naturalization into account; and, second, as in the other contexts in this study, foreign-born students tend to concentrate in certain cities, in particular, Ghent and Antwerp. In addition, as the class composition of the immigrant population would suggest, these students are heavily concentrated in specifically underprivileged schools and, at least insofar as the secondary schools are concerned, in special education classes.[59]

In Brussels, multi-ethnicity is the norm rather than the exception. A recent study showed that in 2005 non-Dutch-speaking students represented respectively at the pre-school, primary, and secondary levels 34.6 percent, 30.3 percent, and 16.7 percent of students attending Dutch-language schools. This growth was dramatic since in the early 1980s the proportion of students of other languages had not even reached 5 percent. The Dutch-speaking sector is now as multicultural as its French-language counterpart, where the foreign presence is 28.4 percent. The popularity of Dutch-language schools with immigrant parents can be explained by a number of factors, including the growing sociolinguistic status of Flemish in Belgian society as a whole and the more abundant resources available to the Dutch-language schools of Brussels. In addition, many parents believe that Dutch schools will help their children become bilingual, since the teaching of French there has an excellent reputation, whereas the teaching of Dutch in the French schools is weak. The fact that the choice of a Dutch-language school at the secondary level is less popular could simply reflect the instrumental motivation of parents who want to help their children master Dutch, and not a choice about integration. However, this data could also indicate that changing attitudes on the part of the immigrant parents are recent and have not yet had the same impact at the secondary level as at the primary level.[60]

Linguistic Integration

THE DEBATE   Paradoxically, given the centrality of the role that language plays in Flemish identity, it is surprising that the public debate on immigration, until recently, has accorded so little importance to the issue. On the one hand, the opposition organized against immigration, partly under the auspices of the extreme right-wing Vlaams Blok (Flemish Bloc) party, recently renamed Vlaams Belang (Flemish Interest), tended to reject immigration wholesale as a social, economic, and identity threat rather than to develop a discourse in which the linguistic integration or non-integration of immigrants would be central. The image of "the immigrants that we would voluntarily accept if they were to learn the language" is sometimes invoked in public debate, but this is not as frequent among Flemish nationalists as among their Québécois peers. On the other hand, in centrist and left-wing political parties, the long dominant preoccupation has been with socio-economic integration and the fight against racism.[61]

Demographic and sociolinguistic realities partly explain this situation. Indeed, as we saw above, the immigrant and allophone population of Flanders is small. In addition, Flanders is a unilingual territory where Dutch is the sole language of schooling. The conflicts and anxieties about the choice of the language spoken or used for schooling, which the other two societies have experienced to some degree, are largely absent. In addition, as elsewhere in Europe, it was assumed for a long time that the presence of immigrants was temporary. Besides, in Brussels, while it may be true that the immigrant population plays a central role in the linguistic balance, the dominance of French is such that aspirations to turn Dutch into the common, public language are unlikely to be fulfilled. At the very least, one can rejoice at (or in some cases, deplore) the new attraction that Dutch-language schools are exerting on the immigrant population.[62]

For several years, however, the government has acted on linguistic integration, partly to counter the discourse of the extreme right. The Inburgering policy, adopted in 2004, is theoretically a policy of civic integration designed to allow foreigners to become acquainted with their new social environment, accelerate their access to work, and facilitate society's recognition of them as fully fledged citizens. However, the essential part of the policy has to do with the offer of Dutch courses, which also includes an initiation into the values and characteristics of Belgium and of Flanders. Language training is an obligation for all foreigners residing in Flanders for less than a year, except for the elderly, handicapped persons, and citizens of the European Union. Immigrants who have been living in Belgium for a longer time may also register for these civic integration courses, but they are not required to do so. Nor does the obligation extend to immigrants who reside in Brussels and, because the Flemish community has no jurisdiction over admission to citizenship, the penalty for persons who refuse to do language training is nothing more than an administrative fine.[63]

The Inburgering policy, especially its coercive dimension, has given rise to numerous debates. Its detractors, especially in the francophone community, have alleged that it reveals the true nature of Flemish nationalism – obsessed by linguistic and cultural survival, disrespectful of individual rights, and closed to diversity. However, its supporters, a large part of the Flemish public, argue to the contrary that this strategy should be an inspiration for all of Belgium, even of Europe. Indeed they see Inburgering as the concretization of an authentically integrative approach, which is going to allow the entire Flemish population, in the words of the government slogan, "to live together in diversity." Although this goal may still be far off, a recent analysis suggests that they are partly correct, insofar as the immigrant population's perception of the new policy and its impact on the learning of Dutch are concerned. Indeed, 80 percent of newcomers who participated in the program from 2004 to 2007 declared themselves to be very satisfied with the initiative. Of note as well is the exponential increase in the number of civic integration contracts concluded by the reception offices throughout Flanders, which were around fifteen thousand in 2008, while the number of persons learning Dutch doubled from 1999 to 2008.[64]

PROGRAMS AND INTERVENTIONS   From the early 1980s, a few initiatives to teach Dutch to newcomer students were undertaken in Flanders. However, it was not until 1991 that a structured program – the *Onthaalklas voor anderstalige nieuwkomers* (Reception Class for Non-native Speaking Newcomers), or OKAN for short – was implemented and the mid-1990s that these efforts were dissociated from aid programs to disadvantaged areas, which in Flanders were called the Equal Opportunity Program. OKAN targeted, with a few slight variations, the students with less than a year in the country, whose mother tongue was not Dutch and who lacked an adequate grasp of the language. At the primary level, the approach adopted was simple: to avoid ghettoization of the students, they were not to be separated from the other students for more than twelve hours a week. At the secondary level, however, the closed-class model dominated, for practical and pedagogical reasons. On the one hand, the students had to acquire a better grasp of Dutch and, on the other, the rapid learning pace rendered partial integration problematic. However, at both levels, the OKAN teacher is responsible for raising the awareness of the regular teachers to prioritize the students' integration after their time spent in reception class and to better understand their needs. In addition, a detailed plan of study, including a long-term integration strategy, must be created for each student. Since 2006, OKAN has developed markedly, both quantitatively and qualitatively. In 2007–08, 1,450 primary students in 133 schools, and 1,749 secondary students in 38 schools had access to these services, which cost five million euros annually. In addition, the minimum number of non-Dutch-speaking students required to justify the opening of a class was lowered.[65]

Important academic initiatives were also approved, partly through the Centrum voor taal en onderwifs (Centre for Language and Education), which developed a detailed program for secondary schools, targeting disciplinary and cross-cutting objectives such as language mastery, and social and academic participation. This centre, whose funding the Ministry of Education has recently questioned, developed many pedagogical materials based on the pragmatic international approach called "Task-Based Language Education" and conducted many training activities for both future and current teachers. Also, very recently, the Ministry of Civic Integration, in collaboration with the Ministry of Education, launched a new project proposing Dutch courses for foreign-language parents while their children are at school. Indeed, though courses offered in the context of Inburgering facilitate social integration, they do not help parents to better understand their children's academic experience or the challenges associated with it. By means of this initiative, which will be evaluated shortly, it is hoped that their participation at the school will be encouraged.[66]

However, efforts to follow up on students who had attended a reception class are seemingly less systematic. At the secondary level a support system was implemented; it is based on the presence of an animator responsible for the circulation of information about the student and for the establishment of regular contacts with his or her former reception teacher. Nonetheless, a gap remains between the OKAN program and the special measures subsequently put in place by the schools.

In Brussels and the surrounding Flemish areas, the situation is more complex, given the large number of children whose mother tongue is not Dutch and the fact that most of them are francophones, not newcomers. The primary schools receive supplementary resources that allow them to organize various services and interventions that can target both newcomers and francophones and can take different forms. At the secondary level, the so-called "Brussels curriculum" has been developed since 2004–05; it enables students to cover the first-cycle program in three years instead of two, or to adapt it by inserting more activities designed for the learning of Dutch or the promoting of multilingualism. But, unlike at the primary level, no additional resources have been made available.[67]

Dutch-language schools in Brussels also distinguished themselves by their long-standing commitment to heritage languages and cultures and, more specifically, to trilingual education. This commitment was concretized by the *Foyer* (Home) initiative implemented in 1981 with the goal of attracting allophones to Dutch-language schools. The program, which brought together Flemish students and, as the case may be, Italian, Spanish and Turkish students, is based on the model of transitional bilingual and bicultural education. The teaching of the language of origin is maximal at the preschool level and during the first two years of the primary level; it decreases gradually, starting with the second cycle of primary school, in which students from the two groups are integrated for more than 90 percent of the time. In addition to the usual subjects taught in Dutch, the students share a common teaching of French and of their language of origin. At the height of its popularity around the mid-1990s, this program was operating in nearly one-third of the Dutch-language primary schools in Brussels. However, as Dutch-language schools became more attractive to other populations, and in a context of opposition from the extreme right-wing and a large portion of the public to multilingualism, a non-official moratorium was imposed on the Foyer program's growth. But, in 2008, some five hundred students in six schools still benefitted from the program.[68]

In the whole of Flanders outside of Brussels, the traditional approach to teaching heritage language prevailed, in part through agreements with the countries of origin. In 2007, this approach was used with 2,900 students in twenty-seven primary and two secondary schools. The fact that the teachers are foreigners has had negative effects: often they did not speak Dutch and had a poor understanding of the values and characteristics of Belgium and its educational culture. In addition, they knew very little about the reality of the immigrant students they were teaching. This is why foreign embassies are now expected to recruit their teachers in Belgium. But the Flemish government has not yet taken steps, as the two other societies under study have done, to organize the teaching of heritage languages itself with a view to promoting multilingualism as an integral part of Flemish identity. Nonetheless, language awareness education, targeting all students and inspired by the European approach to language learning, is beginning to take hold in certain primary and secondary schools, especially in Brussels. In addition, six Flemish institutes of higher education are engaged in awareness-raising activities with future teachers in this area.[69]

THE RESULTS With the exception of general data pertaining to the academic success of foreign-born students, which we will discuss later, we have little that allows us to make an assessment of the linguistic integration of immigrant-origin students in Flanders or in Belgium. Concerning the mastery of Dutch, the evaluation of the OKAN program, conducted from 2003 to 2005, revealed that spending one year in a Dutch training program was not enough to allow students to enter the school system and function normally. Students suffered significant setbacks and were very often oriented toward the least prestigious academic programs.[70]

These findings prompted the authorities and a large segment of public opinion to insist that measures be taken, as was done in 2006, to strengthen the teaching of Dutch. But many analysts believe that giving the students more of the same thing will not resolve the problem. They reckon that, beyond tackling the socio-economic problems that foreign students share with other underprivileged students, schools must absolutely give better recognition to their languages and cultures of origin.[71]

The evaluation of the trilingual Foyer program, conducted in the 1990s, suggests they are partially correct. It showed that foreign students who received a trilingual education had a better command of Dutch than their peers schooled solely in that language. Nonetheless, the outcomes for allophone students continued to be inferior to those of Dutch-speaking students, even though the gap does become smaller with years of schooling. In addition, their use and appreciation of Dutch remains limited.[72]

As to this second dimension, evaluative data are desperately needed, for the whole of Flanders and for Brussels. In Flanders, academics and decision-makers largely agree that immigrant-origin students' adoption of Dutch as the language spoken at school and, in large measure, in their social life outside the family, is widespread. In this regard, 150 testimonies were presented to the Intercultural Dialogue Commission, a public consultation conducted by the federal government – a subject

we will return to in the next chapter. More than half of these testimonies, which came from associations or experts based in Flanders,
are extremely enlightening. Concerns about immigrants' knowledge
of Dutch or of their linguistic habits, both in the wider society and
in the school, were seldom expressed. There were, of course, demands for more resources to support the foreign students in their
efforts to learn the language, but no one questioned their motivation
or expressed anxiety as to their language choice in the long term. In
addition, when multilingual practices were reported, competition
with Dutch was not coming from French, which is almost absent in
Flanders, but from the immigrants' languages of origin, which play
a more or less important role depending on the families' degree of
integration or marginalization. In spite of these largely positive data,
various strategies of resistance to Dutch have been documented
among immigrant students. But these appear principally to be protests about the lower status they experience in several schools rather
than a collective social phenomenon.[73]

In Brussels, the impact of promoting the learning of Dutch on the
linguistic situation would be marginal, given the clear dominance of
French as the common language. Indeed, in Brussels 51.5 percent
have French as their mother tongue, 10.3 percent are bilingual
French-English, 9.3 percent are Dutch-speakers, 9.1 percent are bilingual French-other language, and 19.8 percent speak other languages. However, 96 percent of the city's inhabitants know French
well, while this is the case for only 31 percent insofar as Dutch is
concerned. Among allophones, the predominance of French is even
more pronounced. According to a study done in 2001, the knowledge of Dutch among the Moroccans and Turks of Brussels only
reaches 8.5 percent and 4.5 percent respectively. The percentage is
higher among Northern Europeans (19.5 percent), but this includes
many immigrants from the Netherlands and from Southern Europe
(9.3 percent). Conversely, the knowledge of French within all groups
is more than 70 percent, reaching 97.3 percent among Northern
Europeans.[74]

The impact of schooling in Dutch, which has increased only since the
late 1990s, should make itself felt within the next ten years on the respective knowledge of Dutch and French. But it is not at all certain that
there will be an effect on language use. Indeed, an important transmission of the language of origin can be observed among immigrant-
origin populations since 1980, with spouses and children, particularly

among the Turks. In addition, it is not evident that Flemish will be adopted as the language of public use, first because of the strength of French and, second, because the choice of schooling in Dutch is often limited to primary school. As well, research on linguistic identities, though sill limited, suggests that young immigrants schooled in Dutch in multilingual Brussels develop hybrid identities and show little interest in taking a position on the traditional allegiance conflict pitting francophones against Dutch-speakers.[75]

Equality of Opportunity and Academic Success among Immigrant Students

The data suggesting a significant problem of academic success among immigrant-origin students in the whole of Belgium, and in Flanders and Brussels, are largely consistent. One analysis of the evolution of the educational levels attained between the censuses of 1991 and of 2001 showed that the disparities in university access are flagrant as is the over-representation of ethnic minorities among those who did not get past the first cycle of secondary school. In the case of persons whose parents had immigrated from Turkey or Morocco, the percentages were only 3 percent and 4 percent respectively. In addition, even when they did reach the second cycle of secondary school, immigrant-origin students tended to be concentrated in the vocational sector. The profile for immigrant-origin girls is more positive on the whole, but the gap between them and native-born girls is just as important. What is more, this study, like the others, showed that the cultural and educational capital of the families did not entirely explain the disparity. Indeed, even when the social class and educational level of the parents in 1991 are taken into account, an unexplained ethnic residual, particularly apparent in Flanders, remains, including for the Turkish minority. Possible explanations for this include the pronounced residential segregation of this population and its particularly weak grasp of French or Dutch.[76]

Several phenomena at the origin of these problematic findings have been identified. First of all, a study conducted in Brussels showed that 37.3 percent of students who spoke a language other than Dutch at home suffered an academic setback at the time of entering the second cycle of secondary school, while this was the case for only 11.8 percent of Dutch-speaking students. In addition, the concentration of foreign populations on the sidelines is prevalent.

According to some observers, this is explained by a tendency to underestimate the competencies of immigrant students at the time of orientation and placement, when the parents are most often poorly informed and ill-equipped to point out the interests of their children. In addition, the more prestigious schools employ diverse strategies for attracting the most desirable students, who usually belong to the majority group and the privileged class, to the detriment of immigrant or disadvantaged families.[77]

However, the negative academic mobility of immigrant students in Belgium and Flanders is also explained by deficiencies in their knowledge and skills. This was revealed by the PISA study of 2003, and its controversial findings stirred up a heated national debate. Indeed, Belgium was one of three countries where the gap between students of the second generation or beyond and first-generation students was the highest, as much in mathematics and science as in reading and writing. In addition, when the two communities are compared, it was noted that even if the Dutch schools were getting far better results than the French schools, the gap between native-born students and first- or second-generation students was always greater in Flanders. The gap was 122 points in mathematics, 102.5 in reading, and 115 in science.[78]

The pecking order of academic success in Flanders largely reflects the socio-economic inequality existing globally and locally. It is essentially the North Africans, the Africans, and, above all, the Turks who are weak in mathematics and reading. However, paradoxically, the scores for the North Africans in reading are better in Flanders than in the French community. This could be linked to the socio-economic characteristics of this group in Flanders or to the particular relationship they are developing with the Dutch language, which they have to learn and for which they receive help to do so, but which is not the case, mutatis mutandis, for French in the other school system.

Also, linear regression analysis showed that the language spoken at home, the parents' education, and the type of school attended played an important role in academic success. Nonetheless, even after these factors are taken into account, the impact of origin remains a very important variable. According to the authors, this variable points toward the existence of diverse systemic factors, such as concentration in certain schools, differential access to the top schools, or differentiated expectations on the part of the teachers.[79]

The findings described above in large part seem to justify the relevance of Flanders's approach to combating academic failure since the mid-1990s, even if it has yet to bear fruit in an obvious way. The policy of equal opportunity, confirmed by order-in-council in 2002, in fact has two components. The first, the fight against ethnic concentration, ensures that all parents have access to the school of their choice and that the different school authorities and principals work together to harmonize their strategies for attracting and retaining a diverse student population. The second, the addition of supplementary resources to schools beset by academic and social problems, enables the schools to put in place various measures (to which we will return in the next chapter) that, among other things, foster their adaptation to cultural diversity. However, a study conducted in 2002 showed that the program was suffering from a lack of precise quantitative goals and a tendency to define the educational problems of immigrant students mostly in terms of the language gap. Other measures have also been implemented following the shockwave caused by the PISA findings, including the intensification of cooperation between the family and the school, the establishment of tutorial programs for immigrant students, integrated into teacher training, and, finally, an intensification of teaching Dutch to preschoolers.[80]

THE BALANCE SHEET: COMMON ELEMENTS AND UNIQUE FEATURES

As one can see from this brief overview, the school systems of a society where the status of the majority language is ambiguous face significant challenges with respect to linguistic integration and equal opportunity for immigrant-origin students.

In the case of linguistic integration, fragile majorities must first decide if they want to impose common schooling and the sharing of their language or, on the contrary, respect the freedom of parents and students who are often drawn to the other language. In the three societies under study, the use of a certain amount of coercion was favoured. This seems to be the choice, especially when certain factors are present, including the importance of immigration, the degree to which the majority language can realistically aspire to be the language of public use, and, lastly, the central role that allophones play in overall language equilibrium. However, various constitutional provisions can limit the actions of public authorities, as the case of Brussels illustrates. In addition, the need to adopt policies aimed specifically at the schooling choices of immigrant populations imposes itself less when the school system as a whole is not structured as two subsystems.

Once the question of integration in common structures is settled, so to speak, the challenge of ensuring the knowledge, mastery, and use of the language remains unresolved. Our analysis of the three societies illustrates the importance of their investment in the development of programs and interventions targeting allophone students, though to various degrees depending on the history and size of immigration. Universal access to linguistic services and the subsequent follow-up of allophone students seems better insured than in societies of single ethnic dominance. In addition, the expansion of interventions and initiatives supports the development of targeted educational strategies, teacher training, and relations with parents. Still, whether the reception models are old or recent, the three societies experienced the same debates on the desirable balance between specific services and direct integration into regular classes as well as on the place of heritage languages. The reaction to this latter challenge suggests that no unique feature exists. There was as much resistance to this in Quebec and Flanders as there was openness in Brussels and, to a lesser degree, in Catalonia. Fears linked to the fragility of the host language seem to play out in a contradictory way depending on the persons and the place. Still, contexts where the attraction of the allophone community to the schools of the majority is not a sure thing are favourable to the implementation of programs that valorize multilingualism.

With regard to results, assessment in these three societies with a fragile majority is mixed. As to the allophone populations' knowledge of the language, the three educational systems studied largely reach their objectives or, at least, do not experience problems different from those in simpler sociolinguistic contexts. However, the specific mastery of school language has led to more debates. Several indicators suggest that the levels attained are often inadequate to enable the pursuit of educational opportunities or entry into job sectors where language proficiency is high. It is still difficult to identify to what extent these problems are shared with all immigrant-receiving societies, or if they are experienced in a particular way because of the additional obstacle that schooling in a less prestigious language or simultaneous learning in two languages represents for immigrant-origin students. Certain factors would argue in favour of the first response, among these, the significant impact of socio-economic status on academic success. This holds for societies like Belgium and Catalonia, where the link between immigration and poverty is tight, and for societies like Quebec, where it is not. The Quebec context illustrates well to what degree the cultural capital of families, and not the linguistic proximity of their maternal language to French, conditions the academic results and careers of their children.

The large international surveys, among them the PISA study, have demonstrated the existence of a larger disparity between immigrant populations and native-born students in Quebec, Catalonia, and Flanders than is the case in the rest of Canada, Spain, and Belgium respectively. It is critically important to understand better the causes of this specifically negative profile that the three societies share, although their overall results, which are more influenced by the selective nature of their immigration policies and the dynamism of their interventions, are very different. This requirement is very important, because these three societies have been slow to pay proper attention to immigrant students' equality of opportunity and academic success. In Catalonia and Flanders this wait-and-see policy can be mostly explained by the relatively recent nature of significant immigration levels. In Quebec, the priority given to the francophone community's historical catching up on schooling seems to be the issue. But, in all cases, there is awareness of these issues, and interventions are now well underway.

Another complex issue, and largely specific to societies of ambiguous ethnic dominance, is the impact of host language instruction on the linguistic habits of students, in the short and medium term. It is often this objective, implicit or explicit, that most interests decision-makers and the general public who worry about the survival of a fragile community. But it is also the dimension on which public action has the least control. Indeed, with the exception of a few guidelines that can be imposed in the classroom, personal freedom prevails, in both the schools and the wider society. In this regard, the comparison illustrates two paradoxical realities. On the one hand, the results attained are generally satisfactory or, at the least, clearly more favourable than the alarmist discourse, constantly revived and fed by various fantasies, would lead us to believe. The use of French, Catalan, and Flemish these past twenty years has grown significantly in immigrant-origin populations, especially among the young. This progress is largely explained by a better knowledge and a stronger valuing of these languages as a result of schooling. However, the sociolinguistic dynamic of the regions or cities concerned, and even that of specific schools, continues to play an important role in the linguistic choices of young immigrants. On the other hand, this growth in the use of the host language by newcomers is far from leading to the unilingualism that some of its supporters were hoping for. The three societies under study are becoming multilingual, even more so than in societies of single ethnic dominance. Competition between the languages seems to strengthen attachment to and use of the language of origin. In addition, whether or not the government wants a balanced bilingualism, it is clearly a key objective for immigrant families.

For fragile majority societies, the achievement of their goal of linguistic integration thus supposes a redefinition of the connections between knowing and speaking the language, on the one hand, and individual and collective identity, on the other. And they are more or less prepared to do this. The dominance of traditional cleavages in the ongoing linguistic debate in each society testifies to this. The replacement of generations will doubtless have an effect in this regard, but it is still too early to say exactly what it will be. In addition, the achievements and obstacles related to linguistic integration, equality of opportunity, and the valuing of pluralism influence each other in a reciprocal and dynamic way. Hence this fourth chapter, far from ending with a definite conclusion, instead leads into the debate that will be the topic of the fifth and final chapter – the relevance and limits of institutional adaptation to diversity.

5

Adaptation to Diversity: A "Normal" Discrepancy among Normative Models, Practices, and Public Debate?

Following initial integration, equal participation by immigrant-origin populations in the host society entails, to a certain extent, the pluralist transformation of that society. Indeed, if newcomers fully exercise their citizenship, they will necessarily have an impact on the nature of the institutions that welcome them. What is more, to be more effective and inclusive, these institutions will often be involved, on their own initiative, in various forms of adaptation to cultural, linguistic and even religious diversity.[1]

Educational institutions are no exception to this rule. The normative positioning of most modern societies in favour of parental participation and accountability to the public leads to the constant redefinition of academic goals, programs, and practices and their adaptation to specific milieus. The degree to which native-born and immigrant populations are involved equally in the social debate about education and in the schooling of their children constitutes a central challenge in immigrant-receiving countries. In addition, educational activity supposes taking into account the multiple dimensions that influence the personality of the student and his or her integration into the school. In this regard, though the culture of origin should not be treated as a thing unto itself, nor considered a static reality, as social psychologists and sociologists of ethnicity remind us, it cannot be ignored by decision-makers or teachers either.[2]

The development of programs, the conception of educational materials, the training of teachers, the implementation of teaching and training strategies, and the definition of school norms and regulations – these are some of the activities that the new need for relevance and adaptation to the characteristics of a diverse population demand. Making a normative decision about the desirable model for balancing unity and diversity is thus called for, and not just in the schools "affected," as is often said rather negatively, by diversity, but in all schools. For what kind of society are these future citizens of tomorrow being prepared? What role will be played by the languages, cultures, and religions traditionally associated with the majority group and, on the contrary, those of the new immigrant groups? What principles will guide relations between citizens and newcomers, and how students are to be prepared? No immigrant-receiving country can avoid such a debate, which generally elicits more passion than when it is simply a question of encouraging the adaptation of schools to their specific milieu.[3]

In societies where the status of the majority is or was fragile, this question about which model of citizenship and relation to the diversity to promote can be complex. It touches upon identity, and we have seen how the attempt to revisit history and the relationship to the majority Other can create resistance. The relationship to immigrants and to their contribution, however, could be different. In a context where schools are competing for third-party allegiance and sometimes even poaching ethnic students, adaptation to their needs and realities could be considered the best strategy in the national interest, leading to a stronger consensus than would be the case in a simple majority society. Still, whether public attitudes are positive or negative, the complexity of taking into account linguistic, cultural, and religious diversity in the field will not be reduced, and a discrepancy with normative positioning can thus be expected.[4]

In this chapter, as in the preceding one, we will restrict ourselves to the three societies where immigration is important enough that public programs, social debate, and academic activity have developed significantly: Quebec, Catalonia, and Flanders. Indeed, though the government of Northern Ireland has over the past few years developed a relatively coherent discourse on openness to ethnocultural diversity and the fight against racism, both in society and the school, these issues have hardly affected most Northern Irish schools. The three societies under study are distinguished by the central role that immigration plays in the question of identity. This is reflected in their investment in developing a coherent discourse in this regard, the significant efforts made to adapt their schools to cultural and religious diversity, and the extent of evaluation research conducted on these issues.

Three dimensions are considered, to the degree that data are available in each context. First, we look at the official position taken that defined the relation to diversity promoted in the society and the school, mostly in the form of intercultural education policies. Second, we try to identify to what extent the official orientations concerning general guidelines and specific school practices were communicated in the field. Finally, we pose questions about the presence or absence of a more or less heated public debate on the transformation in progress. Based on these three analyses, we conclude by examining the question that serves as the title of this chapter: is there a discrepancy between rhetoric, practice, and public debate, to various degrees, in each of the three societies? We will also try to discern if adaptation to pluralism in the schools of fragile majority societies is unique or, to the contrary, is part of the logic common to all immigrant-receiving societies.

QUEBEC

Interculturalism and Intercultural Education: A Long-Standing Normative Commitment

From the late 1970s, following the reaffirmation of its status as a majority and of its commitment to increased immigration, the francophone community had to define its normative position in the face of the increased pluralism of public institutions and civil society. The Quebec discourse on this subject can be seen as a third way between Canadian multiculturalism and French Jacobinism. The former is criticized for essentializing cultures and isolating them one from the other. The latter, by relegating diversity to the private sphere, is hardly compatible with the normative ideal of acknowledging pluralism, which has been promulgated in Quebec since the Quiet Revolution.[5]

In the 1980s, following the publication of the white paper entitled *The Quebec Cultural Development* and *So Many Ways to Be a Quebecer: Action Plan for Cultural Communities*, the existence of a relatively homogeneous francophone culture distinct from that of other groups was assumed. The emphasis was on intercultural rapprochement between persons whose belonging to distinct groups was taken for granted. A culture of convergence based on the centrality of francophone culture, traditional and modern, was expected to be enriched by the contributions of the cultural communities.[6]

With the adoption in 1990 of the *Policy Statement on Immigration and Integration*, there began to emerge a greater recognition of identity miscegenation, or blending, as a consequence of the changes of the 1980s. Pluralism is thus presented as a fundamental characteristic of Quebec culture and its expression as a right from which Quebecers of all origins can benefit. However, everyone must respect common limits, including the need for inter-community sharing and respect for fundamental democratic values. Equality of the sexes, respect for the rights of children, nonviolence, and the societal choices of Quebec are specifically named. The statement also supports the equal participation and contribution of all citizens, particularly those of immigrant origin.[7]

The *Policy Statement on Immigration and Integration* has remained the official position of successive governments to the present day, though several aspects of it have been debated and contested, especially by nationalists. Indeed, many feel that citizenship cannot rest solely on social participation and equality, but requires the identification of non-negotiable elements that go beyond the general principles of liberal democracy. The Parti Québécois, in power from 1995 to 2003, tried unsuccessfully to create consensus around a new Quebec approach to civic relations more influenced by the French republican model. The Liberal government, which returned to power in 2003, systematically avoided taking a position on identity issues, at least until the major social debate that Quebec experienced in 2007 forced it to drop its wait-and-see approach.[8]

In the schools, despite the many initiatives introduced since the adoption of Bill 101, it was not until 1998 that the Minister of Education made public the *Policy Statement on Educational Integration and Intercultural Education*, in which the relation to diversity was clearly laid out. Along with the general principles of the *Statement* of 1990, intercultural education is defined as knowing how to live together in a francophone, democratic, and pluralistic society. The normative valorization of taking diversity into account is significant, and the limits in this regard are virtually identical: the protection of students' individual rights, the functionality of the schools, and the linguistic choices of Quebec. The document sets itself apart by its complex treatment of the concept of culture. Teachers are encouraged not to focus on the cultural difference in isolation but to consider its origin as one of the factors that can influence integration and academic success. In addition, although the "we/they" division is still perceptible, diversity is generally discussed as a characteristic of the student population, though the specificity of homogeneous regions is recognized.[9]

The policy emphasizes three challenges to intercultural education. First, to increase the representation of ethnocultural diversity in the different job categories, it proposes an active strategy of promoting the teaching profession to cultural communities and of supporting universities in the recruitment of candidates from these communities. Second, as regards the initial and in-service training of teachers, the orientations and actions are located in the context of past activities, that is to say, to make proposed sensitization to these challenges mandatory in the universities and to promote the establishment of an exchange network and peer-training for practicing teachers. The third orientation has sparked much debate. The original statement, which postulated that openness to ethnocultural, linguistic, and religious diversity should be reflected throughout the curriculum and life at school, was modified after consultation. The final statement now stresses that the heritage and common values of Quebec, in particular, openness to ethnocultural, linguistic, and religious diversity should be reflected throughout the curriculum and life at school. This tension between common values and recognition of diversity can also be seen throughout the document, which was subject to a largely cosmetic rewriting to respond to the particular sensibilities of the more nationalistic element in society.

Although the *Policy Statement on Educational Integration and Intercultural Education* was adopted more than ten years ago, governmental discourse has been neither questioned nor updated. The principles put forth continue to guide the action of the ministry and to influence significantly that of the school boards where the majority of immigrant-origin students are concentrated. Thus, the policy of the Montreal School Board, adopted after a wide consultation in 2007, substantially reflects the same search for balance between the promotion of French, the participation and success of students from all backgrounds, and the development of a concept of a pluralist society where the status of the majority and minority cultures is fluid (some would say ambiguous) enough to create a consensus on both sides. However, the adoption of the policy at a time when a major academic reform was mobilizing most of the public interest, along with material and human resources, limited its visibility. In addition, while this was meant to extend concern about diversity into areas where it was not experienced on a daily basis, the record is limited. In ten years, only six school boards outside of Montreal have adopted a policy of intercultural education, and, in the main, these were not in homogeneous milieus but in areas where diversity became a fact of life because of urban sprawl and a certain regionalization of immigrants.[10]

The 2000s witnessed the development of an original Quebec position on secularity and religious diversity. As we saw earlier, after the deconfessionalization of the schools in 1998, the place of religion in schools and curricula arose in acute form. Indeed, although the structures now respected the principle of neutrality, Catholicism and Protestantism were the only religious perspectives taught and so retained their privileged status. Students of other religious persuasions had to content themselves with so-called *moral* education. After examining four options – the maintenance of the status quo, multiconfessional education, no religious education, and the cultural, non-proselytizing teaching of the principles of religion – a governmental committee struck by the minister recommended, in 2000, the fourth option. However, the Proulx Report, named after the president of the committee, was poorly received or, at least, was met with organized opposition from pressure groups mobilized in favour of Catholic education, especially in the regions. This is why the government pushed back its decision for five years and created the Committee on Religious Affairs, with the mandate to continue looking into the matter.[11]

Through its various *Avis* (Advice), there emerged the broad principles of the Quebec model of open secularism: a conception of the neutrality of the public school based on equal treatment of all religions and not to their confinement to the private sphere, a respect for freedom of conscience and the religion of the students, including their right not to believe, which includes the right to display their beliefs in the public school, and the commitment of the schools to support the students' spiritual journey. The Committee also contributed to the reflection on the showing of religious signs and symbols at school. For minority students, its contribution follows upon the benchmarks established by the Policy of 1998, which it further developed and supported with concrete examples. However, its contribution is much more innovative when it comes to the place of majority religious symbols in public institutions, an issue that took on great importance in the 2000s. The perspective proposed is not to exclude from academic practices and activities the cultural aspects of majority religions, for example, feast days and their accompanying symbols or works of art, but to remain vigilant that the teacher does not engage in any proselytization when dealing with these themes. In other words, students who are nonbelievers or adherents of other religions do not have the right to avoid exposure to religious or philosophical content that differs from what they believe, but they can be assured that this will be done in a way that respects their freedom of conscience.[12]

Formal Programs and Interventions

In terms of structural interventions, significant advances initiated by the Ministry of Education and its school board partners should be noted in four areas: the development of more inclusive study programs; the production of teaching materials free from bias and reflecting diversity; the initial training and further education of teachers in intercultural matters; and support for school-team members in dealing with issues such as parental participation, the management of value conflicts, and relations with students.

An analysis of Quebec's primary and secondary education program thus showed that the points of entry for intercultural, antiracist, or citizenship education were numerous, both in the general orientations and in the detailed description of the competencies, training areas, and learning content of the various disciplines. It is in the field of Citizenship and Community Life, which covers the teaching of geography, history, and citizenship education, where one finds the largest number of commitments to diversity education. These include: respecting the Other in their differences; welcoming diversity; maintaining egalitarian relationships; and rejecting all forms of exclusion. This is embodied in a number of key concepts such as involvement, cooperation, solidarity, contributing to a culture of peace, sensitivity to the negative consequences of stereotypes, and learning peaceful management of power relations. Other general fields, such as the media, the environment, and consumer behaviour include elements linked to intercultural education, such as awareness of the interdependence of peoples and the consequences of globalization on the distribution of wealth or the ability to recognize stereotypical media messages. Input to intercultural education also passes through three cross-cutting skills: exercising one's critical judgement, which gives priority to the recognition of prejudices and the importance of putting one's opinions into perspective; structuring one's identity, which calls students to recognize their rootedness in their own culture and to welcome the culture of others; and, finally, cooperation, which rests on respect for differences, a sensitive presence to the Other, and constructive openness to pluralism and nonviolence. Finally, the authors noted that the Quebec program does not use the concept of anti-racist education, but that it prescribes a pedagogy based on equality and the awareness of discriminatory attitudes and behaviours, allowing students to be exposed, though in a still too limited way, to minority and non-Western ways of knowing.[13]

Since this analysis was completed, the government was also involved in the development of a program on ethics and religious culture launched in 2008, which replaced the former confessional education. This program touches on one of the essential dimensions of intercultural relations: interreligious relationships. Throughout their school career, although the focus is on Judeo-Christian and aboriginal traditions, the students will have the opportunity to be exposed to other world religions, such as Islam, Buddhism, Hinduism, and Sikhism. The program has two complementary goals: first, to foster the recognition of all students in their belonging or not belonging to a religious tradition and, second, to promote the sharing of values and community projects in a pluralistic society. Students will learn to reflect on ethical questions, to show an understanding of the religious phenomenon, and, finally, to dialogue with persons who do not necessarily share their beliefs.[14]

To give flesh to such ambitious programs, it was necessary to produce teaching materials free of bias and adequately reflective of diversity. In this regard, Quebec's experience, though not without limitations, is testimony to a positive evolution. Since 1982, there has been a process in place to approve teaching materials designed to assure the nondiscriminatory representation and treatment of persons belonging to ethnocultural minorities. The goal of ensuring a quantitative presence and of eliminating explicit stereotypes was rapidly achieved by the late 1980s. From that time on, it was the qualitative treatment of diversity that became the challenge;

specifically, omissions and ethnocentric bias in textbooks. Indeed, several studies conducted in the 1990s showed that though the textbooks generally valorized cultural diversity, it was often presented in a folkloric fashion and foreign to their intended readership. The contribution of minority groups to Quebec society also received short shrift. Likewise, certain areas of non-Western civilization, among them the Arab-Muslim, were presented in a stereotypical fashion. Although there are no general studies on the evolution of the treatment of cultural, religious, and ethnic diversity in the educational materials developed following the reform, an analysis of history textbooks reveals an increased inclusion of non-Western societies and cultures internationally, and of aboriginal cultures and immigrant groups nationally.[15]

Concerning Islam, the Muslim world, and the Muslims of Quebec and Canada, an exhaustive study of some two hundred textbooks published since 2001 in various disciplines at the primary and secondary levels showed noticeable progress in comparison with the textbooks from the 1990s. Thus, the description of Islam as a religion is clearly more complex, and the contribution of Muslim civilization to world heritage is better recognized. The Crusades and decolonization are treated in a much more balanced fashion, and students have access to a variety of perspectives. Also evident is an increase in the number of Muslim child characters and, more generally, of immigrant children, in the extracts from works of fiction, which are used in the French textbooks and which often prompt reflection on intercultural relations, both nationally and internationally. Certain limitations persist, however, including a focus on issues that are either problematic, such as the lack of human rights, or exotic, such as life in the desert. In addition, if the Muslim community of Quebec has found its way into the textbooks, it is almost exclusively for its contribution to Montreal gastronomy or through the debate over reasonable accommodation and the wearing of the veil! The study's authors also concluded that the new programs have had a positive impact. The improvements are found above all in the disciplines where the treatment of Islam, the Muslim world, or of Muslims in Quebec and Canada is required; but, when the inclusion of such topics is incidental, the biases and omissions are more pronounced.[16]

Advances in the area of training and further education are more modest. Since 1995, the Ministry of Education made intercultural sensitization a requirement of initial training programs. In the ministry's publication *Core Professional Competencies for the Teaching Profession*, at least three competencies include components of an intercultural or anti-racist perspective: transforming the classroom into a cultural place open to a plurality of perspectives in a shared living space; taking into consideration social differences (gender, ethnic origin, and culture) in the development of teaching-learning situations; and, finally, avoiding all forms of discrimination in regard to students, parents, and colleagues. Montreal's two French-language universities adopted policies on adaptation to cultural diversity, which include aspects that relate to teacher training. In addition, they offer a number of mandatory courses on ethnic diversity, inequality, and discrimination and the development of an adapted pedagogy. Other courses, for example, on history instruction or the teaching of French to allophones, approach these issues without making them the main point. However, there is wide agreement, supported by a few studies, that this effort is inadequate or, at least, that its impact on future teachers is not always conclusive. First, the students perceived a lack of connection between theme courses and courses based on psychopedagogical or disciplinary competencies, which they consider more important. Second, the competencies in intercultural matters were not always passed on as part of their placements, including when the host teacher had a more traditional or assimilationist vision of the school's role.[17]

Otherwise, actions intended to increase the representation of minorities in the teacher training faculties and, in the long term, within the ranks of teachers in the school boards, are beginning to bear fruit. This positive development can be explained, in part, by the efforts of certain schools to update plans for equal access in the area of recruitment or employment. However, it is also due to major changes, such as the massive departure of teachers through retirement and the shortage this created, and the increasingly important presence of qualified francophones among recent immigrants.[18]

The Ministry of Education, the school boards, the Human Rights and Youth Commission, and community organizations also offer upgrading courses for practicing teachers. These deal with such topics as intercultural communication, intervention in multi-ethnic schools, and reasonable accommodation. However, none of this training is mandatory. Some people are critical, arguing that these courses appeal mostly to the converted who are already making significant efforts to adapt to diversity. In addition, the popularity of intercultural upgrading will have decreased in ten years or so, in part because of the sentiment of déjà vu and the aging of the teaching population, although there is a certain growth in demand in the outlying regions.[19]

Finally, the support offered to multi-ethnic schools on issues such as parental participation, the management of value conflict, and intercultural relations among students needs to be highlighted. Each year the Ministry of Education finances from two hundred to four hundred projects in twenty-five school boards that, in addition to valorizing French and helping with the schooling of seriously academically delayed students, may concern the partnership of intercultural rapprochement and school, family, and community. Likewise, through programs intended for underprivileged areas – *New Approaches, New Solutions* and *The Montreal School* – various efforts to foster the participation of immigrant parents and the establishment of a dialogue transcending the barriers of language and culture have been initiated. In addition, a spiritual animation and community involvement service, which replaced the traditional pastoral service in all Quebec schools, now plays an important role in intercultural matters. A recent report indicated that many facilitators experience difficulties in clearly defining their role of spiritual animation. They give priority to their community animation mandate. Although they consider themselves inadequately trained to do this, they get significantly involved in extracurricular activities of an intercultural or interreligious nature and in the daily negotiation of tensions that can emerge among students under the pretext or because of differences. As well, they help teachers to better understand religious questions.[20]

For several years the ministry has also been supporting principals in coming to decisions about requests for exemptions from school norms and practices by parents or students belonging to religious or cultural minorities. A training module that permits educational administrators to develop knowledge and competencies regarding the *why, how far*, and *how* of taking religious and cultural diversity into account was developed since 1994. This training, under the auspices of the ministry, school boards, or nongovernmental organizations, involved more than five hundred school principals in the 1990s. More recently, the ministry updated the module to take into account the evolution of jurisprudence and school legislation, intending to launch an enhanced training program on this development. These initiatives are part of the recommendations contained in the report by the Advisory Committee on Integration and Reasonable Accommodation in the Schools (a topic we will return to below), which brought together some twenty representatives from different governmental, quasi-public, and professional organizations involved in education. The report includes a number of guidelines, which largely take up and support the points put forth in the *Policy Statement on Educational Integration and Intercultural Education*, while proposing a structured approach that administrators can use to resolve value conflicts. Based on this report, which was endorsed by the minister in November 2007, the ministry committed itself to developing a practical guide to be distributed in all schools and to creating a referral centre that staff may contact when they have disputes to resolve with families.[21]

Practices in the School

What is happening in the field – in schools and classrooms? An assessment is difficult to make and, without doubt, quite complex. First, there are few large-scale studies, though the ones we have paint a rather favourable picture. Second, a number of studies focusing on specific schools or small samples reveal indifference or resistance among certain teachers as well as tensions among students or between the school and its surroundings.

The first point that emerges is that of a proliferation of activities intended to better adapt the school to its surroundings, particularly though not exclusively, in multi-ethnic environments. For example, according to a survey of Quebec school principals, more than 25 percent stated they had implemented various initiatives in this regard. They also reported more than one thousand examples of successful practices, citing as examples the organization of twinning between francophone parents and allophone newcomers, the translation of a code of conduct into several languages, the organization of weekly meetings with members of ethnocultural communities, and the development of teaching tips on immigration and different cultures. In the area of religion, certain feast days are highlighted, Ramadan is taken into account by adapting the required schoolwork on a case-by-case basis, or students as a whole are allowed to have a meeting place, without assigning one to each religious group. The inquiry also shows that adaptation requests have remained stable for three years and that the schools are not completely defenceless in the face of pressure from communities or parents. Half the requests were accepted, a little less than a quarter were refused, and in slightly more than a quarter alternate solutions were found. In addition, despite the widespread stereotype, they did not come exclusively from newcomers or Muslims. In fact, they were distributed rather equally between Christians and Jehovah's Witnesses, who were generally long settled, and Muslims.[22]

Another study, cited above, surveyed more than twenty programs that promote intercultural and anti-racist activities in a significant number of schools on the Island of Montreal. We should highlight, at the primary level, the program called To the Pacific, which offers strategies for young people to resolve conflicts, including inter-ethnic and racial conflicts, and, at the secondary level, The Caravan of Tolerance, which helps students identify situations of prejudice and racism. The Action Week against Racism and the Quebec Citizenship Week are also occasions for awareness-raising and youth involvement. As well, still according to the same study, nearly half of the conduct codes of francophone secondary schools on the island of Montreal include points related to shared citizenship.[23]

However, taking diversity in Quebec schools into account is not always smooth sailing; rather, it is a work in progress, where advances and retreats are numerous, as are anxieties and tensions. Several communities harbour fears about the impact of adapting to diversity. In the short term, concerns are expressed about the potential contradictions between certain accommodations and legal requirements about school attendance, programs, and security. There are also questions about the long-term impact of certain exemptions on common values, social cohesion, and the future participation of minority young people. In Quebec as elsewhere, over the last few years, the lightning rod for concern over identity has been the Muslim, for whom adaptation to the common values promoted by the school is often considered problematic. Nonetheless, despite their high visibility in the debate, it is not evident that Muslim parents are the ones who experience particularly problematic relations with the school. Indeed, more than any other factor, socio-economic status influences the models of collaboration that develop between the school and immigrant families. Families with high socio-cultural capital, who are generally North African, are highly mobilized for the academic success of their children and participate actively in the school, sometimes to contest its practices but more often because they value its openness. The most underprivileged families also speak favourably about the reception they receive at the schools, although they prefer to participate indirectly by means of community organizations. These organizations help them to understand the school culture and its requirements or to obtain services for their children. In all cases, however, the non-mastery of French is an aggravating factor, which, once again, leaves North African parents in a rather favourable position toward the school.[24]

Concerning pedagogical and extracurricular practices, research reveals a certain indifference, even resistance, to the intercultural perspective. Thus, according to a study conducted on a large sample of francophone respondents in Montreal, Toronto, and Vancouver, the teachers' main priority was the integration of the students into the culture of the school so as to ensure their academic success. Differences are often implicitly acknowledged by the teachers, who adapt their teaching strategies to the students' characteristics, but rarely explicitly by a change to the curriculum and course content. As to anti-racist interventions, they involve crisis management and timely conflict resolution. When systemic dimensions are discussed, the focus is often on what happens elsewhere in the world rather than in Quebec or in the school. Many of these observations apply to all multi-ethnic societies. But other research reveals a unique feature of minorities, or fragile majorities, in what the Quebec teachers were saying. There is the persistence of an "us/them" division opposing, implicitly or explicitly, French Canadians/Quebecers to foreigners/immigrants. Likewise, adaptation to diversity is experienced as a threat to traditional Quebec identity among a minority of respondents, although they often also invoke a civic discourse that stresses the defence of values such as equality of the sexes or democracy.[25]

Paradoxically, the observation of class practices showed a significant number of activities valorizing pluralistic citizenship. Two logics seem to be at work here: one in which the teachers essentially position themselves as citizens and another in which their professional identity prevails. In four Montreal schools observed in 1999, primary-school teachers largely dealt with the laws and issues having to do with intercultural relations in the classroom, while secondary-school teachers addressed world inequality, the peaceful management of conflict, and the cooperation needed in all parts of society. Likewise, extracurricular activities included many innovative experiments fostering intercultural rapprochement, student participation in defining their school's code of conduct, and their involvement in the transformation of their immediate community. However, these practices were not without ambiguity. For example, researchers observed some stigmatization of minority students during discussion about the absence of human rights internationally, and the difficulty that teachers had, when dealing with inequality and differences, to take into account the dynamics of pedagogical relations in their classroom.[26]

Studies of youth confirm this observation about the glass being half empty or half full. Thus, a somewhat dated study of 10,800 young Montrealers found that they largely shared the same values of what could be called liberal individualism and democratic egalitarianism. They identified first and foremost as youth and they took a critical distance from their parents' values, especially in the area of inter-ethnic relations. In addition, immigrant-origin students expressed strong feelings of belonging to Quebec society, though less strong than that of third-generation students. Likewise, a more recent study of conceptions of citizenship among young immigrants and Quebecers found that the convergences in the definition of citizenship and priority social problems were clearly more important than the divergences. The values of tolerance, liberty, and social solidarity are widely shared by the two groups, who also valorize education against prejudice and the implementation of intercultural rapprochement projects. In addition, where differences do exist, they come more from socio-economic status than from ethnicity. Moreover, other studies showed resistance to us/them divisions among the children of Bill 101 as well as the persistence of ethnic markers in defining certain conflicts in the school. However, these divisions seem to be decreasing, especially in Montreal, where the extremely multi-ethnic character of the schools, paradoxically, fosters shared citizenship.[27]

The absence of pronounced conflict between young francophone Quebecers of long-standing and immigrant-origin youth at school, and the generally positive assessment of the latter about their schooling, does not mean that the implicit desire of many Bill 101 supporters to turn them into Quebecers first and foremost has been realized. Several studies show that Quebec identity remains weaker than Canadian identity among the children of Bill 101. Nationalist spokespersons believe that this situation stems from the ambiguity of Quebec's current status and can only be resolved by attaining independence. However, other explanations have been advanced.

Canadian identity could be positively associated with openness to accommodations and with cultural and linguistic diversity, while Quebec identity continues to be associated exclusively with French-Canadian heritage. Some youth who live in French, who share many characteristics of Quebec culture, and who know no other province but Quebec, have adopted a Canadian identity because it seems to them to be more civic and thus more likely to include them than the Quebec identity. Whatever the case may be, it is risky to make pronouncements about the eventual impact of education and consequent pluralistic adaptation of the schools, in a context where influences on the identity of youth are many and where efforts at institutional transformation are still recent.[28]

The Public Debate

In 2007–08, Quebec experienced a heated collective debate about its identity and the place that diversity should occupy within it. Primed by the Supreme Court's judgment about the wearing of the kirpan at a public school in April 2007, this controversy was dubbed, quite unduly when one considers the real meaning of the concept, the crisis of *reasonable accommodation*. In fact, the debate touched upon many other issues during the Commission's hearings into accommodation practices linked to cultural differences.[29]

Without trying to analyse here the depth of this crisis, three aspects relevant to our study will be highlighted. First, the controversy on reasonable accommodation developed extremely rapidly from a debate, broadly shared by all Western societies, on the place of religious diversity in public institutions to a questioning of the transformation of the majority group's identity and of its pre-eminence as a characteristic of citizenship. The eruption of the linguistic issue, right in the middle of this, also testifies to the fluidity of this debate, whose focal point never ceased to shift. A second interesting aspect was the division between those persons living diversity on a daily basis and those who were reacting solely from their perception of the state of integration and intercultural relations. A strong majority of formally written briefs and testimonies from urban residents of all origins reported a generally harmonious coexistence, especially in light of the recent integration of immigrants, who are mostly francophone, and of the complexity of the linguistic, cultural, and religious challenges that have to be met. Inversely, the regional areas are more divided: their formal submissions positioned them clearly in favour of increasing immigration, in part for reasons linked to regional development. But their population expressed strong anxiety about the too rapid transformation of the social fabric that could result because of it, or which, according to some persons, had already taken place in Montreal. Finally the debate about reasonable accommodation also permitted the re-emergence in the Quebec political landscape of traditional definitions of identity, based on French-Canadian origin and the Catholic religion, which had not been heard since the progressive neo-nationalism of the 1970s became dominant. According to some, the relative space occupied by the traditionalists was made possible by an improbable coalition with a fringe of persons championing French republicanism and preoccupied with defending the neutrality of public space. Although most could not be suspected of playing the card of ethnic discrimination, some, whose position was less articulated theoretically, continually shifted from the defence of civic values to the defence of ethnic values, thus intertwining the two logics.[30]

Concerning the adaptation of the school to diversity, these two positions were generally distinct. Among the Republicans, the issue of the Islamic veil was most troublesome. One would have thought that the major controversy Quebec experienced in 1995 had made possible the creation of a relative consensus on the toleration of symbols within the limits defined by the Commission on Human Rights and Youth, including legal access to school activities and the freedom of choice for the student, or for the parent in the case of a young child. In 2008, these aspects were effectively included in the briefs written by school authorities, but largely absent in the testimonies from the public at large. Many of them again established a connection between the oppression of Muslim women and the wearing of the veil. In addition, following the relative success in the recruitment of teachers and future teachers of all origins, the wearing of religious symbols by teaching personnel was now the main concern. The openness of the Commission on this point also elicited many negative comments. As to the traditionalists, their pet peeve was the new course on ethics and religious culture. They criticized the program for putting all religions on an equal footing, which did not reflect the central role of the Catholic religion in the development of Quebec identity, or even its current demographic weight. As well, they stressed that the cultural teaching of religion could be a violation of young children's religious freedom: children are not in a position to make the distinction between the facts reported on various religions and the beliefs that their parents want them to adopt.[31]

Still, through all the written submissions and public statements, the role of education in the transformation of Quebec's identity was deemed positive on the whole. Even the most worried or negative speakers often mentioned that the generation of children of Bill 101 hardly resembled them, because the latter had first-hand experience in living diversity. Several youth had also come to reprimand their elders and call them to more subtlety and moderation when making their comments. Moreover, most informed positions, including those coming from the educational community, presented a complex portrait of the advances and limits noted above.

It is difficult to say to what extent the positions expressed during the debate on reasonable accommodation represent the entire spectrum of Quebec public opinion. The positive attitudes about immigration and diversity, which remain high in comparison to European societies, have shown a slight decline for the past two years, particularly within the francophone group. Other studies reveal greater reservations about Muslims or Arabs and other visible minorities than about immigrants of European origin. In addition, Quebecers show less openness to various ways of acknowledging diversity in the public space than do other Canadians. This tendency includes the youth as well, according to a 2003 study of 1,200 francophone and anglophone CEGEP students, though openness to immigration and diversity in general are very high among all groups.[32]

Nonetheless, it will be interesting to watch the evolution of the public debate on pluralist redefinition and Quebec identity in the coming years. Overall, the Bouchard-Taylor Report provided a positive assessment of the state of the model of integration and of intercultural relations and of its concretization, in part, by convincingly dismantling the mechanisms used by the media to produce the recent crisis. Its recommendations are based, for the most part, on the initiatives undertaken over the past thirty years. The pluralist camp benefitted more from this than did the hard-line secularists and the ethno-nationalists especially. The controversy is thus not over, either in the society or in the school, though the expertise developed in this area is considerable.

CATALONIA

The normative Model: Interculturalism Recently Reaffirmed

Of the three societies under study, Catalonia distinguishes itself by a national identity in which diversity is deeply rooted. The pluralist discourse, or the melting pot theory as it was once known, which recognizes that the Catalan population is mixed and that its identity is the result of successive waves of immigration, was articulated at an early stage. This collective image was also influenced by a well-organized political Left, which exerted strong leadership, even when in hiding during the Franco dictatorship. Inclusivity, not ethnicity, was put forth as the basis for Catalonia's claims for recuperation of autonomous power. These principles were reaffirmed during the promulgation of the new autonomous state in 1977 and in the platforms of various political parties, including Convergència i Unió (Convergence and Union), which was to dominate the political scene for more than twenty years.[33]

Still, it was not until the early 1970s that the presence of foreign immigrants gave rise to collective reflection, first about integration and, subsequently, about the principles underlying shared citizenship in Catalan society. The first report, the *Interdepartmental Immigration Plan*, implemented from 1993 to 2000, was intended for the most part to support the integration of the immigrant population by developing better coordinated policies among the various ministries and with civil society. However, it was with the creation of the Immigration Secretariat in 2000 that an approach more specifically focused on citizenship emerged. The second report, *Plan 2001–2004*, tried to define a Catalan path to integration that included both respect for diversity and the sense of belonging to a specific community. The model, which brings to mind the Quebec moral contract of 1990, stressed the importance for immigrants to respect the democratic framework and Catalan language and culture, both defined as pluralistic. Conversely, the host society should protect the rights of immigrants and permit them to preserve different aspects of their culture of origin.[34]

The change in government in Catalonia in 2004, after more than twenty years of Convergencia i Unió rule, would speed up developments in these matters. In fact, the coalition in power included the Socialist Party of Catalonia, which was keen to develop a counter-discourse to that of the Right then in power in Spain, and a pro-independence party, the Esquerra Republicana de Catalunya

(Republican Left of Catalonia), which articulated a vision of the national state it wanted to establish. The *Citizenship and Immigration Plan 2005–2008* was a much more developed document that proposed certain reorientations. The identification of Catalonia as a space of citizenship and the importance of the Catalan language as conditions of participation and the fight against exclusion were strengthened. The allegiance of newcomers to a nation under construction, while simultaneously committed to the defence of a Catalan identity in the process of redefinition, was also stressed. As to civil society, interculturalism should be based on empathy and mutual understanding. However, at the institutional level, the taking into account of diversity, here called *accommodation*, should be guided by the guarantee and progressive extension of human rights, including nondiscrimination between men and women, secularity, and a culture of citizenship permitting the maintenance of long-term social cohesion.[35]

Concerning education, developments were largely similar. Until the mid-1990s, a compensatory perspective inspired by programs for the Roma was the rule. No specific document dealt with intercultural education until 1996. It gave priority to a vision, widely shared at that time in Europe, of distinct cultures coexisting in the same territory, no doubt influenced by the *return myth*. It was about encouraging persons from different cultural groups to communicate better, although the document invoked the perspective of a new Catalan culture in which the people would participate by mediating their diverse national origins. Four goals are specifically proposed: develop positive intercultural attitudes and fight against prejudice within the entire school population; support a positive identity among immigrant students; promote harmonious togetherness; and, finally, support equal educational opportunity for students. However, the report did not propose administrative frameworks or concrete measures that would come under the Ministry of Education. Rather, it was a question of supporting schools so that they themselves could develop their own intercultural practices, through the openings that the curriculum already provided. The degree to which such activities were implemented is questionable. Thus, in a report on the schooling of students from immigrant families in 1996, intercultural education occupied three pages of material on what should be accomplished, but no evaluation of the program's impact.[36]

With the publication of the *Language and Social Cohesion Plan* in 2003, following the *Citizenship and Immigration Plan*, a true action plan emerged. The development of intercultural education founded on equality, solidarity, and respect for diverse cultures in an atmosphere of dialogue and conviviality is, in effect, one of the three principles that structure the *Linguistic Policy Plan*. As we saw above, the other two have to do with the strengthening of the Catalan language as the foundation for a multilingual society and the promotion of equal opportunity to avoid situations of marginalization and exclusion. However, intercultural education occupies a very small portion of the document – all of one paragraph, which barely defines it but affirms that it affects the entire population. An annex repeats, for the most part, the objectives of 1996. However, in the work plan, several actions are given priority. Most aim at the sensitization and training of teams at educational centres so they can develop a coherent intercultural approach, in their educational plans and activities. This work is carried out in part with the help of professionals at the Servei d'Interculturalitat i Cohesió social (Interculturalism and Social Cohesion Service). Most of the work, however, is done by territorial coordinators and facilitators and by coordinators and reception teachers in the schools themselves.[37]

The ministry has taken on a leadership role for a number of measures: the development of programs and materials better adapted to intercultural values; the revision of existing materials to eliminate discriminatory or racist stereotypes; and the creation of materials facilitating knowledge of Catalan culture among immigrant families. On the subject of school-family connections, as in the Quebec case, it is a problem that one also finds elsewhere in the *Action Plan*, under the goal of promoting equal opportunity.

Since then, the Sub-Directorate General for Language and Social Cohesion published several documents to support the implementation of the *Linguistic Policy Plan*. However, these documents mostly deal with the reception of newcomers, learning the language, and compensatory services to help immigrant students and their families to narrow certain gaps. Progress on intercultural education is modest. However, two guides on shared citizenship at school, one for the primary level and the other for the secondary level, have been published.[38]

Programs and Formal Interventions

Though the commitment to intercultural education is recent, a series of measures have been implemented to make it a reality. Some flow from the *Language and Social Cohesion Plan*, while others are based on past actions or Spain's education guidelines. The most important one is without doubt the development of the new curriculum in 2007.

One of the goals of primary education is to form citizens able to: acknowledge the pluralism proper to a democratic society; know, comprehend, and respect different cultures, differences among persons, and equality of rights between men and women; and fight against all types of discrimination. At the secondary level, goals are formulated around a concept of democratic citizenship in which familiarity with the historic, cultural, geographic, and social characteristics of Catalan society plays a more important role. The entry points for an intercultural education for all students are found in cross-curricular competency 8, *Social and Citizenship Competency*, and in three subject-based programs: citizenship and human rights education; the social sciences, geography, and history; and a course in religious culture offered at the secondary level as an option of the religion course. Citizenship and human rights education has three goals: learn to be and to act in an autonomous fashion; learn to live in a community; and, finally, learn to be a citizen in a global world. The first contains aspects pertaining to the student's own identity in a context of multiple influences; the second an initiation to rights and liberties and to cultural differences and the development of skills at negotiating conflicts; and the third a sensitization to inequality locally and globally and a commitment to the establishment of a cohesive and equitable society.[39]

As to the course in religious culture, in addition to presenting the great religions, it endeavours to: understand them in their political, social and cultural context; valorize freedom of thought and respect for religion and secularity; and, finally, promote shared citizenship among individuals who hold many differing religious and nonreligious beliefs and practices. In addition, it points out the significant contributions of diverse religions to the history and culture of Spain and Catalonia. However, its content is only proposed as optional. Indeed, in Spain, the right of parents of all faith communities to receive a confessional education corresponding to their values has been guaranteed since 1994 by the Constitution and a royal decree. This has had the effect of making Spain one of the rare European countries where, in principle, Islam is treated on an equal footing with Catholicism. However, in the whole country, but more specifically in Catalonia, Muslim parents are ill informed of their rights and seldom take advantage of them. According to a recent study, in primary schools, students are taught the Catholic religion (85 percent) or no religion (15 percent), while at the secondary level, a meagre 4 percent of schools offer minority religion courses: 2.5 percent for the evangelical Protestantism and 1.5 percent for Islam. Reading the program, it is clear that the Catalan government is not too keen on the confessional teaching of diverse religions, which is imposed on it by Madrid. While giving lip service to the importance of respecting the law, it clearly stresses that ghettoization must not occur as a result of promoting the religion courses. In addition, there is a strong encouragement for the schools to better publicize the religious culture option to parents, majority and minority, who do not want their children to receive confessional teaching at the school. Since the reform will only be implemented progressively in the twelve years of mandatory schooling, the popularity of this new course is not yet known.[40]

Although there are no large-scale studies in Catalonia or even Spain on the treatment of cultural and religious diversity in textbooks and teacher training, the observation that emerges from the smaller studies is rather mixed. The most ideologically conservative, nationalist, and stereotyped content that used to be found in manuals from the Franco era has disappeared. Nevertheless, as opposed to Quebec and other North American societies, there are no guidelines for authors and publishers of textbooks in these matters. Hence apparently praiseworthy goal of valuing cultural diversity can actually create perverse effects by crystallizing differences or highlighting boundaries between groups.[41]

Turning specifically to Islam and the Muslim world, an analysis of 246 textbooks and teacher's guides, inspired by the Quebec study presented above, revealed a distinctly problematic situation. The main finding is the weakness in, and often even the absence of, content in the textbooks dealing with the actual presence of Muslims in Catalonia and Spain and their historical contribution, which is certainly surprising in the Spanish context, to say the least. Influenced by orientalism, the focus of the textbooks is strongly on exotic and folkloric aspects. In addition, although the study's authors noted the inclusion of critical perspectives on colonialism, they suggested that the treatment of other historical events, such as the Crusades, were marked by numerous biases.[42]

To overcome these limitations, teachers have access to supplementary material developed by the Ministry of Education, various private foundations, and the Council of Europe. This material has been widely used and is given high marks by teachers who are familiar with it. However, all agree that the teaching material currently available do not sufficiently foster real intercultural education.[43]

The initial training and continuing education of teachers are equally inadequate. In the first case, which falls under the jurisdiction of the Spanish central state, a recent study showed that despite the statement about various European requirements or recommendations, the treatment of cultural diversity in the mandatory classes for future primary-school teachers is limited. Only in a course on the sociology of education are ethnic groups named. But the study of the content of the various courses shows that the focus is on disadvantage rather than diversity. There are nevertheless optional courses in various universities, including in Catalonia, that approach the systemic adaptation to pluralism from a broader, more positive perspective. No particular study has looked at the secondary level. Nevertheless, there is no reason to believe that the training for this level is any more positive. Indeed, in Spain as in Catalonia, training is for the most part by discipline, and the psychopedagogical and social components are reduced to the bare bones.[44]

Likewise, a study conducted in 2000 with a representative sample of primary and secondary schoolteachers in Catalonia showed that 57.5 percent of them had no training in cultural diversity, while 40.3 percent stated that they had received some limited upgrading on various subjects such as intercultural education, conflict resolution, and the diverse characteristics of certain cultures. The results were a little more positive for teachers under thirty years of age, which seems to indicate that recent initial training is having an impact. In any cases, a strong majority of teachers said they were inadequately prepared and would like to enrol in specific courses. Several initiatives have been developed recently in response to this need, by the Ministry of Education and by private and professional organizations like the Bofill Foundation and Aula Intercultural (literally, the intercultural classroom).[45]

As to the participation of parents and the management of school-family conflict, the actions taken appear to be equally as limited. Indeed, while parent organizations benefit from a highly developed support system in Catalonia, they have only recently become aware of the increasingly multicultural nature of the persons they represent. However, Catalonia sets itself apart by a particularly innovative program of intercultural mediators. The program initially targeted the Roma community but was extended since the mid-1990s to serve immigrant families. Some thirty mediators, funded by the Ministry of Education or local school authorities, now work in seventy schools. Their tasks relate to linguistic and cultural contact with the families, mediation in value conflicts, raising the awareness of teachers to the realities experienced by their students, and the encouragement of minority parents to participate more at the school and in parent associations. At the present time, the mediator jobs are not permanent and are performed by people with extremely diversified profiles who, for the most part, belong to the communities themselves. A debate about the relevance of the certification of this position is currently underway. Certification would contribute more stability, to the persons and the communities concerned, but it could also restrict access to the profession to persons holding Catalan or Spanish diplomas. In addition, the resource persons, assigned to the schools by virtue of the Compensatory Education program aimed at students experiencing academic difficulties, often spur efforts to promote the involvement of immigrant parents in school life, even though their mandate is not first and foremost connected to cultural diversity.[46]

Practices in the Schools

The situation in the field is more positive than the recent articulation of the government position on intercultural education and the general limitations of the guidelines would lead us to believe. The weaknesses listed hardly differ from those we have seen in other societies like Quebec, where government intervention has been long-standing and more consistent.

Thus, according to the study cited above, more than half the teachers reported that their school educational plan contained elements fostering common, concerted action on cultural diversity. There were, however, important differences between primary schools, which are clearly more adapted, and secondary schools and, not unexpectedly, between schools with a strong immigrant presence, especially in Barcelona, and schools in the more homogeneous regions. And, in the school educational project, where the choices as to various educational materials and activities are more spelled out, the results are equally positive. Indeed, 55 percent of teachers say that the need to take diversity into account is stated in this document. However, bottlenecks seem to appear when translating these orientations into concrete actions. Thus, only 44 percent of teachers believe that the plan's guidelines allow them to integrate an intercultural perspective into their teaching. When questioned about school practices, such as the organization of awareness-raising days on the intercultural or the adaptation of menus in light of religious differences, the percentages remain equally low.[47]

The results concerning relations with immigrant families and their participation at the school are also somewhat paradoxical, according to a study conducted in 2003. Parents stated that they were generally very satisfied with the reception and the services they received at the school and with the support given to their children. Although they mentioned certain problems linked to the language barrier or to their religious practices, few reported conflicts or incidents. In addition, when necessary, the mediation in this regard had been excellent. Conversely, teachers complained about the weak participation by a large proportion of immigrant parents, as much in community activities and as in those directly concerning their child. In addition, they reported several problems with communication, even conflicts, which they associate with the low educational level of the families, their lack of knowledge about the educational system, and their insistence that the children respect the special features of their culture of origin. The problems are more serious at the secondary schools where participation is weaker for all parents and where the gap between the values of the families and the school are more pronounced. Given these results, the authors concluded that there is some bridge-building required between the respective perspectives on what is happening. Teachers' expectations are largely unrealistic and need to be better adapted to the reality experienced by immigrant families. Conversely, immigrant parents are not sufficiently aware of the fact that their minimal contact with the school is likely to inhibit the success of their children even if, in comparison to the situation experienced in the country of origin, the schooling seems to be unfolding in a positive way.[48]

A more recent study suggests that relations between the school and Muslim families are particularly problematic. In addition to the issues identified above, teachers believe that the influence of religion widens the value gap. They mentioned the inferior status of girls, certain clothing and food requirements, the demands about adapting the curriculum, and even untimely visits by certain orthodox imams. A well, teachers hold a negative image of Islam and Muslims in general and know little about the distinctions among the many cultures from which their students come. As to Muslim parents, although positive on the whole, they are less satisfied than other parents about how the schools take their culture into account, in particular concerning food, respect for the modesty of their daughters, and the possibility of learning Arabic or other heritage languages.[49]

The same logic of the glass half full or half empty seems to intrude on teaching and educational relations in the classroom, although the results in this regard are less favourable than at the institutional level. According to the same study cited above, half of the teachers feel that adapting to cultural diversity is unnecessary, either because there are no immigrant-origin students in the class, or because their presence is not problematic; 40 percent of teachers in classes with a strong multi-ethnic presence share this view. Among the activities reported by the other half of the respondents, the most popular are presentations on immigrant cultures, adaptations to the academic program, sometimes of an intercultural nature but more often of a compensatory nature, and discussions with the student body on tolerance. Here, too, primary school teachers showed more dynamism and openness to diversity.[50]

In 1997, an ethnographic study in three schools noted the coexistence of several models, but the most frequent was that of compensatory education in which cultural diversity was taken into account only when the normal and habitual approach did not yield the hoped-for results with immigrant-origin students. Some authors suggest that the compensatory model is still the dominant one today. Others argue, to the contrary, that there has been a significant evolution of practices, at least toward the model of ad hoc valorization of diversity. The teachers' positive responses, when they were asked to evaluate the presence of North Africans (82 percent) or sub-Saharan African students (85 percent), seem in part to confirm this assessment. However, their contribution is formulated in vague and largely politically correct terms, while the identification of difficulties created by their presence is much more precise, including the slowing down of the teaching pace or the emergence of cultural conflicts. The teachers' ambivalence is confirmed by the extremely high percentages of those who feel that intercultural education should be recommended for all schools in Catalonia (96 percent), but also that this ideology is difficult to put into practice in a concrete way on a daily basis (75 percent).[51]

Though professional considerations are a key consideration in all this, one cannot exclude the more emotional relation of certain teachers to cultural diversity. Thus, an already dated study of future teachers identified three large groups that were approximately equivalent. The first, in which an assimilationist perspective dominated, was characterized by fear of the Other, but especially of the social transformations linked to European integration and globalization. The second, while denouncing stereotypes and promoting tolerance, showed themselves to be concerned about the *cultural incompatibility* of certain communities. Finally, the third group was characterized by its anti-racist commitment and its openness to the inclusion of newcomers, while supporting the defence of Catalan identity and betraying a certain hesitation between integration and assimilation.[52]

As to the students, few studies have dealt with the way in which they experience, or did experience, their schooling, especially in the case of newcomer populations, where the focus of the research was on reception and linguistic integration. However, a few studies of limited scope do illustrate the complexity of identity construction among young immigrants in a context of double exposure, as in Catalonia. Latin American students, for example, had difficulty expressing a coherent historical narrative. Indeed, on the one hand, what they had learned about Spain in their country of origin was partially contradicted by Catalan teaching and, on the other, their actual situation in Catalonia did not correspond to the discourse about civic belonging in the programs. Similarly, students living in the suburbs of Barcelona generally developed mixed identities, where, depending on the context, it is the identity of origin, Spanish identity, or Catalan identity that predominates. Some live this situation easily, while others experience insecurity in such a fluid context. Nevertheless, for the majority of young immigrants, it is not the traditional rivalry between Spain and Catalonia that is most problematic, but the often impervious boundaries between natives and immigrants, especially when they are members of racialized minorities who immigrated at adolescence.[53]

The Public Debate

Until now, adaptation to diversity has not generated debate beyond the circle of concerned decision-makers, stakeholders, and experts. Several elements can explain this weak development. First, it has to do with the recent character of significant immigration from abroad and of the articulation of a policy on matters of integration and intercultural relations. Several experts argue that the questions of national identity and immigration remain largely dissociated in Catalonia, in both the university and political worlds. Only the Catalan People's Party talks about immigration as a threat to identity, security, and social and economic well-being. However, as it is a party that also opposes Catalan nationalism and linguistic normalization, its support in Catalonia is limited and concentrated within the Spanish-speaking population. It has also created a negative reaction within Catalan nationalist parties, which are less inclined to take a position opposing national development and immigration. As to educational policies, the media sometimes refer to challenges such as the concentration of immigrant students in certain schools, the relevance of the school taking over the teaching of religion, and the adequacy of the new citizenship and human rights program to community diversity. But one cannot speak of major controversies.[54]

Nonetheless, certain anxieties over immigration are quietly expressed by decision-makers and stakeholders directly concerned by the issue. A recent study identified two major preoccupations: the too rapid and uncontrolled increase in immigration levels and the diversification in the origins of the immigrants. More conservative persons make a direct link between these phenomena and various social problems, such as criminal activity or the emergence of racism in the host population. More progressive respondents, socialists, and Catalan nationalists are less likely to blame the immigrant population for these problems or to stress the role of cultural determinism in explaining them. A strong majority of respondents also feel that the Catalan state lacks the required means to concretize the generous (according to some, idealistic) model proposed in the *Citizenship and Immigration Plan 2005*. However, as opposed to the Spanish state, most acknowledge that it is to Catalonia's advantage to have a well-articulated, overall vision, even if it does not have the means to implement it. In the school, there is concern mostly about inequality and marginalization, but few indications of any talk about institutional adaptation to diversity as a threat. Increasingly, though, some worry that certain adjustments granted to Muslims could constitute a questioning of sexual equality or of the secularism of the schools. This topic could take on increased visibility in the medium term, since teachers are beginning to talk about, as noted above. But at this point in time, it is not a subject of much concern or debate in the public square.[55]

FLANDERS

Ideologies: From Multiculturalism to Integration in Diversity

Although its actions on linguistic integration grabbed the headlines, the involvement of the Flemish government in the area of diversity is also significant. Flanders first defined a coherent and specific approach to diversity in the early 1990s. Reacting in large part to the emergence of the Vlaams Blok, and in response to the Royal Commission on immigration policy, the Flemish government gave priority to a multicultural model of society, insisting that intercultural exchange be encouraged. It was a vision of the future since, at the time, the immigrant proportion of the population was smaller than it is today. The government's actions especially supported the organization of communities to become part of a more structured and efficient conversation with the authorities. Nevertheless, parallel with this new promotion of pluralism, immigration continued to be largely defined as a socio-economic problem. This generated a number of compensatory measures in the schools, not targeting immigrants specifically but affecting them significantly.[56]

In 1996, still with the recognition of immigrant populations in mind, the Flemish government revised its policy, now called the Policy on Minorities. For foreign-born citizens legally living in Belgium and for traveller communities, mostly the Roma, it was designed to do away with the barriers to full participation in the host society. In the schools, as we saw above, this goal was concretized by the Equal Opportunity Policy, which aimed to foster a greater academic mobility by students of certain communities strongly concentrated in ghetto schools. Two other aspects of the Policy, reception and accompaniment, were intended for newcomers in regular and irregular situations respectively. The Policy, confirmed by Royal Decree in 1998, also strengthened the political recognition of minorities, in part by the creation of the Ethno-Cultural Minorities Forum, an instrument for the defence of their rights.[57]

In 2003, a first evaluation uncovered numerous gaps in its implementation: the evaluation criticized some effects of ethnic categorization and the almost exclusive focus on newcomers at the expense of the host society. In addition, the political context had also changed, on the one hand, with the constant rise in support for the Vlaams Blok and the emergence of language concerns and, on the other, the questioning of multiculturalism in the Netherlands, a society having an important influence on Flemish public policies. This is why, in 2004, in its new strategic plan, *Living Together in Diversity*, the Flemish government took a certain distance from its multicultural conception of Flemish society, now defining it as a pluralistic society. The time for each community to retreat into itself was over. The goal was now for each community to interact and be transformed. The promotion of cultural diversity in the whole society thus became a central component.[58]

When the document is analysed, however, one notes some ambiguity concerning the values that should underlie this new citizenship, as well as some wavering between a communitarian and an individualistic model of relating to diversity. The values enunciated are essentially civic in nature: respect for the Other; contribution to society by work and effort; respect for the fundamental rights and freedoms of the Constitution and the law; and rejection of exclusion or discrimination on the basis of ethnicity, religion, or culture. However, the content of the Inburgering program itself includes much more substantive elements linked to Flemish history and culture. This tension, which we encountered in the other two societies, is without doubt inevitable. Yet, in the Flemish case, this was not tackled head on, and the content of that, which could serve as a common heritage, such as its pluralistic nature, was not defined. In addition, although it put forth a paradigm of individuals' multiple diversities, the new document is marked by the rhetoric of the former Policy on Minorities. For example, the complex relationship of individuals with their cultural roots is not discussed, nor the means of resolving rights conflicts which could emerge in such cases, for instance, among minority women.[59]

Concerning intercultural education, the Flemish government did not publish an exhaustive document that contained normative positions or specific goals. During the 1990s, initiatives taking diversity into account flowed from either a compensatory perspective aiming to bridge the gap experienced by immigrant students, or from a multicultural perspective based on the belief that students would retain their language and culture and later return to their country of origin. Nonetheless, both government and its partners in education would pass various declarations with intercultural content, such as the Non-discrimination Pact of 1993 or the Equal Opportunity Policy of 1996. Thus, among the various indicators of socio-economic or educational barriers allowing schools to receive supplementary financial support was, in primary school, the fact of having students who did not speak Dutch at home and, in secondary school, the fact of having students who had attended a reception class the year before. In addition, the integration of an intercultural dimension into their practice is one of the bases of support for multi-ethnic schools.[60]

No official frame of reference on the nature of the actions to take or their target audience is proposed. The Flemish government prefers to leave the initiative for this to subsidiary organizations that it largely funds, including the Intercultural Point of Ghent, recently renamed the Centre for Diversity and Learning. As of the late 1990s, this institution, whose funding was recently questioned by the Minister of Education, supported schools in the implementation of their policy of equal educational opportunity and published several documents presenting an original concept of intercultural education. Refusing to concentrate on the ethno-cultural question, the Centre conceives diversity as a multiform, daily reality that teachers should learn to deal with when it emerges in class interactions or exchanges, without crystallizing it by overly structured approaches based on cultures of origin, or on undue blame for racism and inequality.[61]

More recently, the document *Living Together in Diversity* spoke to the role of education in intercultural matters. It mentions, among other things, that diversity should be taken into account in the diverse mandates and activities of the school with a view to promoting equality and the full participation of all students. In addition, the Ministry of Education published a short document on its website, where it presented its vision of diversity. Diversity is now to be considered an integral component of Flemish society and schools; it should not be defined as a problem, unless it creates exclusion. The document also reiterates the importance of the school being a place that promotes *shared citizenship* and a conception of interculturalism that not only includes ethnic and religious issues but also addresses other types of discrimination and exclusion, such as those based on age, gender, and disabilities.[62]

In addition, the Pact to Promote Non-discrimination in Education was renewed in February 2003 by a very broad grouping of partners from the world of education, including the various organizational pillars of education in Flanders, professional associations, parent committees, and the Ministry of Education. While positioning itself on the issue of combating exclusion, the document in now pertinently named *Diversity as Added Value* and has as a first premise that diversity in Flemish society is increasing. All are committed to working for a society that is more tolerant, more open, and more respectful of differences, and to promoting an education free of discrimination, exclusion, segregation, and racism. The core of the measures proposed and of the involvement of diverse groups depends, however, on full participation and equality in education, and, while the taking diversity into account is mentioned, it is as a means of concretizing these goals.[63]

Programs and Formal Interventions

The Flemish approach to adapting schools to diversity does not proceed from a vision as articulated as those of the other two societies, but in its broad framework most of the elements described above are present.

Thus the mandatory curriculum for the primary and secondary schools includes a number of goals, under crosscutting themes or diverse disciplines that foster raising awareness to diversity and the development of skills to live in a pluralistic society. At the end of primary school, students expected to be able to show how different social and cultural groups have different norms and values and to be aware that racism is often founded on a lack of knowledge and a fear of those who are foreign. At the end of secondary school, through the cross-cutting theme of citizenship education, students will be trained to respect the opinions, arguments, and dignity of others in a multicultural society and in a pluralist debate. They will also know how to recognize the existence of prejudice and discriminatory behaviour in themselves, in others, and in the media. In addition, they will react in a tolerant manner to cultural differences. There are similar statements in other disciplines like history and geography. For example, students will learn to respect individuality but also the specific lifestyles of persons of other cultures, including in our multicultural society.[64]

However, two aspects of the school system limit the impact of such statements. On the one hand, it is only general objectives that the various organizational pillars and schools are expected to implement and adapt to their specific context. On the other, the intercultural content is found for the most part in the cross-cutting themes, which are not subject to evaluation. One may therefore ask what priority teachers will give to them, since in Flanders there are no specific courses on citizenship education.[65]

Nonetheless, the teaching of religion clearly places Belgium, and especially Flanders, at the cutting edge of diversity promotion. Indeed, though the relations between Muslim leaders and the Belgian state have not always been easy, the granting of recognized religious and philosophical confessional status to Islam dates from 1974. Since that time, it has been theoretically possible for any parent or student to ask the school to organize a course on the Muslim religion, which would be financed by the Ministry of Education, as are courses on the other five recognized religions and moral education. However, the application of this right has not always been effective. Indeed, because of political turbulence, which we need not go into here, it was necessary to wait until 1999 so that the organization representing the Muslim faith could be completed by the election of a Belgian Muslim executive. Now this organization is responsible for the nomination of Muslim teachers and inspectors.[66]

In 2004–05, 26,777 Muslim students in primary and secondary schools – enrolled largely in the official, subsidized community boards – had access to the teaching of their religion. In fact, the decree did not apply to free subsidized, or Catholic, education, although the Catholic schools were sometimes involved in teaching the Muslim religion, in part to keep their numbers up. The Belgian and Flemish governments also made significant efforts to assure the continuing education of the teachers, most of whom were foreigners. More recently, a program designed to train Muslin teachers of Belgian nationality at the secondary level was also implemented at the Erasmus Graduate School of Brussels. After creating much debate, the teaching of Islam now seems to be accepted today, in part because it is thought to be a strategy for integrating Muslim students, whose families could be tempted to enrol in ethno-specific schools if this service did not exist.[67]

Still concerning the religious dimension, it should be pointed out that in 2003 the *Education Act* was amended to permit students to be absent from school during feasts constituting a central element of the Anglican, Catholic, Jewish, Muslim, Orthodox, and Protestant faith communities, which are recognized by the Belgian constitution. However, beyond that issue, the ministry did not adopt a particular position on the adaptation of the norms and practices of schools to religious diversity.[68]

The broader efforts to train teachers in intercultural matters were also significant, though more recent. Indeed, though the institutes of higher learning and the education faculties, which are jointly responsible for teacher training in Belgium, had taken several initiatives in this regard, it would be necessary to wait until 2007 for the intercultural dimension to be explicitly named in the competencies required of future teachers by the Flemish state. The *Decree of the Flemish Government on Fundamental Teaching Competencies* of 5 October 2007 mentions that teachers must be aware of the lifestyles of children and adolescents and the cultural differences among social groups. In this regard, an inventory completed in 2006 by the Ministry of Education showed that a significant number of training programs for future teachers contained components or activities connected to raising intercultural consciousness. However, given certain gaps, the document recommended that taking diversity into account be the subject of a better defined strategy in each institution and that it be more systematic throughout their training, including their placements.[69]

The ministry also timidly tried to encourage the recruitment of minority teachers. In the mid-1990s, an experimental project to support eighty immigrant women in the theoretical and practical training required for teaching kindergarten was implemented. However, this measure was challenged by certain school officials, especially Catholics, in the name of freedom of education and the fact that these women, all Muslims, could not teach religion. Although the Court of Appeal sided with the Flemish government, once their training was completed, these teachers encountered great difficulties in finding employment. More recently, the focus is instead on the *natural* presence of second-generation students in teacher training institutions, but no particular program has been developed.[70]

As to continuing education of practising teachers, for the most part, it again falls under the Equal Opportunity Policy. In addition to funding specific upgrading programs, the Ministry of Education supports the Centre for Diversity and Learning and a Brussels initiative, the Voorrangsbeleid Brussel (Priority Policy Brussels), which deals with five major issues: learning the language, managing diversity and intercultural education, differentiating educational strategies, cooperating with parents, and coordinating with other partners in the world of education. These two centres sometimes intervene directly in the team-teaching classes with teachers and develop educational materials based on taking differences into account.[71]

For several years, however, a specific intercultural component seems to be emerging in departmental programs. One example is the development of a resource base on diversity on the ministry's website, where there are more than two hundred references, and the annual organization of Diversity Week. In addition, the Flemish government launched in 2006 an action plan aimed at the "interculturalization" of the culture and sports sectors, targeting youth in particular. This action plan, which fosters consultation with other sectors, such as education, led to the implementation of many after-school and extracurricular programs prioritizing rapprochement among youth of all origins. As in the formal educational sector, a website gives interested persons access to a large repertoire of best practices.[72]

The ministry, however, has refrained from forcing the publishing industry to eliminate discriminatory stereotypes or to provide a better treatment of diversity in textbooks. Some incidents that caught media attention in 2003, dealing with examples of blatant racism in primary school textbooks, led the Evens Foundation, in collaboration with the Centre for Diversity and Learning, to do an initial analysis of the intercultural content, or lack thereof, in educational materials. The analysis of the twelve most popular collections for various primary and secondary courses resulted in a mixed report. Despite the recent controversy, the textbooks are largely free from prejudice and explicit stereotypes and place great importance on the denunciation of discrimination and stereotypes and on the promotion of multiple perspectives in the analysis of these phenomena. However, they include few minority characters, and the diversity of cultures and lifestyles is barely included. In addition, when diversity is depicted, it is generally in specific subthemes rather than in the work as a whole. Multiple identities, differences within groups, and interaction among students of different origins are also seldom discussed. As to the pedagogical treatment of diversity, like the other elements in the textbooks, few active learning situations are proposed. The authors recommend that better support be given to publishing houses so they can develop more adequate textbooks and to schools and teachers so that they can adapt the materials they already have. However, it is not evident that the Ministry of Education will do this, given the long tradition in Belgium and Flanders of respecting local freedom in the area of education.[73]

School Practices

Faced with a relatively cautious discourse, in part because of political tensions, and a multitude of generally favourable initiatives for institutional adaptation, one may wonder what is happening in the field. Are Flemish schools really involved in an intercultural shift, or is the movement largely cosmetic? This is difficult to answer, even more so than in the other two contexts, because large data sets are not available. In addition, the conclusions are generally inconsistent. Decision-makers and academics involved in applied research present a complex portrait that leans more toward the positive elements, while sociologists and anthropologists, focusing on broader trends or observations of particular schools, are more pessimistic.

As to the schools themselves, a 2003 evaluation of the implementation of the Equal Opportunity Policy shows that 50 percent of Flemish primary schools, but only 10 percent of secondary schools, were engaged in structured approaches to better adapt their services for their multi-ethnic clientele. The projects undertaken in this regard are extremely varied: the production of an intercultural curriculum; the intensification of rapprochement with the families; and initiatives for staff training. Their impact was generally evaluated very positively.[74]

However, several problematic dimensions seem to persist. First of all, the policy did not foster a balanced redistribution of the students as a whole. This failure had an impact on the wider availability of intercultural education and on the perception of its relevance as a way of dealing with the *problem* of immigrant students. In this regard, several briefs presented before the Commission on Intercultural Dialogue are extremely consistent, although it is not always possible to distinguish between the reality of the Dutch-language and French-language schools.[75]

The Commission's report also noted the emergence of uneasiness in several schools at the transformation of norms and practices created by the presence of students of diverse cultures and, especially, religions. Of particular concern was the refusal to mix and interact with female teachers and administrators, the objection to some of the content in biology, philosophy, and physical education courses,

and the pressure exerted on young Muslims who refused to participate in Ramadan or wear the veil. Certain school administrators
also noted the existence of tensions between students and their
Belgian or European parents and students and their parents from
other parts of the world. Given the international context and the
content of the xenophobic Belgium discourse, the negative reaction
was primarily to the Muslim community, although anti-Semitism
was also present. Administrators and teachers are demanding more
training, support, and guidelines to deal with intercultural and interreligious conflicts, even though their main concern is academic marginalization and failure.[76]

The participation of immigrant-origin parents is also likely to be
weaker than that of native-born parents, although there is little
quantitative data on this. Factors explaining this state of affairs
include their low level of schooling, their extremely demanding
work schedules, the inability to speak Dutch, and a culture of origin
that does not value sustained interaction with school personnel.
Administrators and teachers have very negative things to say about
non-Western immigrant parents, especially Moroccans and Turks.
Thus, according to a study of some fifty Dutch-speaking teachers in
Brussels in 2002, they reproached the parents for not being interested in the schooling of their children and for delegating most of
their responsibilities to the school. In addition, they mention the lack
of discipline or the different treatment of boys and girls within the
family and the pressure exerted by parents to maintain their own
language, culture, and religion as factors slowing down the integration of the children as well as their academic success. Some teachers
are more positive; they show a much stronger sensitivity to the reality experienced by the parents as well as a commitment to an anti-
racist perspective.[77]

As in the other two contexts, the perspective of the parents, though
mixed, is more positive, according to a series of studies conducted in
the late 1990s. A majority of the parents say they appreciate the educational services offered in Belgium and Flanders and are optimistic
about the positive impact of schooling on the future life opportunities
for their children. However, several concerns were expressed by the
people interviewed. The main one was the concentration of their
children in specific schools, which is obvious, even for persons who
do not know the ins and outs of the school system. A strong majority
of parents thus support the action of the Flemish government to

encourage a better distribution of immigrant students, even if this irritates them sometimes when they try to enrol their children in schools where the quota has already been reached. Cultural questions also interest the parents. Thus, in 2003, the Ethnic Minorities Forum took up a position in favour of strengthening the teaching of heritage languages and cultures, whereas many Moroccan and Turkish parents felt that the school is not collaborating enough with them and, above all, does not take sufficient account of their values.[78]

Concerning the taking into account of diversity in the classroom, the past ten years have witnessed a multitude of experiments and pilot projects in Flemish schools. Many are influenced by the cooperative learning movement in multicultural groups, a Flemish adaptation of "Complex Instruction," a pedagogy developed by the American researcher Elizabeth Cohen. This approach aims at the redefinition of relationships between teachers and students, the valorization of interaction among peers, and the implementation of a curriculum favouring multiple skills. It is assumed that, in the context of complex, less linear learning, diversity will naturally emerge and above all be treated in a more complex, less stereotypical way by the teachers. However, achieving such a goal supposes the advanced sociological training of teachers. They should be able to analyse the sociogram of their class and the unequal social and academic statuses of the students in order to assure that inequalities are not reproduced in the work of the team and informal interactions.[79]

Evaluations of the impact of the wider application of Complex Instruction activities on intercultural education are divided. Its supporters argue that it has weakened the traditional objection to an interculturalism or anti-racism conceived as too guilt-inducing or as an activity to do *in addition to* the academic program. As well, this approach helps schools to practise the intercultural concretely rather than philosophize about it benignly. Others, conversely, feel that its success resides precisely in the fact that it prevents teachers from actually taking into account the ethnocultural or anti-racist dimension in their teaching. Other forms of diversity, individual or tied to gender or lifestyle, would be clearly preferred. In addition, many teachers would not have the necessary training to correct the effects of reproducing the inequalities that so open a pedagogy would create.[80]

A study, conducted in fifteen schools in 2003 on the effective implementation of intercultural education through Complex Instruction seems in part to support the sceptics. It shows that, first, as opposed to the normative model, interactions in the great majority of classes remain dominated by a traditional conception of the role of the student and by the tendency of teachers to homogenization when they are reacting to the comments or contributions of students who do not fit the mold. The variety of cognitive styles, experiences, and modes of interaction were barely considered. As well, a troubling observation of this study is the tight link between the tendency to homogenization and the degree of ethnic concentration in the schools. In schools with a smaller immigrant population, teachers would take more account of the diversity of their students and would foster relationships based on individualisation. In schools with high immigrant concentrations, the way of relating would be much more formal, and teachers and students would each stick to their respective roles, leaving little opportunity for the expression of their social backgrounds. It was nonetheless in schools of medium density where diversity received the least consideration, a situation the study's authors explain by the strong pressure that teachers experience in such contexts to respect the pace of learning expected by the program. These differences were also observed with regard to knowledge of the neighbourhood where the school is located and to openness to integrating its diverse characteristics into teaching practices. Administrators of low-density schools generally know their milieu better; they describe it in historical, geographical, and artistic terms and consider it a favourable place in which to learn. In schools with medium, and especially high, concentrations of immigrant students, negative ethnic and socio-economic aspects are stressed. They show themselves less open to the organization of activities based on the reality of the neighbourhood, even though links with the community are precisely the priority of many projects.[81]

The attitudes of teachers are nevertheless largely similar from one school to the next. They continue to define intercultural education for the most part as the transmission of knowledge about different cultures, though the promotion of openness, respect, and tolerance is also identified. In addition, essentialist conceptions assigning each person to a unique culture are still the norm. Also, the same gap was observed as in the Quebec context between what the teachers say about diversity, which is quite negative and based on political conviction, and their professional and ethical position in class, which leads them to give more attention to the diversified needs and characteristics of their students.[82]

Research on student experience and identity is still rather limited. Several ethnographic studies using small samples illustrate the realities experienced in other migratory contexts, such as the feelings of alienation of young Turks and North Africans in the face of stereotypes and discrimination encountered at school, or the development of identities that combine elements of the heritage and host cultures among Muslim girls. However, there are no overall data on the relations that young immigrants develop with Flemish identity, or on the impact of schooling in this regard. We also do not know to what extent intercultural education could have contributed to a redefinition of traditional Flemish identity among native-born students, a goal that, in any case, has only been discussed in public politics since 2004.[83]

The recommendations enunciated by the Intercultural Dialogue Commission partially confirm this complex portrait. They especially emphasize the importance of academic valorization of immigrant memory, language, and culture as integral parts of the Belgian heritage and not as some additional content related to the Other. The necessity to understand better the needs of second-generation youth, whose multiple identities are often reduced to one of their two identity poles by decision-makers and stakeholders, is also highlighted. As well, teachers seem not to be fully aware of the linguistic and cultural potential of their minority students because they often describe them, for the most part, by starting with their weaknesses.[84]

The Public Debate

Of the three societies under study, Flanders is the one where the politicization of the immigration issue is most visible. Indeed, the Vlaams Belang, which year in and year out receives around 25 percent of the vote, promotes a nationalism based on blood ties rather than territorial affiliation, and a static and traditional idea of identity and culture. The party rejects any pluralistic definition of Flemish society and holds to a clearly assimilationist integration model in which the immigrant should have more duties than rights. Rather unconvincingly defending itself against charges of being racist, the Vlaams Belang blames the increase of intercultural conflicts on the perverse effects of multicultural policies and on the substantial cultural distance of new immigrants, who are often considered as "non-integratable." In this regard, Muslims, and Third-World immigrants generally, are particularly targeted. Though this rhetoric may be shared with other like-minded parties in Europe, the position of the Vlaams Belang is influenced by the historical memory of the Flemish people, or, more precisely, the most nationalistic interpretation of that history. Immigrants are frequently presented as natural allies of francophones, who for this reason would prefer a more relaxed policy of immigration control. As well, an analysis of the vocabulary used by the leaders of this movement shows a significant occurrence of concepts such as suffering, domination, menace, uncertainty, and the need to protect a fragile language and culture against the threat posed by the Other.[85]

However, the vitality of the extreme right in Flanders tends sometimes to obscure an obvious mathematical reality, namely, that most of the Flemish population votes for parties favourable to immigration and to taking diversity into account. Some Flemish analysts also criticize the press and certain francophone spokespersons of exploiting legitimate concerns that the extreme right arouses, as proof of the civic nationalism and openness that characterizes their own community. Regardless, the commitment of the Flemish elite of the left and the centre in support of multiculturalism has persisted, although several language policies and programs seem to have been adopted in reaction to the popularity of the extreme right. The debate on the model of integration, secularism, and intercultural relations to put forth has nevertheless remained muted. For some leftist intellectuals, any criticism of the multicultural ideology is a flirtation with racist ideology. For other observers, it is better to let sleeping dogs lie than to risk unleashing strong passions.[86]

However, a debate at once social and educational seems to have been launched recently on how far institutional adaptation should go, although it was begun mostly by the federal government and thus reflects the concerns of both French- and Dutch-speakers. This new concern was particularly obvious during the presentations made before the Intercultural Dialogue Commission, but traces of it could be detected in other documents and consultations. A relatively easy consensus, at least among those who support immigration and the recognition of diversity, seems to have emerged around the concept of inclusive citizenship that would be based on the great founding values of Belgium, such as social consensus, ideological and philosophical pluralism, and federalism. There is also agreement that the rights of all should be well defined in order to respect, among other things, the equality of men and women. The importance of putting forward policies that do not stigmatize immigrants and that recognize the dynamic character of their identity is also agreed upon.[87]

Still, on the difficult question of religion's place in the public square, the positions are much more polarized. Thus, the Commission refused to formulate precise recommendations on respect for religious symbols, on the part of either students or teachers, by noting the multiplicity of ideologies, practices, and opinions. There are three positions. At one extreme, some called for a general ban on the wearing of any religious symbols, since the neutrality of the school ensures the peaceful coexistence of students of different religions or philosophies. However, the Commission was not inclined to go in this direction, considering that such a ban would risk creating exclusion and that, above all, it would be difficult to enforce in light of the jurisdiction of the respective communities and the broad autonomy that the Belgian educational authorities exercise. At the opposite extreme, others were demanding a legislative intervention that would guarantee the freedom to display religious symbols in the schools, in virtue of an inclusive conception of neutrality and of their association with diversity. However, this option was not retained either, out of concern for the negative effects of community pressure to conform, especially on students who do not want to practise their religion or to show it by these symbols. It is thus, the third position, which insists on the importance of respecting autonomy and dialogue in each school, de facto prevails today in the absence of a clear decision by the Commission. However, several school principals have requested that guidelines be formulated that would ensure respect for fundamental democratic values when taking into account religious diversity and consistent interventions from one school to the next. In the absence of these guidelines, many have lamented the feeling of insecurity that is currently rampant in the schools.[88]

Recently, this issue again stirred up strong feelings following the decision of several Flemish school authorities to ban the wearing of the veil. Still, many schools seem to live easily enough with a nonregulation that allows them to adopt various solutions depending on the nature of the challenge concerned and the persons associated with it. It is therefore difficult to predict if the debate on school adaptation to diversity is going to take off in the years to come or if it will mostly remain focused on social problems. Besides, it is still obviously far too early for the impact of intercultural education on the eventual transformation of the Flemish community's identity to be a subject of concern.

DYNAMICS AND TENSIONS IN COMPARATIVE
PERSPECTIVE

Of all the issues looked at in this volume, adaptation to ethnocultural diversity is the most difficult to assess clearly. Indeed, like any initiative using education to bring about social transformation, it involves complex iterative dynamics where the tensions can be assets as much as obstacles. Thus we do not intend to judge if the intercultural shift is well underway in each context or to classify them on a continuum. Indeed, the three societies do not perform in the same way, depending on the indicator used. For example, if it is the degree of consensus that gives rise to the transformations underway, Catalonia is located at one extreme of the continuum while the situation in Quebec and Flanders appears as more problematic. Inversely, with regard to institutional commitment and the effective implementation of measures, Quebec, with more than thirty years of experience, clearly stands alone. But Catalonia and Flanders set themselves apart from each other by the quality of the clear normative discourse or the intensity of the action in the field respectively. We will therefore rely upon the foregoing analysis to answer two central questions. First, is the discrepancy among normative models, practices, and public debates, experienced to differing degrees in the three societies, tied to the specificity of the ethnic relations that predominate in each? Second, do the differences encountered enable the identification of conditions likely to maximize the impact of educational interventions on the pluralistic transformation of traditionally homogeneous groups whose identity is fragile?

Concerning the first issue, remember, as the title of this chapter indicates, that a certain discrepancy between policies, programs, practices, and perceptions was foreseen. Indeed, whatever the reality studied, there is never perfect consistency among the diverse spheres of institutional change. The task that interests us here is to identify to what extent the dynamics and tensions encountered between these spheres of public action and citizen reaction can be ascribed to the particular historical trajectory of fragile majorities.

A first observation emerging from the comparative analysis is that of a remarkable dynamism in terms of normative models and overall frameworks designed to facilitate the adaptation of schools to diversity. Commitment in this regard seems significant and clearly stems, although in varying degrees, from awareness of the need to transform traditional ethnic relations. As well, the comparison of

Quebec, Catalonia, and Flanders with their respective sister society shows no systematic advantage or particular disparity.[89]

When we turned our attention to the connections between the normative models and overall frameworks, on one hand, and the practices and relations of the stakeholders in the field, on the other, we did find a great deal of tension. In all three contexts, teachers experience difficulties fully integrating an intercultural perspective in the norms of the school and the classroom. Relations with immigrant parents, though generally positive, generate cultural misunderstandings and great anxiety when religious issues are involved. Finally, if relationships among students create a social bond, parallel identity development is still largely the norm. It would be difficult, given the magnitude of the data required, to compare the record of these three societies with those of other societies in which ethnic relationships are more routine and uneventful. Admittedly, several of the dynamics identified are also experienced there, but it is difficult to state if they are of the same intensity. Nonetheless, our analysis demonstrates that specificity, as an explanatory factor, is marginal in the studies reviewed, although this has been used in the three contexts to explain some resistance on the part of teachers.

Most striking is the pronounced dissonance between the generally favourable assessment one can make of institutional efforts at adapting to diversity and the state of public discourse on this reality. The three societies, though less so in Catalonia, experienced important debates, and in some cases political mobilization, around the issue of the identity transformations underway and their impact on the school. Certain points raised have substantial echoes elsewhere, such as the place of religion in the schools and the connection with Muslim students and parents, or, at least in Europe, the academic and social marginalization of a large proportion of second-generation students. As well, though these concerns are at times expressed rather strongly, as we saw the Quebec debate over reasonable accommodation, this is by no means always the case.

However, in the three societies, the controversies are clearly marked by the historical memory of victimization and the present feeling of fragility. Identity anxiety, even in some instances the resurgence of language questions in debates that have little or nothing to do with it, characterizes many of the views expressed. In Flanders, as we have said, this anxiety even constitutes the base of an extreme right-wing party's popularity. In the more moderate cases of Quebec, and to a lesser degree of Catalonia, there is evidence of a certain difficulty in delimiting the "us" boundary in order fully to accommodate ethnocultural diversity. The resilience of ethnic boundaries is also observed among minorities. The identity dynamics of young immigrants and of the second generation more often reveal a refusal to take part in the historical conflict opposing the two majorities than a clear identification with the group that welcomed them into its institutions. This phenomenon seems to be more pronounced in Quebec, Catalonia, and Flanders than in English Canada, Spain, and Wallonia. As well, the concerns expressed, often exploited artificially in clearly dominant-majority societies, seem to be better inscribed in the historical and present realities of fragile-majority societies. This could explain, among other things, the more pronounced coexistence than elsewhere of discourses and practices of openness and resistance to diversity within the same persons, especially in a professional context. Genuine adherence to the project of social transformation piloted by the school enters into conflict with anxieties, also very real, inherited from individual and community history.

In looking at the complex challenge of integrating pluralism into traditionally homogeneous school systems, it is possible to identify, from our analysis, the conditions facilitating such a development. Some conditions are givens of each society and are therefore very unlikely to be the object of public action. Thus the relative ease with which Catalonia approached pluralistic transformation in a consensual spirit in large measure reflects the deep roots that diversity already had as a constitutive component of Catalan identity. Conversely, the current clearly dominant status of the former fragile majority, as in Flanders, seems to act as a brake to raising awareness about the importance of institutional adaptation to pluralism and to the desire of public authorities to explicitly enunciate such a goal. Openness to diversity thus gives rise to a stronger consensus in Brussels and Montreal than in Flanders or in the outlying area, although the involvement of Quebec and Flanders in this matter is disproportionate: indeed, Quebec clearly has a greater need for immigrants than Flanders or even Belgium.

Beyond these dominant trends, our analysis illustrates the importance of a clear and repeated commitment by public authorities in support of adaptation to diversity, in society and in the school. For if the school is to play a role in identity transformation, with all the challenges this implies, it would be better to say so explicitly and to repeat it often. As well, this normative commitment must be concretized in overall frameworks and especially in resources enabling the change to have an impact on those in the field. On this last point, the three societies studied, like numerous others, have many limits. Nevertheless, the Quebec and Catalan governments have a head start on the Flemish government in their ability to express clearly to their population the collective challenges that await them and to which the school is asked respond, given its central role in the socialization of future generations. Nothing guarantees that the ambitious goal of transforming ethnic relations enunciated in these two societies will be reached, but at least the stakeholders who deal with this on a daily basis can visualize the horizon. In the Flemish case, the goal is more blurred, although significant resources are dedicated to it.

Some could argue that to cope with contentious issues, a cautious, stage-by-stage strategy is better than the proclamation of society-wide mobilization. Our analysis does not lean in this direction, nor does it confirm the predictions of the English Canadian, Spanish, and Walloon prophets of doom about the inability of Quebecers, Catalans, and Flemings to go beyond the heritage of homogeneity and closed attitudes toward the Other. However, only the future will tell how far each of these societies can proceed in their desire to adapt schools to diversity, in light of their specific sociohistoric contexts and the challenges that all immigrant-receiving countries share today.

Conclusion

In this book, we have dealt with openness to pluralism in Belgium, and more specifically in Flanders, Catalonia, Northern Ireland, and Quebec, societies that, despite their differences, can be characterized as living the common dynamic of ambiguous ethnic dominance. The relationship maintained by the group in the process of becoming a majority, what we have called a fragile majority, with the majority Other and the minority Other, was explored by examining diverse issues, such as the structure of schooling, rapprochements initiatives, the teaching of history, the linguistic and academic integration of immigrants, and the adaptation of school practices and norms to ethnocultural diversity. What conclusions can we draw?

Can fragile majorities open themselves to the ethnocultural pluralism emanating from the past or present history of their respective societies? What is the role formal education in this regard? We will begin by saying that, beyond the conclusions about the specific issues presented at the end of each chapter, it seems to us presumptuous, even silly, to try to respond categorically to these questions. Indeed, all the steps we have taken illustrate, as one would expect, that fragile majorities can move toward a pluralistic transformation of the school's habitus – or traditional and acquired schemes of perception, thought, and action – and a redefinition of the identity traditionally associated with it. The four societies studied have in large part redefined their history curriculum, made more room for immigrant languages and cultures, and, even though this last dimension gives rise to more controversy, redefined the traditional links they maintain, in many cases, with a particular religious heritage. All of them have also, to varying degrees, accorded great importance to the role of education as an agent of social engineering and the transformation of ethnic relations. The choice is largely explained by the important mandate of schools in modern societies to teach, socialize, and qualify students, especially through compulsory schooling.

In this regard, it would be doubtful that the four societies studied, all liberal democracies caught up in the complex dynamics of modernity and globalization, have not moved ahead. However, have these societies, their educational system, and their pedagogical practices evolved sufficiently for one to infer the irreversible character of the process embarked upon? Or, conversely, can one detect resistance and obstacles large enough that one can think the opposite – that, like other societies, they will eventually stagnate?

To offer a satisfying and exhaustive response to these questions, it would be necessary to define a new threshold, which would make it possible to determine that a process of identity transformation is significant, or a point of no return from which the dynamics initiated would not likely be called into question. But, even in societies with a simple dynamic, this type of indicator does not exist. We have seen, to the contrary, especially in the second section, dealing with relations to the minority Other, to what extent the obstacles and limits met in the four societies studied were far from calling attention to some unique feature.

In this conclusion, then, we will emphasize two general findings that emerge from our analysis concerning the discontinuities in the dynamics of change. As well, we will identify three conditions supporting openness to pluralism in the school systems of fragile-majority societies.

Our first observation relates to the fact that initiatives aiming at transforming the traditional relations of the fragile majority with the majority Other are less popular than those targeting the minority Other. As well, when the former are undertaken, they stir up stronger resistance. In the four societies studied, with the exception of Catalonia, where inter-group boundaries are more blurred, each community strongly endeavours to keep control of specific institutions and to cross educational boundaries on a non-permanent basis for utilitarian purposes. Moreover, although the societies that have experienced pronounced conflict seem more open, each group remains much attached to its own history. Confronted by communities of immigrant origin, creativity and dynamism are more evident. Societies, like Québec, that receive large numbers of immigrants, and more recently Catalonia and Flanders, are admittedly not free of populist or even overtly racist discourses. But the integration of various languages, cultures, and heritages in school policies, programs, and practices enjoys significant support. However, we have observed that the two problems are not always distinguished, including in public debate. The memory of past victimization often serves to legitimate the discourse of exclusion of third groups and makes more difficult the acknowledgement, by the new majority group, of its now favourable power balance, including in the area of academic success.

Our second observation relates to the difficulty, apparently more pronounced than elsewhere, that members of fragile majorities seem to have in recognizing the undeniable gains of the transformation in progress. This tendency, particularly obvious during certain controversies, tends to perpetuate a feeling of anxiety about the results achieved. This feeling is not supported by the research and could have negative consequences on the mobilization of the social actors most immediately involved, among others, the teachers. These fears obviously reflect, in part, the much greater complexity of the challenges experienced in contexts of sociolinguistic ambivalence and competition for allegiance. Thus, common schooling has clearly had a less immediate impact on the linguistic usage and attitudes of young immigrants and the development of a shared identity by students of all origins. However, the persistence of a certain defeatist and nostalgic discourse also reveals an inability of the group in the process in becoming a majority that fully acknowledges its new status, including the responsibilities of acceptance and openness that go with it. It still remains to be seen, something our analysis does not allow, if this instrumental use of past victimization is fundamentally different from other types of resistance to identity transformations worldwide, even among groups whose dominance of the national state is unquestionable.

Certain significant differences from one context to the next also help to identify the conditions that seem to facilitate openness to pluralism in educational institutions. The first concerns the necessity of agreeing to revisit the normative presuppositions and inherited choices of the past. Paradoxically, the process seems easier in societies that, like Northern Ireland, are marked by a difficult legacy of ethnic relations. However, the ability to take a critical distance from the knee-jerk protection of gains also shows itself, especially as concerns relations with the minority Other, in contexts where this heightening of awareness is less dictated by the urgency of the situation. This is particularly the case in Catalonia, where the legacy of the past is more open to pluralism than in the other societies. Nonetheless, in all the contexts, there remains much distance to cover before this first facilitating condition of pluralistic transformation can be fully actualized.

The fragile majority's ability to control, if not totally, at least significantly, the nature and pace of change also reveals a very important dimension. Indeed, if the pluralistic transformation seems to be imposed from outside and serve the interests of the majority Other, resistance will increase. In addition, opponents of any pluralist transformation use this discursive strategy when they want to stir up emotional reactions to certain issues. We saw this during the debates surrounding the redefinition of the History program in Quebec or during the controversies over the role of immigration in the sociolinguistic dynamics of Brussels. Our analyses show, to the contrary, that in these four societies, with some qualification to the statement in Northern Ireland, the majority group largely initiated the process of using education to bring about social change. Moreover, although it likely did not foresee all the consequences of this transformation, this group largely maintained control of the educational agenda and the public debate. Some may deplore it, including persons belonging to minority communities who would sometimes like to see their concerns take centre stage more often. However, these points explain, in large measure, the significant progress achieved, both in terms of the results of the actions specifically targeting the school and identity transformation more generally.

Finally, a last favourable condition lies in a positive but realistic vision of the challenges associated with pluralist transformation. In all cases, initially, this condition was not entirely fulfilled. The fragile majorities of the four societies have committed themselves to social or educational initiatives to transform unfavourable ethnic relations without being fully aware of the eventual consequences of their actions. As well, whereas common sense would suggest that failure is to be feared, paradoxically, it is often success that arouses anxiety. In the contexts where the central marker was language, it is fascinating to see to what extent the normative and cultural changes flowing from every successful linguistic policy were underestimated, including changes to relations with immigrant populations. To a lesser extent, although much less was done on this front, the transformation of relations with the majority Other is unsettling, no doubt because it calls into question the comfort of mutual ignorance and cultural isolationism. Examples of this are the ambivalence of school staff confronted by the unplanned crossing of boundaries by francophones in Brussels and anglophones in Montreal, and the relative stagnation of integrated education in Northern Ireland.

Perhaps it is in the nature of things for reformist politicians to announce a better tomorrow to their constituents rather than to paint a complex picture of the difficulties that await them. Nevertheless, in order to better support the stakeholders in the field and better manage citizens' anxieties, the authorities need to show more leadership in stating clearly the important challenges facing the educational systems and, more generally, all institutions in societies whose traditional identity being questioned.

In any event, we hope that this book will help the reader become aware of the complexity of the educational issues associated with opening up to pluralism, not only for fragile majorities and their institutions but also in large measure for all societies today confronted by globalization, increased immigration, and the emergence of new citizenship paradigms more respectful of diversity and human rights.

Notes

INTRODUCTION

1 Barth (1969); Juteau (1996); McAndrew (2003a).
2 Schermerhorn (1970); Juteau (2000a).
3 Bousetta (2000); Cochrane (2000); Juteau (2000b); Solé (2000).
4 Bourhis and Marshall (1999); Dunn (2000); McAndrew (2002a).
5 Leman (1999); McAndrew and Lemire (1999); Verlot and McAndrew (2004).
6 Irwin (1992); Kymlicka (1996); Thornberry and Gibbons (1997); Potvin et al. (2004).
7 Solé (1982); Laperrière (1989); McAndrew (2000); Mehdoune (2000).
8 Samper (1996); Figueroa (1999); Hohl and Normand (2000); Bourgeault et al. (2004).
9 Levine (1990); Juteau (2000b); Commission des États généraux sur la situation et l'avenir de la langue française au Québec (2001).
10 Mercadé and Hernandez (1988); Vila (1995); Keating (1996).
11 Farrell (1976); Darby (1997); Mitchell (2003).
12 Martiniello and Swyngedouw (1998); Witte and Van Velthoven (1999); Verlot and McAndrew (2004).
13 Boussetta (2000); Cochrane (2000); Juteau (2000b); Solé (2000).
14 Barth (1969); Juteau (2000a).
15 Juteau (1993); Martin, 1994; O'Murchei (1999).
16 Zapata (2004); Office of the First Minister and Deputy First Minister for Northern Ireland (2005); Khader et al. (2006); McAndrew (2007a).

CHAPTER ONE

1 Lê Than Khoi (1981); Gallagher (2004); McAndrew and Janssens (2004).

2 Holmes (1981); Homan (1992); Thornberry and Gibbons (1997).

3 Irwin (1992); McAndrew and Lemire (1994); Gallagher (2003).

4 Laferrière (1983); Behiels (1986); Levine (1990); Proulx and Woerhling (1997).

5 Lamarre (1997); Association des commissions scolaires anglophones du Québec (2006); Ministère de l'Éducation, du Loisir et du Sport (2006c).

6 Jedwab (1996); Martel (1996).

7 McAndrew and Eid (2003a); Béland (2006); Ministère de l'Éducation, du Loisir et du Sport (2007a).

8 McAndrew (2001 and 2002a); Ministère de l'Éducation, du Loisir et du Sport (2006a).

9 Chambers (1992); Proulx (1998).

10 Lamarre (1997); Association des commissions scolaires anglophones du Québec (2006); Ministère de l'Éducation, du Loisir et du Sport (2006c).

11 Lamarre and Laperrière (2005); McAndrew and Eid (2003a and b).

12 McAndrew and Eid (2003a and b).

13 McAndrew (2006b).

14 Smith et al. (2003); McAndrew et al. (2006).

15 Lamarre (2007 and 2008); McAndrew (2001); Jedwab (2002).

16 Commission des États généraux sur la situation et l'avenir de la langue française au Québec (2001); Martel (1996); Marois (2008).

17 Smith et al. (2003); Association des commissions scolaires anglophones du Québec (2006); McAndrew et al. (2006).

18 Lamarre (1999).

19 Zanazanian (à paraitre 2009).

20 Clément et al. (2001); Adsett and Morin (2004); Côté (2005).

21 Martiniello and Swyngedouw (1998); Glenn (1999); Witte et al. (1999); Witte and Van Velthoven (1999).

22 Lindemans et al. (1981).

23 Witte and Van Velthoven (1999); McAndrew and Janssens (2004).

24 Parlement Belge (1963); Brigouleix (1983); Leclerc (2008).

25 Van de Craen and D'Hondt (1997); Medhoune and Lavallée (2000); Koppen et al. (2002); Verlot et al. (2003).

26 Institut National de la Statistique (1999); Medhoune and Lavallée (2000); Communauté française de Belgique (2007); Ministère de la Communauté flamande (2007c).

27 Van Velthoven (1981); Witte and Van Velthoven (1998, 1999).

28 Deprez et al. (1982); De Vriendt and Willemyns (1987); François (2004); Mettewie (2004).

29 Janssens (2001); Janssens and Van Mensel (2006); Mawet and Van Parijs (2007).

30 Braun (2002); Van Mensel et al. (2005); Mettewie and Janssens (2007).

31 Fondation Roi Baudoin (2003a and 2006); De Mets (2004).

32 De Schutter (2001); Mettewie (2007); Vlaamse Gemeenschapscommissie (2008).

33 Akenson (1973); Darby (1976); Farren (1995).

34 Dunn (1990); Gallagher et al. (1993, 1994).

35 Her Majesty's Stationery Office (1989); Morgan et al. (1992, 1993); Department of Education of Northern Ireland (1998); Dunn and Morgan (1999).

36 Department of Education of Northern Ireland (1997); Smith (2001); McGlynn (2003).

37 Cormack (1992); Gallagher et al. (2003); Gallagher (2004).

38 McPoilan (1997); Comhairle na Gaelscolaïochta (2007); Department of Education for Northern Ireland (2007a).

39 Office of the First Minister and Deputy First Minister for Northern Ireland (2005b); Department of Education for Northern Ireland (2006).

40 Gallagher et al. (2003).

41 Morgan and Fraser (1999); Morgan (2000); Gallagher et al. (2003); McGonigle et al. (2003).

42 Darby et al. (1977); Department of Education for Northern Ireland (1999); Morgan (2000); O'Connor et al. (2002 and 2003).

43 Ewart and Schubotz (2004); Jarman (2005).

44 Gallagher (2004); Sinn Féin (2009); Council for Catholic Maintained Schools (2006); Northern Ireland Council for Integrated Education (2006).

45 Smith and Dunn (1990); Abbott et al. (1999); Dunn and Morgan (1999).

46 Murray (1985); Department of Education for Northern Ireland (1999, 2006); Smith (2003).

47 McClenahan et al. (1996); McAndrew (2002c); Cairns (1989).

48 Stringer et al. (2003).

49 Solé (1982); Siguan (1984); Keating (1996).

50 Grant and Doherty (1992); Samper et al. (2000).

51 Arenas (1985); Laitin (1987); Flaquer (1996).

52 Direcció General de Politica Lingüistica (1983); Artigal (1991);
    Strubell (1996); Garcia (1997).
53 Direcció General d'Ordenació Educativa (1999); Vila i Moreno
    (2004a); Generalitat de Catalunya (2006c).
54 Miller and Miller (1996); Samper et al. (2000); Vila i Moreno (2004a).
55 Bartolomé Pina et al. (1997); Subirats (2002); Vila i Moreno (2004b).
56 Rees (1996); Comes et al. (1995); Puig-Salellas (2000); Samper et al.
    (2000).
57 Artigal (1991); Vila (1995); Serra (1997); Consell Superior d'Avaluació
    del Sistema Educatiu (2006).
58 Romani (1999); Vila i Moreno (2004a, b, and c).
59 Vila i Moreno and Galindo (2006).
60 Boix (1993); Vila (1995); Romani (1999).
61 Lê Than Khoi (1981); Farrell (1976); Rust et al. (1999).
62 McAndrew (1999, 2003a).
63 Nagel (1994); Hargreaves (1996); Walford (1996); Tomlinson (1997).
64 Carens (1995); Taylor (1992); Bull et al. (1997).

CHAPTER TWO

1 McAndrew and Lemire (1994); McAndrew (1996); Donnelly (2006).
2 McGlynn and Bekerman (2007); Junne and Verkoren (2005).
3 Allport (1954); Pettigrew (1998); Côté (2005); Dovidio et al. (2003).
4 Tajfel (1982); Bourhis and Leyens (1994); Brewer and Miller (1996);
   Dovidio et al. (2003).
5 Wilder (1984); Stephan and Stephan (1985); Pettigrew (1998).
6 Allport (1954); Tajfel and Turner (1986).
7 Rothbart and John (1985); Johnston and Hewstone (1992); Brewer
   and Miller (1996).
8 Gaertner et al. (1996); Anastasio et al. (1997).
9 Wilder (1984); Biernat (1990); Desforges et al. (1991); Biernart and
   Crandall (1994).
10 Wilder (1984); Brewer and Miller (1988); Insko et al. (1987); Biernat
    (1990).
11 McAndrew and Eid (2003b); Mettewie (2007).
12 McAndrew and Janssens (2004); Côté and Mettewie (2008); McGlynn
    et al. (2009).
13 Laperrière and Lamarre (2004, 2005); McGlynn et al. (2009).
14 McAndrew and Lemire (1994); McGlynn (2007); Côté and Mettewie
    (2008).

15 Janssens (2007 and 2008).

16 Ponjaert-Kristoffersen, Van Braak, and Lambrecht (1998); Deckers (1999); Schrauwen and Van Braak (2000); Devlieger and Goossens (2006).

17 Housen et al. (2002); Housen et al. (2004); Mettewie (2007).

18 Mettewie (2003, 2004); Mettewie et al. (2004).

19 Montgomery et al. (2003).

20 Morgan et al. (1993); Abbott et al. (1999); Morgan (2000); Gallagher et al. (2003).

21 Montgomery et al. (2003); McGlynn (2007); McGlynn et al. (2009).

22 McGlynn (2001).

23 Wicklow (1997); Abbott et al. (1999); Dunn (2000).

24 Morgan et al. (1993); McGlynn (2001); Montgomery et al. (2003); Bryan and Gillepsie (2005).

25 McGonigle (2000); McGonigle et al. (2003); Donnelly (2004); Northern Ireland Council for Integrated Education (2006).

26 Dunn and Morgan (1999); McGlynn (2003); Donnelly (2006); McGlynn et al. (2009).

27 McClenehan et al. (1996); McGlynn (2001); Stringer et al. (2003).

28 Smith (2003); Gallagher (2004); McGlynn et al. (2004).

29 McCully et al. (2003); McAndrew et al. (2003a).

30 Côté (2009a, b); Pagé et al. (2007).

31 Smith et al. (2003); Côté (2005); Pagé and Côté (2006); Pagé et al. (2007).

32 McAndrew et al. (2003a); Kirk et al. (2006).

33 McAndrew et al. (2003b).

34 O'Connor et al. (2002, 2003).

35 McCully et al. (1999); Speak Your Piece (1995).

36 Smith and Robinson (1996); Connolly (1998); Department of Education for Northern Ireland (1999, 2007b).

37 McAndrew (2003a); McCully (2006).

38 Mc Cully (2006).

39 Smyth and Scott (2000); Hugues and Donnelly (2002); Ewart and Schubotz (2004).

CHAPTER THREE

1 Tonkin et al. (1989); Juteau (1996); Jenkins (1997).

2 Connerton (1989); Straub (2005); Vickers (2005).

3 Ricœur (2000); Simon (2004); Angenot (1997).

4 Davis (1989); Seixas (2004); Rüsen (2005).
5 Fullwinder (1996); Lantheaume (2003); Laville (2004).
6 McAndrew, Tessier, and Bourgeault (1997); McDonough and Feinderg (2003); Lenoir and Xypas (2006).
7 Phillips et al. (1999); Smith (2003); Chastenay and Niens (2008).
8 Phillips (1998); Smith (2005); Government of Northern Ireland (2007).
9 Council for the Curriculum Examinations and Assessment (2003a, b; 2007a, b).
10 McCully et al. (2002); Kitson and McCully (2005); Council for the Curriculum Examinations and Assessment (2007b); McCall (2007).
11 Council for the Curriculum Examinations and Assessment (2007a, c).
12 Council for the Curriculum Examinations and Assessment (2003c).
13 Council for the Curriculum Examinations and Assessment (2007d).
14 Smith (2003); McAndrew (2006b); Chastenay and Niens (2008).
15 Conway (2004); Smith (2005), Kitson (2007).
16 Thompson (2007).
17 McCombe (2006).
18 Council for the Curriculum Examinations and Assessment (2006).
19 Barton et al. (2003); Niens and Chastenay (2005).
20 Barton (2005); Barton and McCully (2005 and 2006); McCully et al. (2003).
21 Niens and Chastenay (2005); Council for the Curriculum Examinations and Assessment (2006).
22 Labio (2002); Van Dam and Nizet (2002); Van den Braembussche (2002); Bailly and Sephiha (2005).
23 La Libre Belgique (2007); Sept sur Sept Canal Infos (2007); *Le Soir* en ligne (2007).
24 Wils (2003); Bouffioux (2005); Fondation Roi Baudoin (2003b, 2007a, b).
25 Ministère de la Communauté française (1998, 1999b, 2002); Commission d'observation et de pilotage de l'Enseignement (2006).
26 Ministère de la Communauté française (1997, 1999a); Jadoulle, Bouhon, and Nys (2004).
27 Fédération de l'enseignement secondaire catholique (2000); Communauté française de Belgique (2007).
28 Ministry of the Flemish Community, Education Department (2002a).
29 Ministry of the Flemish Community (2001, 2002b, c, d).
30 Ministry of the Flemish Community (1997, 2001).
31 Létourneau (2000); Maclure (2000); Pagé and Chastenay (2002)
32 Trudel and Jain (1970); Durocher (1996).

33 MEQ (1983, 1986); Lévesque (2004); Charland et al. (2006).

34 Martineau (1998); McAndrew (2001).

35 Ministère de l'Éducation du Québec (1996, 1998a).

36 Ministère de l'Éducation du Québec (1997); Cardin (2004); McAndrew (2006c).

37 Ministère de l'Éducation du Québec (1982, 2001a).

38 McAndrew (2004); Chastenay and Niens (2008).

39 Ministère de l'Éducation, du Loisir et du Sport (2003, 2007b).

40 Éthier et al. (2008); Zanazanian (2008).

41 Ministère de l'Éducation, du Loisir et du Sport (2006b).

42 Boileau (2006); Bouvier and Lamontagne (2006); Robitaille (2006).

43 Cardin (2006); Laville (2006); Létourneau (2006).

44 Ministère de l'Éducation, du Loisir et du Sport (2007b).

45 Éthier (2004); McAndrew (2004, 2006a); Éthier et al. (2008).

46 Zanazanian (2005 and 2008).

47 Létourneau and Moisan (2004a, b).

48 Llobera (1989); Montés (1999); Facal (2003).

49 Fernandez (1997); Pagès i Blanch (2003a, 2004a).

50 Real Academia de la Historia (2000); Pagès i Blanch (2001).

51 Prats (2000); Montes (2004); Segura et al. (2000, 2001).

52 Prats (1999); Pagès i Blanch (2003b, 2004b, 2005).

53 Generalitat de Catalunya (2005).

54 Puig Rovira et al. (2005).

55 Generalitat de Catalunya (2007c, d).

56 Pagès i Blanch (1999a, 2004b); Ministerio de Educación y Ciencia (2004).

CHAPTER FOUR

1 Ministère des Affaires internationales, de l'Immigration et des Communautés culturelles (1994); McAndrew and Weinfeld (1997); Commissions des communautés européennes (2007); Fix (2007).

2 Ballantine (2001); McAndrew (2007c).

3 Inglis (2008); McAndrew et al. (2008a); McAndrew (2009a).

4 Humet et al. (2005); Vila i Moreno et al. (2006).

5 McAndrew and Gagnon (2000); Bayley and Schecter (2003).

6 Ministère des Communautés culturelles et de l'Immigration (1990a); Gagné and Chamberland (1999); McAndrew (2007a).

7 Ministère de l'Immigration et des Communautés culturelles (2005, 2008a, 2009).

8 McAndrew (2001); Ministère de l'Éducation, du Loisir et du Sport (2006a, 2008a).

9 Mallea (1977); Levine (1990).

10 Gouvernement du Québec (1977); Harvey (2000); McAndrew (2002a).

11 Conseil de la langue française (1987a, b); Ministère de l'Éducation du Québec (1988); Plourde (1988).

12 Comité interministériel sur la situation de la langue française (1996); Commission des États généraux sur la situation et l'avenir de la langue française au Québec (2001); El Kouri (2001).

13 McAndrew (2002b); Lisée (2007); Bouchard and Taylor (2008).

14 McAndrew (2001); Ministère de l'Éducation, du Loisir et du Sport (2007c).

15 McAndrew and Cicéri (1998).

16 Armand and Dagenais (2005); Chamberland (2008); McAndrew (2009a).

17 Commission scolaire Marguerite Bourgeois (1999); Commission scolaire de Montréal (2006); Sévigny (2008).

18 Paillé (2002); McAndrew and Eid (2003b); Ministère de l'Éducation, du Loisir et du Sport (2008a).

19 McAndrew (2006d); Ministère de l'Éducation, du Loisir et du Sport (2008b).

20 McAndrew et al. (1999); McAndrew et al. (2000).

21 Rossell (2005, 2006).

22 Ministère de l'Éducation, du Loisir et du Sport (2007d); McAndrew (2008a); Office québécois de la langue française (2008).

23 Girard-Lamoureux (2004); Castonguay (2005); Statistique Canada (2007).

24 Ministère de l'Éducation du Québec (1998a); Anisef et al. (2004); McAndrew (2006d).

25 McAndrew (2001); Ministère de l'Éducation, du Loisir et du Sport (2007e).

26 McAndrew (2006d) McAndrew et al. (2008b).

27 Bussières (2004); Organisation de Coopération et de Développement Économiques (2006); Statistique Canada (2008).

28 Potvin et al. (2004); Potvin et al. (2006); Ministère de l'Éducation, du Loisir et du Sport (2007e, f); Chamberland (2009).

29 Palaudàrias and Serra (2007); Instituto Nacional de Estadística (2009).

30 Generalitat de Catalunya (2006a); Generalitat de Catalunya (2007e); Secretaría de Estado de Inmigración y Emigración (2008).

31 Generalitat de Catalunya (1979, 2006b); Zapata et al. (2005); Garreta (2007).

32 Generalitat de Catalunya (2008, 2009a).

33 Querol (2001); Jou (2002).

34 Boix (2004); Vila i Moreno (2004a, c); Bastardas (2007).

35 Esquerra de Catalunya (2003); Generalitat de Catalunya (2003a, 2004a, 2005).

36 Subirats and Gallego (2003); Zapata et al. (2005); Generalitat de Catalunya (2006c); Garreta (2008).

37 Generalitat de Catalunya (2007b); Pueyo (2007).

38 Vila and Perera (1997); Generalitat de Catalunya (1999); Garreta and Llevot (2001).

39 Generalitat de Catalunya (2004b, 2006c); Vila (2004, 2006); Àngel Alegre (2005).

40 Generalitat de Catalunya (2003a).

41 Generalitat de Catalunya (2004a); Vallcorba (2009).

42 Generalitat de Catalunya (2007c, d, 2009b); Masats (2001).

43 Àngel Alegre (2005); Àngel Alegre et al. (2006); Generalitat de Catalunya (2006c).

44 Boix (2004); Vila i Moreno (2004b); Vila i Moreno and Galindo (2006).

45 Torres (2006),

46 Generalitat de Calatunya (2006c).

47 Vila i Moreno (2004c).

48 Fukuda (2009).

49 Comajoan (2008); Bretxa (2009).

50 Huguet et al. (2005).

51 Vila i Moreno (2004a); Torres (2005).

52 Ferrer et al. (2006); Huguet and Navarro (2006).

53 Llosada et al. (2005); Palaudàrias (2008).

54 Consell Superior d'Avaluació del Sistema Educatiu (2005); Garreta (2006); Huguet and Navarro (2006); Schleicher (2006).

55 Blaise et al. (1997); Gsir et al. (2005); Loobuyck and Jacobs (2006).

56 Lennert and Decroly (2001); Timmerman et al. (2006).

57 Institut National de la Statistique (2008).

58 Gsir (2006); Khader et al. (2006); Van Robaeys and Perrin (2006).

59 European Commission (2004); Centre pour l'égalité des chances et la lutte contre le racisme (2004); Communauté flamande (2006).

60 European Commission (2004); Janssens (2007); Vlaamse Gemeenschapscommissie (2008).

61 De Witte and Klandermans (2000); Erk (2002); Jacobs (2004).

62 McAndrew and Janssens (2004); McAndrew and Verlot (2004); Humet et al. (2005); Van Parys and Wauters (2006).

63 Ministère de la Communauté flamande (2003a, 2008a, b).

64 D'Hondt (2006); Lamberts et al. (2007); Keulen (2008); Pulinx (2008).

65 European Commission (2004); Ministère de la communauté flamande (2004b, 2006b, c, 2008d, e).

66 Bogaert and Goossens (1996); Verhelst (2005); Van den Branden et al. (2006); Steunpunt GOK (2009).

67 Gatz (2004).

68 Byram and Leman (1990); Le Foyer (2008).

69 Le Foyer (2008); Roekens (2008).

70 Centrum voor Taal en Onderwijs (2006).

71 Manço and Crutzen (1999); Hambye and Lucchini (2005); Roosens (2007).

72 Byram and Leman (1990); Leman (1999).

73 Van Avermaet and Klatter-Folmer (1998); Delruelle and Torfs (2005); Jaspers (2005); Spotti (2008).

74 Verlot and Delrue (2004); Van Parijs (2005); Janssens (2006); Van Parys and Wauters (2006).

75 Leman (1999); Manço (1999); Janssens (2006).

76 Phalet et al. (2007).

77 De Rycke and Swyngedouw (1999); Verlot (2000a); Centre pour l'égalité des chances et la lutte au racisme (2004); François (2004, 2005).

78 De Meyer et al. (2005); Organisation de Coopération et de Développement Économiques (2006); Jacobs et al. (2007);

79 Fondation Roi Baudoin (2007a); Jacobs et al. (2007).

80 Ministère de la Communauté flamande (2002, 2006a); Centre pour l'égalité des chances et la lutte contre le racisme (2004); Fondation Roi Baudoin (2007b).

CHAPTER FIVE

1 Black et al. (1998); Pagé and Gagnon (1999).

2 Bourhis and Leyens (1994); Hohl and Normand (1996); Juteau (2000a); Kanouté and Vatz Laaroussi (2008).

3 McAndrew (2003a); Suárez-Orozco (2007); Inglis (2008) Keating (1996); McAndrew (2000); Zappata et al. (2005).

4 Keating (1996); McAndrew (2000); Zappata et al. (2005).

5 Juteau et al. (1998); Salée (2007).

6 Gouvernement du Québec (1978, 1984).

7 Ministère de l'Immigration et des Communautés culturelles (1990).

8 Labelle (2000); Juteau (2002); Ministère de l'Immigration et des Communautés culturelles (2008b).

9 Ministère de l'Éducation du Québec (1998b); McAndrew (2001).

10 Commission scolaire de Montréal (2006); Comité consultatif sur l'intégration et l'accommodement raisonnable en milieu scolaire (2007).

11 Proulx (1999); Racine (2008).

12 Comité sur les affaires religieuses (2003, 2006).

13 Ministère de l'Éducation du Québec (1997, 2001a); Ministère de l'Éducation, du Loisir et du Sport (2003); Potvin, McAndrew and Kanouté (2006).

14 Ministère de l'Éducation, du Loisir et du Sport (2005); Racine (2008).

15 McAndrew (1986, 1987, 2001); Éthier et al. (2008).

16 Oueslati et al. (2004); Oueslati (2009).

17 Ministère de l'Éducation du Québec (2001b); Kanouté et al. (2004); Potvin et al. (2006); Potvin and Crarr (2008).

18 Kanouté et al. (2002); Kanouté and Chastenay (2009).

19 Potvin et al. (2006).

20 Lefebvre (2007); Ministère de l'Éducation, du Loisir et du Sport (2007e, f); Fortin (2008).

21 Comité consultatif sur l'intégration et l'accommodement raison-nable en milieu scolaire (2007); McAndrew (2008b); Ministère de l'Éducation, du Loisir et du Sport (2008c).

22 Comité consultatif sur l'intégration et l'accommodement raison-nable en milieu scolaire (2007).

23 Potvin et al. (2006).

24 McAndrew (2003b, 2009b); Comité consultatif sur l'intégration et l'accommodement raisonnable en milieu scolaire (2007); Kanouté and Llevot (2008).

25 Hohl and Normand (2000); Potvin et al. (2006); Gérin-Lajoie (2007).

26 Tessier and McAndrew (2001); Normand and Hohl (2000).

27 McAndrew et al. (1997); Laperrière and Dumont (2000).

28 Laperrière et al. (1994); Pagé et al. (1997); Laperrière and Dumont (2000).

29 Bouchard and Taylor (2008); Woehrling (2008).

30 McAndrew (2007b); Maclure (2008); Potvin (2008).

31 Commission des droits de la personne (1995); McAndrew (2006e); Bouchard and Taylor (2008); Ouellet (2008).

32 Jolicoeur et al. (2004); Montreuil and Bourhis (2004); Chastenay and Pagé (2006); Duchesne (2006).

33 Pujol (1976); Generalitat de Catalunya (1979); Solé (1982, 2000).

34 Garreta (2007 and 2009b); Generalitat de Catalunya (1993, 2001).

35 Esquerra Republicana de Catalunya (2003); Generalitat de Catalunya (2005).

36 Generalitat de Catalunya (1996, 1999); Samper et al. (2001).

37 Generalitat de Catalunya (2003a, 2004b).

38 Generalitat de Catalunya (2003b, 2007f); Vallcorba (2008).

39 Generalitat de Catalunya (2007c, d).

40 Garreta (2000); Garreta et al. (2007); Generalitat de Catalunya (2007b).

41 Segura et al. (2001); Garreta and Llevot (2002); Valls (2005).

42 Samper and Garreta (2009)

43 Garreta (2006); Aula Intercultural (2009); Edualter (2009).

44 Centro de Investigación y Documentación Educativa (2000); Samper and Garreta (2007).

45 Garreta and Llevot (2002); Centro de Recursos para la Atención a la Diversidad Cultural en Educación (2009); Fundació Jaume Bofill (2009).

46 Llevot (2004); Garreta (2008).

47 Garreta and Llevot (2002).

48 Garreta (2008 and 2009b); Kanouté and Llevot (2008).

49 Garreta et al. (2007).

50 Garreta and Llevot (2002).

51 Bartolomé Pina et al. (1997); Pascual (1998); Palaudàrias and Garreta (2008).

52 Samper (1996).

53 Romani (1999); Besalú and Climent (2004); Vázquez (2004).

54 Subirats and Gallego (2003); Aubarell et al. (2004); Zapata et al. (2005).

55 Garreta (2008).

56 Leman (1991); Jacobs (2004); Gsir (2006).

57 Ministère de la communauté flamande (2003b, 2004a); Jacobs (2004).

58 Ministère de la communauté flamande (1998, 2002); Gsir et al. (2005).

59 Ministère de la communauté flamande (2003a, 2004a).

60 Leman (1997); Verlot (1998); European Commission (2004); Communauté flamande (2006).

61 Fondation Evens (2001); Paelman (2005); Centre for Diversity and Learning (2008).

62 Ministère de la communauté flamande (2004a, 2007a).

63 Ministère de la communauté flamande (2003c).

64 Ministry of the Flemish Community (2001, 2002a, b, c, d).

65 Conseil de l'Europe (2008).

66 Rea (1999); Bousetta and Maréchal (2003).

67 Boender and Kanmaz (2002); El Battiui and Kanmaz (2004); Brébant and Schreiber (2006).

68 Delruelle and Torfs (2005).

69 Soetart and van Heule (1999); Ministère de la communauté flamande (2006d, 2008f).

70 Verlot (1998, 2000a); Ministère de la communauté flamande (2005, 2007a).

71 Fondation Evens (2001); Centre for Diversity and Learning (2008); Vlaamse Gemeenschapscommissie (2009).

72 Ministère de la communauté flamande (2007b, 2008c)

73 Verstraete (2006).

74 Centre pour l'égalité des chances et la lutte au racisme (2004); European Commission (2004).

75 Verlot (2000b); Delruelle and Torfs (2005).

76 Delruelle and Torfs (2005); Carpentier de Changy et al. (2006).

77 De Mets (2005); Merry (2005).

78 Hermans (2004, 2006); Carpentier de Changy et al. (2006); Roosens (2007).

79 Verlot and Pinxten (2000); Verlot and Suijs (2000); Fondation Evens (2001).

80 Van den Branden and Van Gorp (2000); Ernalsteen (2002); Roosens (2007).

81 Verlot (2000b); Verlot et al. (2000).

82 Verlot (2002).

83 Timmerman (2000); Phalet and Swyngedouw (2002); Stevens (2008).

84 Delruelle and Torfs (2005).

85 De Witte and Klandermans (2000); Somers (2005); Zapata et al. (2005).

86 Maddens et al. (2000); Jacobs (2004); Loobuyck and Jacobs (2006).

87 Delruelle and Torfs (2005); Carpentier de Changy et al. (2006).

88 Delruelle and Torfs (2005).

89 Garreta (2006); Verhoeven (2006); McAndrew 2010).

Bibliography

Abbott, L., S. Dunn, and V. Morgan. 1999. "Integrated Education in Northern Ireland: An Analytical Literature Review." *Research Serial* 15. Ulster: Northern Ireland Department of Education Report.

Adsett, M., and M. Morin. 2004. "Contact and Regional Variation in Attitudes Towards Linguistic Duality in Canada." *Journal of Canadian Studies* 38(2): 129–51.

Advisory Committee on Integration and Reasonable Accommodation in the Schools. 2007. *Inclusive Québec Schools: Dialogue, Values and Common Reference Points.* A report presented to Madame Michelle Courchesne, Minister of Education, Recreation and Sport (Quebec) by Bergman Fleury.

Akenson, D.H. 1973. *Education and Enmity: The Control of Schooling in Northern Ireland, 1920–1950.* Newton Abbot: David and Charles.

Aldrich, R., and D. Dean. 1991. "The Historical Dimension." In *History in the National Curriculum*, edited by R. Aldrich. London: Kogan Page.

Allport, G.W. 1954. *The Nature of Prejudice.* Cambridge, MA: Addison-Wesley Publishing Company.

Anastasio, P.A., B. Bachman, S. Gaertner, and J. Dovidio. 1997. "Categorization, Recategorization, and Common Ingroup Identity." In *The Social Psychology of Stereotyping and Group Life*, edited by R. Spears, P. Oakes, N. Ellemers, and A. Haslam, 236–56. Malden, MA: Blackwell Publishers.

Àngel Alegre, M. 2005. *Educació i immigració: l'acollida als centres educatius.* Barcelona: Editorial Mediterrània.

– R. Benito, and S. González. 2006. *Immigrants als instituts. L'acollida vista pels seus protagonistes.* Barcelona: Editorial Mediterrània.

Angenot, M. 1997. *Les idéologies du ressentiment.* Montreal: XYZ Éditeurs.

Anisef, P. et al. 2004. *Academic Performance and Educational Mobility of Youth of Immigrant Origin in Canada: What Can We Learn from Provincial Data Banks?* Ottawa: Department of Citizenship and Immigration Canada.

Arenas, J. 1985. *Absència I Recuperació de la Liengua Catalana a l'Ensenyament a Catalunya (1970–1983).* Lleida: Quarderns d'Escola 5.

Armand, F., and D. Dagenais. 2005. "Languages and immigration: Raising awareness of language and linguistic diversity in schools." *Journal of the Canadian Studies Association,* special issue 99–102. www.im.metropolis.net/research-policy/research_content/bilans_02_05/CITC_Armand_article_eng.pdf.

Artigal, J.P. 1991. *The Catalan Immersion Program. A European Point of View.* Translated from Catalan by J. Hall. Norwood, NJ: Ablex Publishing Corporation.

Association des commissions scolaires anglophones du Québec/Quebec English School Boards Association (2006). QESBA Advisory Council on the Future of English Public Education in Quebec: Final Report. QESBA: Montreal.

Aubarell, G., A. Nicolau-Coll, and A. Ros, eds. 2004. *Immigració i qüestió nacional. Minories subestatals i immigració a Europa.* Barcelona: Editorial Mediterrània.

Aula Intercultural. 2009. Website of Aula Intercultural, the intercultural education portal. www.aulaintercultural.org.

Bailly, O., and M. Sephiha. 2005. "La crise belge vue de Wanze et de Kruibeke: cloisonnement identitaire entre Flamands et Wallons." *Le Monde diplomatique.* www.monde-diplomatique.fr/2005/06/bailly/12521.

Ballantine, J.H. 2001. *The Sociology of Education: A Systematic Analysis.* 5th ed. Upper Saddle, NJ: Prentice Hall.

Bartolomé Pina, M., F. Cabrera Rodríguez, J. del Campo Sorribas, J.V. Espín López, Á. Marín Gracia, D. del Rincón Igea, M. Rodríguez-Lajo, and P. Sandín-Esteban. 1997. *Diagnóstico a la escuela multicultural.* Barcelona: CEDECS Psichopedagogía.

Barth, F., ed. 1969. *Ethnic Groups and Boundaries.* Boston: Little, Brown & Co.

Barton, K. 2005. "Best Not to Forget Them: Adolescence Judgment of Historical Significance in Northern Ireland." *Theory and Research in Social Education* 33: 9–44.

Barton, K., and A. McCully. 2005. "History, Identity, and the School Curriculum in Northern Ireland: An Empirical Study of Secondary

Students' Ideas and Perspectives." *Journal of Curriculum Studies* 37(1): 85–116.

– (2006). "Secondary Students' Perspectives on School and Community History in Northern Ireland." *European Social Science History Conference.* March. hdl.handle.net/2428/6038.

Barton, K., A. McCully, and M. Conway. 2003. "History Education and National Identity in Northern Ireland." *International Journal of Historical Learning, Teaching and Research* 3(1): 31–43.

Bastardas, A. 2007. *Les polítiques de la llengua i la identitat a l'era "glo-cal."* Generalitat de Catalunya: Departament d'Interior, Relacions Institutcionals i Participació, Institut d'Estudis Autonòmics.

Bayley, R., and S. Schecter. 2003. *Language Socialization in Bilingual and Multilingual Societies – Bilingual Education and Bilingualism.* Clevedon: Multilingual Matters.

Behiels, M.D. 1986. "The Commission des écoles catholiques de Montréal and the Neo-Canadian question: 1947–1963." *Canadian Ethnic Studies/ Études ethniques au Canada* 18(2): 38–64.

Béland, P. 2006. *La fréquentation du réseau scolaire anglophone. Une étude exploratoire des statistiques de 2000 à 2004.* Montreal: Conseil supérieur de la langue française.

Besalú, X., and T. Climent, eds. 2004. *Construint identitats. Espais i processos de socialització dels joves d'origen immigrat.* Catalonia: Editorial Mediterrània.

Biernat, M. 1990. "Stereotypes on Campus: How Contact and Liking Influence Perceptions of Group Directiveness." *Journal of Applied Social Psychology* 20(18): 1485–513.

Biernart, M., and C.S. Crandall. 1994. "Stereotyping and Contact with Social Groups: Measurement and Conceptual Issues." *European Journal of Social Psychology* 24: 659–77.

Black, J.H., P.H. Glenn, D. Juteau, and D. Weinstock. 1998. *Les enjeux de la citoyenneté: un bilan interdisciplinaire.* Working paper no. 3. Montreal: Centre Metropolis du Québec et Immigration et métropoles.

Blaise, P., M.T. Coenen, R. Dresse, V. de Coorebyter, C. Kesteloot, J. Leunda, R. Lewin, T. Manghot, M. Martiniello, N. Ouali, K. Peleman, A. Rea. T. Roesems, and M. Vandemeulebroucke. 1997. *La Belgique et ses immigrés. Les politiques manquées.* Collection Pol-His. Brussels: De Boeck University.

Boender, W., and M. Kanmaz. 2002. "Imams in the Netherlands and Islam teachers in Flanders." In *Intercultural Relations and Religious*

Authorities: Muslims in the European Union, edited by W.A.R. Shadid and P.S. Van Koningsveld, 169–80. Leuven: Peeters.

Bogaert, N., and G. Goossens. 1996. "Tasks accomplished? Implementation of an Analytic Approach to Language Teaching in Secondary Schools." In *Second Language Acquisition in Europe: Proceeding of the International Conference on Second-Language Learning in Secondary Education, Veldhoven, the Netherlands, 17–19 May 1995*, 171–81. Hertogenbosch: KPC

Boileau, J. 2006. "Dérives du socioconstructivisme." *Le Devoir,* 28 April, A-8.

Boix, E. 1993. *Identitat i llengua en els joves de Barcelona*. Barcelona: Edicións 62.

Boix, E. 2004. "El camí fins a la situació contemporània del català i del castellà a Catalunya: entre la complexitat i la fragilitat." In *Les Llengües a Catalunya*, edited by L. Payrató and F.X.Vila, 13–27. Barcelona: Sabadell.

Bouchard, G., and Taylor, C. 2008. *Fonder l'avenir. Le temps de la conciliation*. Québec: Rapport du Comité de consultation sur les pratiques d'accommodement reliées aux différences culturelles.

– 2008. *Building the Future: A Time for Reconciliation*. Québec: Report of the Consultation Commission on Accommodation Practices Related to Cultural Differences.

Bouffioux, M. 2005. "À propos de la Belgique." *Ciné-Télé Revue,* 17 March.

Bourgeault, G., M.H. Chastenay, and M. Verlot. 2004. "Relations ethniques et éducation dans les sociétés divisées: comparaison Belgique-Canada/Ethnic Relations and Education in Divided Societies: Comparing Belgium and Canada." Études ethniques au Canada/ Canadian Ethnic Studies. Special issue. 36(3): 25–60.

Bourhis R.Y, and J.J. Leyens, eds. 1994. *Stéréotypes, discrimination et relations intergroupes*. Liège: Mardaga.

Bourhis R.Y, and D.F. Marshall. 1999. "The United States and Canada." In *Handbook of Language and Ethnic Identity*, edited by J.A. Fishman, 244–64. Oxford University Press.

Bousetta, H. 2000. "Intégration des immigrés et divisions communautaires: l'exemple de la Belgique." In *Relations ethniques et éducation dans les sociétés divisées: Québec, Irlande du Nord, Catalogne et Belgique*, edited by M. McAndrew and F. Gagnon, 89–122. Montreal: L'Harmattan.

Bousetta, H., and B. Maréchal. 2003. *L'Islam et les musulmans en Belgique. Enjeux locaux et cadres de réflexion globaux*. Brussels: Fondation Roi Baudoin.

Bouvier, F., and L. Lamontagne. 2006. "Quand l'histoire se fait outil de propagande." *Le Devoir*, 28 April, A-9.

Braun, A. 2002. *Rapport relatif à la problématique de l'enseignement/apprentissage des langues en communauté française de Belgique*. Brussels: Parlement de la Communauté française.

Brébant, É., and J.P. Schreiber 2006. État de la formation des enseignants de religion islamique dans l'enseignement officiel en communauté française. Brussels: Université Libre de Bruxelles and Centre Interuniversitaire de Recherche en Education de Lille. www.ulb.ac.be/philo/cierl.

Bretxa, V. 2009. " El salt a secundària: els preadolescents, consum cultural i llengua." *Zeitschrift für Katalanistik*, 22: 171–202.

Brewer, M.B., and N. Miller. 1988. "Contact and cooperation: When Do They Work?" In *Eliminating Racism: Profiles in Controversy*, edited by P.A Katz and D.A. Taylor, 315–28. New York: Plenum Press.

Brewer, M.B. and N. Miller. 1996. *Intergroup Relations*. Buckingham: Open University Press.

Brigouleix, B. 1983. "Une vaillante petite nation." *Le Monde diplomatique*, 1 November, 21–3.

Bryan, D., and G. Gillespie. 2005. *Transforming Conflicts: Flags and Emblem*." Belfast: Institute of Irish Studies, Queen's University.

Bull, B., R. Fruehling, and V. Chattergy. 1997. *The Ethic of Multicultural and Bilingual Education*. New York Teacher's College.

Bussière, P., F. Cartwright, T. Knighton, and R.W. Todd. 2004. *Measuring Up: Canadian Results of the OECD PISA Study. The Performance of Canada's Youth in Mathematics, Reading, Science and Problem Solving. 2003 First Findings for Canadians Age 15*. Ottawa: Statistics Canada.

Byram, M., and J. Leman. 1990. *Bicultural and Trilingual Education*. Clevedon, England: Multilingual Matters.

Cairns, E. 1989. "Social identity and intergroup conflict in Northern Ireland: A developmental perspective." In *Growing Up in Northern Ireland*, edited by J.I. Harbison. Belfast: Stranmillis College.

Cardin, J.F. 2004. "Le nouveau programme d'histoire au secondaire: le choix d'éduquer à la citoyenneté." *Formation et profession* (December): 44–8.

– 2006. "Les programmes d'histoire nationale: une mise au point," *Le Devoir*, 29 April, B-5.

Carens, J.H. 1995. "Complex justice, cultural difference, and political community." In *Pluralism, Justice and Equality*, edited by D. Miller and M. Walzer. Oxford University Press.

Carpentier de Changy, J., F. Dassetto, and B. Maréchal. 2006. *Musulmans et non-musulmans: les noeuds du dialogue*. Brussels: Fondation Roi Baudoin.

Castonguay, C. 2005. "La force réelle du français au Québec," *Le Devoir*, 20 December.

Centre for Diversity and Learning. 2008. www.steunpuntico.be.

Centre pour l'égalité des chances et la lutte contre le racisme. 2004. *National Focal Point for Belgium: Analytical Report on Education*. Brussels.

Centro de Recursos para la Atención a la Diversidad Cultural en Educación. 2009. www.mepsyd.es/creade/index.do.

Centrum voor Taal en Onderwijs. 2006. *Wat is er nog van onze dromen?* Eindrapport van een onderzoek naar de doorstroming van anderstalige nieuwkomers in het secundair onderwijs in de eerste drie jaar na de onthaalklas in Vlaanderen (2003–2005). www.cteno.be/doc=190&nav=3,5,1.

Chamberland, C. 2008. "Le point sur l'intégration des jeunes immigrants dans les écoles québécoises," presented at the *Immigration, Social Cohesion, and the School* conference, on 24 November at the University of Lleida.

– 2009. Response to the author from the *Directrice des Services aux communautés culturelles du Ministère de l'Éducation, du Loisir et du Sport (Gouvernement du Québec)*, 1 April.

Chambers, G., ed. 1992. "Report to the Minister of Education for Quebec." Task Force on English Education.

Charland, J.-P., M.-A. Éthier, and J.-F. Cardin. 2006. "L'enseignement de l'histoire et la conscience historique des élèves au Québec." *LISA* 3(2).

Chastenay, M.-H., and U. Niens. 2008. "L'éducation à la citoyenneté dans des contextes de division: les défis au Québec et en Irlande du Nord." Éducation et Francophonie 36(1): 103–22.

— and M. Pagé. 2006. "L'ouverture à la diversité culturelle chez les jeunes collégiens québécois." *Vivre ensemble* 13(46): 13–16.

Centro de Investigación y Documentación Educativa. 2000. *El sistema educativo español*. Madrid: Gobierno de España.

Clément, R., K, Noels, and B. Denault. 2001. "Interethnic Contact, Identity, and Psychological Adjustment: The Mediating and Moderating Roles of Communication." *Journal of Social Issues* 57(3): 559–77.

Cochrane, F. 2000. "Guerre et paix: l'évolution des relations ethniques en Irlande du Nord." In *Relations ethniques et éducation dans les sociétés divisées: Québec, Irlande du Nord, Catalogne et Belgique*, edited by M. McAndrew and F. Gagnon, 39–62. Montreal: L'Harmattan.

Comajoan, L. 2008. *La diversidad (lingüística) en entornos multilingües: Observaciones durante el periodo de prácticas de psicopedagogía, I*

Jornadas sobre Lenguas, Currículo y Alumnado Inmigrante. Bilbao: Deusto Publicaciones.

Comes, G., B. Jiménez, and V. Alcaraz. 1995. *La llengua catalana i els alumnes castellanoparlant de 10 a 15 anys.* Barcelona: Columna.

Comhairle na Gaelscolaíochta. 2007. "Response of Comhairle na Gaelscolaíochta to the Strategic Review of Education, carried out by Professor Georges Bain." www.deni.gov.uk/cnag_response-2.

Comité interministériel sur la situation de la langue française. 1996. *Le français langue commune, enjeu de la société québécoise.*

Comité sur les affaires religieuses. 2003. *Religious Rites and Symbols in the Schools: The Educational Challenge of Diversity.* www.meq.gouv. qc.ca/sections/publications/index.asp?page=fiche&id=1659.

– 2006. *Secular Schools in Quebec: A Necessary Change in Institutionl Culture.* www.mels.gouv.qc.ca/sections/publications/index.asp?page= fiche&id=1654.

Commissions des communautés européennes/european commission. 2007. *Third Annual Report on Immigration and Integration.* ec.europa.eu/ justice_home/fsj/immigration/docs/com_2007_512_fr.pdf.

Commission des droits de la personne. 1995. *Religious Pluralism in Québec: A Social and Ethical Challenge.* Montreal: Gouvernement du Québec.

Commission des États généraux sur la situation et l'avenir de la langue française au Québec. 2001. *Le français, une langue pour tout le monde. Une nouvelle approche stratégique et citoyenne.* Québec: Rapport Larose. www.etatsgeneraux.gouv.qc.ca.

Commission d'observation et de pilotage de l'Enseignement. 2006. "Éveil – Formation historique et géographique." Special issue. *Les Nouvelles de l'Observatoire* 55(1).

Commission scolaire de Montréal. 2006. *Politique interculturelle de la Comission scolaire de Montréal.* www.csdm.qc.ca/Csdm/ Administration/default.asp?csdm-diversite_culturelle.

Commission scolaire Marguerite Bourgeois. 1999. *Politique d'intégration scolaire des élèves non francophones, d'éducation interculturelle et d'éducation à la citoyenneté.* www.csmb.qc.ca/fr/politiques.html.

Communauté flamande. 2006. *Statistical Jaarboek 2006–2007. Aantal leerlingen van vreemde nationaliteit* TOV *de totale schoolbevolking in het basis- en secundair onderwijs.*

Communauté française de Belgique. 2007. *L'enseignement en chiffres: 2006–2007.* Service des statistiques de l'ETNIC. www.statistiques.etnic. be/publications.php.

Connolly, P. 1998. *Educational Research on Schools and Community Relations in Northern Ireland: A Critical Evaluation.* International Sociological Association XIV World Congress, 26 July to 1 August, Montreal.

Connerton, P. 1989. *How Societies Remember.* Cambridge: Cambridge University Press.

Conseil de l'Europe. 2008. Éducation à la citoyenneté démocratique et aux droits de l'homme. Communauté flamande de Belgique. www.coe.int/t/dg4/education/edc.

Conseil de la langue française. 1987a. *Réfléchir ensemble sur l'école française pluriethnique.* Québec: CLF.

– 1987b. *Vivre la diversité en français. Le défi de l'école française à la clientèle pluriethnique.* Québec: CLF.

Conseil scolaire de l'île de Montréal. 1991. *Les enfants des milieux défavorisés et ceux des communautés culturelles.* Memorandum to the Minister of Education for Quebec on the situation of the school boards on the Island of Montreal. February.

Conseil Superior d'Avaluació del Sistema Educatiu. 2005. *Dades de resultats de llengua catalan i de llengua castellana a l'educació primària i secundària.* Generalitat de Catalunya: Departament d'Educació.

– 2006. "El coneixement de llengües a Catalunya." *Quaderns d'Avaluació* 6 (Septembre): 4–55.

Conway, M. 2004. "Identifying the Past: An Exploration of Teaching and Learning Sensitive Issues in History at Secondary School Level." *Educate* 4(2). www.educatejournal.org.

Cormack, J. 1992. "Curriculum Access to Grammar Schools and the Financing of Schools: An Overview Paper." Belfast: Standing Advisory Commission on Human Rights, HMSO.

Côté, B. 2005. Étude des rapports entre jeunes "francophones" et "anglophones" dans des collèges anglophones du Québec. Doctoral dissertation. Montreal: Department of Psychology: University of Montreal.

Côté, B. 2009a. "Intergroup Contacts: From Theory to Practice." www.peliq-an.qc.ca.

Côté, B. 2009b. *PELIQ-AN 2008–2009: Rapport de recherche.* Final report submitted to the Ministère de l'Éducation, des Loisirs et du Sport du Québec. University of Sherbrooke.

Côté, B., and L. Mettewie. 2008. "Les relations entre communautés linguistiques en contexte scolaire et communautaire: regard croisé sur Montréal et Bruxelles." *Éducation et francophonie* 36(1): 5–24.

Council for Catholic Maintained Schools (CCMS). 2006. *Response from the Council for Catholic Maintained Schools to the Independent Strategic Review of Education.* July.

Council for the Curriculum Examinations and Assessment (CCEA). 2003a. *Proposals for Curriculum and Assessment at Key-Stage 3, Part 1: Background Rational and Details.* Belfast: CCEA.

– 2003b. *Proposals for Curriculum and Assessment at Key-Stage 3, Part 2: Discussion Papers and Case Study.* Belfast: CCEA.

– 2003c. *Local and Global Citizenship Teacher's Note.* Belfast: CCEA.

– 2006. *Local and Global Citizenship at Key-Stage 3: Preliminary Evaluation Findings.* Belfast: CCEA.

– 2007a. *The Statutory Curriculum at Key-Stage 3: Supplementary Guidance.* Belfast: CCEA.

– 2007b. *Program of Study for History at Key-Stage 3.* Belfast: CCEA.

– 2007c. *Learning for Life and Work: Local and Global Citizenship, Staturory Minimum Requierements at Key-Stage 3.* Belfast: CCEA.

– 2007d. *Key-Stage 4, Guide Material, Local and Global Citizenship.* Belfast: CCEA.

D'Hondt, D. 2006. "La Flandre impose la gratuité, Merchtem impose le néerlandais." *Alter Educ.* www.altereduc.be/index.php?page=archiveList &content=article&list_p_num=8&lg=1&s_id=11&art_id=14972& display=item.

De Mets, J. 2004. *Vers un programme en plusieurs étapes?* Roundtable and evaluation of secondary schools' non-participation in the *Trèfle* program. Mission du Fonds Prince Philippe, 31 May.

De Mets, J. 2005. *Partenaires dans l'éducation: Familles issues de l'immigration et école.* Report of the study day on the diffusion of field expertise. 18 May. Fondation Roi Baudouin. www.kbs-frb.be/publication. aspx?id=178274 &LangType=2060.

De Meyer, I, J. Pauly, and L. Van de Poele. 2005. *Learning for Tomorrow's Problems. First Results from PISA 2003.* OECD, PISA, Ministry of the Flemish Community, Education Department, and University of Ghent.

De Rycke, L., and M. Swyngedouw. 1999. "The Value of Concentration Schools as Appreciated by Morrocans, Turks, and Unskilled Belgians in Brussels." *International Journal of Educational Research* 31: 267–81.

De Schutter, H. 2001. "Taalpolitiek en multiculturalisme in het Brussels Nederlandstalig onderwijs." In *19 keer Brussel. Brusselse Thema's 7,* edited by E. Witte and A. Mares. Brussels: VUB Press.

De Vriendt, S., and R. Willemyns. 1987. "Sociolinguistic aspects. Linguistic research on Brussels." In *The Interdisciplinary Study of Urban Bilingualism in Brussesl,* edited by E. Witte and H. Baetens-Beardsmore, 195–231. Clevendon: Multilingual Matters.

De Witte, H., and B. Klandermans. 2000. "Political Racism in Flanders and the Netherlands: Explaining Differences in the Electoral Success of Extreme Right-wing Parties." *Journal of Ethnic and Migration Studies* 26(4): 699–717.

Daoust, D. 1990. "A Decade of Language Planning in Québec: A Socio-Political Overview." In *Language Policy and Political Development,* edited by B. Weinstein. Beverly Hills, CA: Sage.

Darby, J. 1976. *Conflict in Northern Ireland: The Development of a Polarized Community.* New York: Barnes and Noble Books.

– 1997. *Scorpions in a Bottle* London: Minority Rights Group.

Darby, J., D. Batts, S. Dunns, S. Farren, J. Harris, and D. Murray. 1977. *Schools Apart? Education and Communities in Northern Ireland.* Coleraine: Centre for the Study of Conflict, University of Ulster.

Davis, J. 1989. "The Social Relations of the Production of History." In *Ethnicity and History,* edited by E.Tonkin et al. London and New York: Routledge.

Deckers, M. 1999. *Rapport. Beleidsplan.* Brussels: Voorrangsbeleid Brussel.

Delruelle, E., and R. Torfs. 2005. *Commission du dialogue interculturel: Rapport final.* Brussels: Centre pour l'égalité des chances et la lutte contre le racisme.

Department for Education (DFE). 1995. *History in the National Curriculum: England.* London: HMSO.

Department of Education and Sciences (DES). 1990. *National Curriculum History Working Group: Final Report.* London: HMSO.

– 1991. *History in the National Curriculum (England).* London: HMSO.

Department of Education for Northern Ireland (DENI). 1997. *Integrated Education. A Framework for Transformation.* Bangor: DENI.

– 1998. *Integrated Schools in Northern Ireland.* Bangor: DENI.

– 1999. *Towards a Culture of Tolerance: Education for Diversity,* Report of the Working Group on the Strategic Promotion of Education for Mutual Understanding.

– 2006. *Schools for the Future: Funding, Strategy, Sharing: Report of the Independent Strategic Review of Education.* December.

– 2007a. *Irish Medium Schools and Irish Medium Units in Mainstream Schools in Northern Ireland 2006–2007.* Northern Ireland School Census 2006–2007. DENI.

– 2007b. *Developing Good Relations in the School Community.* Policy Research and Youth Division, Department of Education, Northern Ireland.

Deprez, K., Y. Persoons, M. Struelens and A. Wijnants. 1982. "Anderstaligen in het Nederlandstalig basisonderwijs in Brussel. Wie en waarom?" *Taal en Sociale Integratie* 6: 231–63.

Desforges, D.M., C.G. Lord, S.L. Ramsey, J.A. Mason, M.D. Van Leeuwen, S.C. West, and M.R. Lepper. 1991. "Effects of Structured Cooperative Contact on Changing Negative Attitudes toward Stigmatized Social Groups." *Journal of Personality and Social Psychology* 60(4): 531–44.

Devlieger, M., and G. Goossens. 2006. "Evaluatie van vier jaar Voorrangsbeleid Brussel, een intensieve onderwijsvernieuwing in Brusselse Nederlandstalige basisscholen met een meertalige populatie." In *Artikelen van de Vijfde sociolinguïstische conferentie,* edited by T. Koole, J. Nortier, and B. Tahitu Delft, 126–37. Delft: Eburon.

Direcció General d'Ordenació Educativa. 1999. *Pla d'acció del servei d'ensenyament del català, 1999–2000.* Barcelona: Departament d'Ensenyament, Generalitat de Catalunya.

Direcció General de Politica Lingüística. 1983. *Llei de normalització lingüística de Catalunya.* Barcelona: Departament de Cultura, Generalitat de Catalunya.

Dovidio, J.F., S.L. Gaertner, and K. Kawakami, K. 2003. "Intergroup Contact: The Past, Present, and the Future." *Group Processes & Intergroup Relations* 6(1): 5–21.

Donnelly, C. 2004. "Constructing the Ethos of Tolerance and Respect in an Integrated School: The Role of Teachers." *British Education Research Journal* 30(2): 263–78.

– 2006. "Contact, Culture and Context: Evidence from Faith Mix Schools in Northern Ireland and Israel." *Comparative Education* 42(4): 493–516.

Duchesne, A. 2006. "Des accommodements raisonnables qui incommodent." *La Presse,* 29 December, A1.

Dunn, S. 1990. "A History of Education in Northern Ireland since 1920." *Fifteenth Report on the Standing Advisory Commission on Human Rights (SACHR).* London: HMSO.

– 2000. "L'éducation dans une société divisée: le cas de l'Irlande du Nord." In *Relations ethniques et éducation dans les sociétés divisées: Québec, Irlande du Nord, Catalogne et Belgique,* edited by M. McAndrew and F. Gagnon, 161–82. Montreal: L'Harmattan.

Dunn, S., and V. Morgan. 1999. "A Fraught Path: Education as a Basis for Developing Improved Community Relations in Northern Ireland." *Oxford Review of Education* 25(1–2): 141–53.

Durocher, R. 1996. "La Révolution tranquille." *L'encyclopédie canadienne.* www.thecanadianencyclopedia.com/index.cfm?PgNm=TCE&Params=f 1ARTf0006619.

Edualter. 2009. Edualter website. www.edualter.org/index.htm.

El Battiui, M., and M. Kanmaz. 2004. *Mosquées, imams et professeurs de religion islamique en Belgique. État de la question et enjeux.* Brussels: Fondation Roi Baudoin.

El Kouri, R. 2001. "Des démographes se contredisent aux États généraux sur la langue." *La Presse,* 26 January.

Erk, J. 2002. "Le Québec entre la Flandre et la Wallonie: Une comparaison des nationalismes sous-étatiques belges et du nationalisme québécois." *Recherches sociographiques* 43(3): 499–516.

Ernalsteen, V. 2002. "Does complex instruction benefit intercultural education?" *Intercultural Education,* 13(1): 69–80.

Esquerra Republicana de Catalunya. 2003. "Resum del programa de govern d'ERC. Eleccions al Parlament de Catalunya." www.esquerra.cat.

Éthier, M.A. 2004. "Où va l'éducation à la citoyenneté?" *Traces* 43(3): 10–15.

– F. Lantheaume, D. Lefrançois, and P. Zanazanian. 2008. "L'enseignement au Québec et en France des questions controversées en histoire: tensions entre politique du passé et politique de la reconnaissance dans les curricula." In Éducation et Francophonie, *Rapports ethniques et éducation: perspectives nationales et internationales,* 36(1): 65–85. Edited by M. McAndrew.

European Commission. 2004. *Integrating Immigrant Children into Schools in Europe.* Country Report: Belgium. Eurydice: Directorate-General for Education and Culture.

Evens Fondation. 2001. *Learning for Change in a Multicultural Society.* Laureates Evens Prize 2000. Antwerp: Evens Foundation.

Ewart, S., and D. Schubotz. 2004. *Voices behind the Statistics. Young People's Views of Sectarianism in Northern Ireland.* Belfast: National Children's Bureau.

Facal, R.L. 2003. "La enseñanza de la historia, más allá del nacionalismo." In *Usos Públicos de la Historia,* edited by J.H.J. Carrearas Ares and C. Forcadell Álvarez, 223–56. Madrid: Prensas Universitarias de Zaragoza.

Farrell, M. 1976. *Northern Ireland: The Orange State.* London: Pluto Press.

Farren, S. 1995. *The Politics of Irish Education.* Belfast: Institute of Irish Studies, The Queen's University of Belfast.

Fédération de l'enseignement secondaire catholique. 2000. *Histoire – Formation historique, 2e et 3e degrés. Humanités générales et technologiques. www.fltr.ucl.ac.be.*

Fernandez, G.A. 1997. "La didáctica de las ciencias sociales en la educación básica española. Une tesis doctoral sobre el diseño curricular de ciencias sociales en la educación secundaria obligatoria." *Revista Bibliográfica de Geografía y Ciencias Sociales* 49: 1–15.

Ferrer, F., G. Ferrer, and J.L. Castel. 2006. *Les desigualtats educatives a Catalunya: PISA 2003. Informes Breus de l'Educació. Volume 1.* Barcelona: Fundació Jaume Bofill.

Figueroa, P. 1999. "Multiculturalism and Anti-Racism in a New Era: A Critical Review." *Race Ethnicity and Education* 2: 281–99.

Fix, M. 2007. *Securing the Future: US Immigrant Integration Policy: A Reader.* Washington: Migration Policy Institute.

Flaquer, L. 1996. *El Català, ¿Llengua Pública o Privada?* Barcelona: Empúries.

Fondation Roi Baudoin. 2003a. *Cinq ans Fonds Prince Philippe.* Brussels: Fondation Roi Baudoin.

Fondation Roi Baudoin. 2003b. *Publications.* www.kbs-frb.be.

Fondation Roi Baudoin. 2006a. *Tous nos projets: Prince Philippe (Fonds Prince Philippe)–Trèfle. Intercommunity school exchange.* www.kbs-frb.be.

Fondation Roi Baudoin. 2007a. *Réussite scolaire des jeunes d'origine étrangère. Identification des facteurs critiques de succès dans un contexte européen.* Minutes from workshop Compte held in Brussels on 8 December.

Fondation Roi Baudoin. 2007b. *Le tutorat d'étudiants. Exemples de bonnes pratiques en Belgique.* Brussels: Fondation Roi Baudoin.

Fortin, L. 2008. "La prise en compte de la diversité: bilan des actions gouvernementales." In *L'accommodement raisonnable et la diversité religieuse à l'école publique: normes et pratiques*, edited by M. McAndrew, M. Milot, J.S. Imbeault, and P. Eid, 27–42. Montreal: Fides.

François, K. 2004. "Het Brussels Nederlandstalig secundair onderwijs: kwaliteit wel maar...?" *Samenleving en Politiek* 11: 4–12.

François, K. 2005. "Een kwaliteitslabel voor her Brussels Nederlandstalig secundair onderwijs. Ten koste waarvan?" In *Politiek, Taal, Onderwijs en Samenleving in Beweging. Brusselse thema's 14*, 293–310. Brussels: VUB Press.

Fukuda, M. 2009. "Els usos lingüístics dels nens japonesos i nipocatalans/nipocastellans escolaritzats a Catalunya. El cas dels alumnes del Col·legi

Japonès de Barcelona i de l'Escola Complementària de Llengua Japonesa de Barcelona." *Interlinguistica* 18: 707–16.

Fullwinder, R.K. 1996. *Public Education in a Multicultural Society: Policy, Theory, Critique*. New York: Cambridge University Press.

Fundació Jaume Bofill. 2009. Website of the Jaume Bofill Foundation. www.fbofill.cat/index.php?codmenu=17.01.

Gaertner, S.L., M.C. Rust, M.C. Dovidio, B.A. Bachman, and P.A. Anastasio, 1996. "The Contact Hypothesis: The Role of Common Ingroup Identity on Reducing Intergroup Bias among Majority and Minority Group Members." In *What's Social about Social Cognition? Research on Socially Shared Cognition in Small Group*, edited by J.L. Nye and A.M. Brower, 230–60. Thousand Oaks, CA: Sage Publications.

Gagné, M., and C. Chamberland. 1999. "L'évolution des politiques d'intégration et d'immigration au Québec." In *Les politiques d'immigration et d'intégration au Canada et en France: analyses comparées et perspectives de recherche*, edited by M. McAndrew, A.C. Decouflé, and C. Cicéri, 71–90. Paris and Ottawa: Ministère de l'Emploi et de la Solidarité and the Social Sciences and Humanities Research Council of Canada.

Gallagher, A.M., R.J. Cormack, and R.D. Osborne. 1993. "Community Relations, Equality and Education." In *After the Reforms: Education and Policy in Northern Ireland*, edited by R.D. Osborne, R.J. Cormack, and A.M. Gallagher. Aldershot: Avebury.

– 1994. "Religion, Equity and Education in Northern Ireland." *British Research Journal* 20(5): 507–18.

Gallagher, T. 2003. "Conflict and Young People in Northern Ireland: The Role of the Schools." In *Working with Children and Young People in Violently Divided Societies: South Africa and Northern Ireland*, edited by M. Smyth and K. Thomson, 51–68. Belfast: CCIC (2001).

– 2004. *Education in Divided Societies*. Basingstoke: Palgrave Macmillan.

– A. Smith, and A. Montgomery. 2003. *Integrated Education in Northern Ireland. Participation, Profile and Performance*. Coleraine: Unesco Centre, University of Ulster.

Garcia, C. 1997. "La politique nationaliste et l'identification linguistique en Catalogne." *Revue européenne des migrations internationales* 13(3): 85–98.

Garreta, J. 2000. "Inmigrantes musulmanes en Cataluña. Los retos sociales, culturales y educativos de la diversidad religiosa." *Revista Internacional de Sociología* 25: 151–76.

- 2006. "Ethnic minorities and the Spanish and Catalan educational systems: From exclusion to intercultural education." *International Journal of Intercultural Relations* 30: 261–79.
- 2007. "Continuidad y cambios en la gestión de la inmigración." *Papers* 85: 61–93.
- 2008. "Escuela, familia de origen immigrante y participación/School, immigrant, families and participation." *Revista de Educación* 345: 133–55.
- 2009a. *Sociedad multicultural e integración de los inmigrantes en Cataluña: discursos y prácticas.* Lleida: Publicacions de la Universitat de Lleida.
- 2009b. "Escuela y familias de origen inmigrado: relaciones complejas." *Revista Complutense de Educación* 20(2): 275–94.
- and N. Llevot. 2001. "Immigration, éducation et intégration en Catalogne (Espagne)." *FEI Enjeux* 125.
- and N. Llevot. 2002. *El espejismo intercultural. La escuela de Cataluña ante la diversidad cultural*, Colección Investigación, 155. Ministerio de Educación, Cultura y Deporte.
- L. Samper, D. Mayoral, N. Llevot, F. Molina, C. Lapresta, C. Serra, J.M. Palaudàrias, G. Notario, E. Salinas, X. Monclús and N. Creixell. 2007. *La relació família d'origen immigrant i escola: l'Islam en els centres educatius de Catalunya.* Unpublished report available at the University of Lleida.
Gatz, S. (2004). "Het voorrangsbeleid Brussel. De langverwachte eindevaluatie." Available online at www.gatz.be/page.php/politiek/vierdeweg/2004102901.
Generalitat de Catalunya. 1979. *Escolarització d'alumnat fill de famílies immigrants.* Barcelona: Departament d'Ensenyament, Generalitat de Catalunya.
- 1993. *Pla Interdepartamental d'Immigració 1993–2000.* Barcelona: Departament de Benestar i Familia, Generalitat de Catalunya.
- 1996. Éducació intercultural: *Orientacions per al desplegament del curriculum.* Barcelona: Departament d'Ensenyament, Generalitat de Catalunya.
- 1999. *Estatuto de autonomía.* www.gencat.cat/generalitat/cas/estatut 1979/preambul.htm.
- 2001. *Pla Interdepartamental d'Immigració 2001–2004.* Barcelona: Departament de Benestar i Familia, Secretaria per a la Immigració, Generalitat de Catalunya.

– 2003a. *Pla per a la llengua i la cohesió social.* Barcelona: Departament d'Educació, Generalitat de Catalunya.

– 2003b. *La convivència en els centres docents d'ensenyament secundari.* Departament d'Educació. www20.gencat.cat/portal/site/Educacio/ menuitem.046d33c25faf415a72623b10boc0e1a0/?vgnextoid=e7eff2da 8c305110VgnVCM1000000boc1eoaRCRD&vgnextchannel=e7eff2da8 c305110VgnVCM1000000boc1eoaRCRD&vgnextfmt=default.

– 2004a. *Pla d'acció de política lingüística 2004–2005.* Barcelona: Departament de la Presidència, Secretaria de Política Lingüística, Generalitat de Catalunya.

– 2004b. *Pla d'acollida del centre docent.* Barcelona: Departament d'Educació, Generalitat de Catalunya.

– 2005. *Pla de Ciutadania i Immigració 2005–2008.* Barcelona: Departament de Benestar i Família, Generalitat de Catalunya.

– 2006a. Pla de *Ciutadania i Immigració 2005–2008.* Catalonia: Foreign Population May 2006. Barcelona: Secretaria per a la Immigració, Generalitat de Catalunya.

– 2006b. *Estatuto de autonomía de Cataluña 2006.* www.gencat.cat/ generalitat/cas/estatut/index.htm.

– 2006c. *Consell assessor de la llengua a l'escola: conclusions.* Barcelona: Departament d'Educació i Universitats, Generalitat de Catalunya.

– 2007a. *Pacte Nacional per a l'Educació Debat curricular. Reflexions i Propostes.* Barcelona: Generalitat de Catalunya.

– 2007b. *Pla per a l'actualització de la metodologica d'immersió.* www. gencat/educacio.

– 2007c. *Decret 142, de 26 de juny, pel qual s'estableix l'ordenació dels ensenyaments de l'educació primària.* Barcelona: Generalitat de Catalunya.

– 2007d. *Decret 143, de 26 de juny, pel qual s'estableix l'ordenació dels ensenyaments de l'educació secundaria obligatòria.* Barcelona: Generalitat de Catalunya.

– 2007e. *Moviments migratoris 2006 – Dades comarcals i municipals.* www.idescat.cat/cat/poblacio/migracions/.

– 2007f. *La convivència en els centres d'educació infantil i primària.* Departament d'Educació, Generalitat de Catalunya. www20.gencat.cat/ portal/site/Educacio/menuitem.046d33c25faf415a72623b10boc0e1a0/? vgnextoid=e7eff2da8c305110VgnVCM1000000boc1eoaRCRD&vgnex tchannel=e7eff2da8c305110VgnVCM1000000boc1eoaRCRD&vgnextf mt=default.

– 2008. *Anuari estadístic de Catalunya 2008.* Institut d'Estadística de Catalunya. www.idescat.cat/cat/idescat/publicacions/anuari.

– 2009a. *Indicadors demogràfics*. Institut d'Estadística de Catalunya (Idescat). www.idescat.cat/cat/poblacio/poblfluxos.html.

– 2009b. *Bloc de les llengües d'origen*. Departament d'Educació. blocs. xtec.cat/llenguadorigen/presentacio.

Gérin-Lajoie, D. 2007. Le discours du personnel des écoles sur la diversité de la clientèle scolaire. Communication presented at the 60th Congress of the Association canadienne d'éducation de langue française (ACELF).

Girard-Lamoureux, C. 2004. *La langue d'usage publique des allophones scolarisés au Québec*. Québec: Conseil supérieur de la langue française (CSLF). www.cslf.gouv.qc.ca.

Glenn, C.L. 1999. "The Belgian Model of Peace-Making in Education Policy." In *Le pacte scolaire de 1958. Origines, principes et application d'un compromise belge*, edited by E. Witte, J. De Groof, and J. Tyssens. Brussels: VUB Press.

Gouvernement du Québec. 1977. *The Quebec Policy of the French Language*. Québec: Gouvernement du Québec.

– 1978. *The Québec Cultural Development*. Québec: Gouvernement du Québec.

– 1984. *So Many Ways to Be Quebecers*. Québec: Gouvernement du Québec.

Government of Northern Ireland. 2007. *The Education (Curriculum Minimal Contents) Order, Statutory Rules 2007, no 46, Northern Ireland*. www.opsi.gov.uk/Sr/ sr2007/nisr_20070046_en_1.

Grant, N., and F.J. Doherty. 1992. "Language Policy Education: Some Scottish-Catalan comparisons." *Comparative Education* 28(2): 145–66.

Gsir, S. 2006. "Belgique: integration et cohésion sociale." An exposé in the national newspaper of the Federal Aliens Commission (Commission fédérale des étrangers, or CFE). *Quelle intégration? Welche Integration?* 16 November.

– M. Martiniello, K. Meireman, and J. Wets. 2005. "Belgium." In *Current Immigration Debates in Europe: A Publication of the European Migration Dialogue*, edited by J. Niessen, Y. Schibel, and C. Thompson. Brussels: Migration Policy Group.

Hambye, P., and S. Lucchini. 2005. "Diversité sociolinguistique et ressources partagées. Regards critiques sur les politiques d'intégration linguistique en Belgique." *Noves SL* 6 (summer-spring). www6.gencat.net/ llengcat/noves/hmo5primavera-estiu/hambye1_3.htm.

Hargreaves, D.H. 1996. "Diversity and Choice in School Education: A Modified Libertarian Approach." *Oxford Review of Education* 22(2): 131–41.

Harvey, F. 2000. "Le Canada français et la question linguistique." In *Le français au Québec, 400 ans d'histoire et de vie,* edited by M. Plourde, H. Duval, and P. Georgeault, 139–53. Montreal: Fides/Publications du Québec.

Her Majesty's Stationery Office. 1989. *Education Reform (NI) Order.* Belfast: Her Majesty's Stationery Office.

Hermans, P. 2004. "Applying Ogbu's theory of minority academic achievement to the situation of Moroccans in the low countries." *Intercultural Education* 15(4): 431–9.

Hermans, P. 2006. "Counternarratives of Moroccan parents in Belgium and The Netherlands: Answering back to discrimination in education and society." *Ethnography and Education* 1: 87–101.

Hohl, J., and Normand, M. 1996. "Construction et stratégies identitaires des enfants et des adolescents en contexte migratoire: le rôle des intervenants scolaires." *Revue française de pédagogie* 117: 39–52.

– and Normand, M. 2000. "Enseigner en milieu pluriethnique dans une société divisée." In *Relations ethniques et éducation dans les sociétés divisées: Québec, Irlande du Nord, Catalogne et Belgique,* edited by M. McAndrew and F. Gagnon, 241–58. Montreal: L'Harmattan.

– and Normand, M. 2001. *Savoir, rapport au savoir et éducation à la citoyenneté.* Unpublished report by the Groupe de recherche sur l'ethnicité et l'adaptation au pluralisme en éducation (Research Group on Ethnicity and Adaptation to Pluralism in Education), Faculty of Education, University of Montreal.

Holmes, B. 1981. *Comparative Education: A Study of Educational Factors and Traditions.* London: Routledge and Kegan Paul.

Homan, R. 1992. "Separate Schools." In *Cultural Diversity and the Schools.* Volume 1: *Education for Cultural Diversity: Convergence et divergence,* edited by J. Lynch, C. Modgil, and S. Modgil, 59–72. London and Washington: Falmer Press.

Housen, A., L. Mettewie, and M. Pierrard. 2002. *Taalvaardigheid en attitudes van Nederlandstalige en Franstalige leerlingen in het secundair onderwijs in Brussel.* Rapport Belleidsgericht ondeerzoek PBO/98/2/36. Brussels: Centrum voor Linguïstiek, Vrije Universiteit Brussel.

Housen, A., M. Pierrard, and P. Van de Craen, eds. 2004. *Taal, Attitude en Onderwijs in Brussel.* Brussels: VUB Press.

Hugues, J., and C. Donnelly. 2002. "Ten Years of Social Attitudes to Community Relations in Northern Ireland." In *Social Attitudes in Northern Ireland: The 8th Report,* edited by A. Gray et al. London: Pluto Press.

Huguet, A. and J.L. Navarro. 2006. "Inmigración y resultados escolares: lo que dice la investigación (presentación dél monográfico)." *Cultura y Educación* 18(2): 117–26.

– J. Janés, J.L. Navarro, and J.M. Serra. 2005. *Les actituds lingüístiques de l'alumnat immigrant a Catalunya.* Barcelona: Institut d'Estudis Autonòmics.

Humet, J.S., M.À. Alegre, J. Collet, S. Gonzàlez, and R. Benito. 2005. "Una visió comparada a les polítiques d'acollida i escolarització de l'alumnat nouvingut. Els casos de Baviera, la Comunitat Francòfona de Bèlgica, Quebec i Anglaterra." Unpublished research report, Faculty of Politics and Sociology, Autonomous University of Barcelona.

Inglis, C. 2008. *Planning for Cultural Diversity.* Paris: Unesco.

Insko, C.A., R.L. Pinkley, R.H. Hoyle, B. Dalton, G. Hong, R.M. Slim, P. Landry, B. Holton, P.F. Ruffin, and J. Thibaut. 1987. "Individual versus Group Discontinuity: The Role of Intergroup Contact." *Journal of Experimental Social Psychology* 23: 250–67.

Institut National de la Statistique. 1999. *Census.* Bruxelles: INS.

– 2008. "Statistiques sur la population – Structure de la population." www.statbel.fgov.be/figures/d21_fr.asp.

Instutito nacional de estadistica. 2009. *Encuesta Nacional de Inmigrantes 2007: una monografía.* www.ine.es/prodyser/pubweb/eni07/eni07.htm.

Irwin, C. 1992. "L'éducation intégrée: de la théorie à la pratique dans des sociétés divisées." *Perspectives* 22: 75–89.

Jacobs, D. 2004. "Alive and kicking? Multiculturalism in Flanders." *International Journal on Multicultural Societies* 6(2): 280–99.

Jacobs, D., A. Rea, and L. Hanquinet. 2007. *Performance des élèves issus de l'immigration en Belgique selon l'étude PISA: une comparaison entre la Communauté française et la Communauté flamande.* Brussels: Fondation Roi Baudoin.

Jadoulle, J.-L., M. Bouhon, and A. Nys. 2004. *Conceptualiser le passé pour comprendre le présent: Conceptualisation et pédagogie de l'intégration en classe d'histoire.* Collection Apprendre l'histoire, n° 7. Louvain-la-Neuve: Unité de didactique et de communication en histoire.

Janssens, R. 2001. *Taalgebruik in Brussel. Taalverhoudingen, taalver-schuivingen en taalidentiteit in een meertalige stad. Brusselse Thema's 8.* Brussels: VUB Press.

Janssens, R. 2006. "L'impacte de la immigració estrangera sobre l'ús lingüístic a Brusselles." In *Integrar, des de la fragilitat? Societats plurilingües davant els reptes de les immigracions multilingües: Suïssa, Brussel-les, Luxembruge, Quebec i Catalunya,* edited by F.X. Vila i

Moreno, E. Boix-Fuster, and N. Alturo i Monné, 23–8. Barcelona: Institute of Catalan Studies.

Janssens, R. 2007. *Van Brussel gesproken. Taalgebruik, taalverschuivingen en taalidentiteit in het Brussels Hoofdstedelijk Gewest (Taalbarometer III). Brusselse Thema's 15.* Brussels: VUB Press.

– 2008. "L'usage des langues à Bruxelles et la place du néerlandais. Quelques constatations récentes." *Brussels Studies* 13 (January): 1–16.

– and L. Van Mensel. 2006. *Publieksonderzoek Gemeenschapscentra. Een onderzoek naar het profiel van de bezoekers van de Vlaaamse gemeenschapscentra in Brussel.* Brussels: Vrije Universiteit Brussel.

Jarman, N. 2005. *No Longer a Problem? Sectarian Violence in Northern Ireland.* Institute for Conflict Research, March. *www.patfinucanecentre.org/policing/violence.pdf.*

Jaspers, J. 2005. "Linguistic sabotage in a context of monolingualism and standardization." *Language & Communication* 25: 279–97.

Jedwab, J. 1996. *English in Montreal. A Layman's Look at the Current Situation.* Montreal: Les Éditions Images.

– (2002). *The Chambers Report, Ten Years After: The State of English Language Education in Quebec, 1992–2002.* Montreal: The Missisquoi Institute. www.chssn.org/en/pdf/Education%20report.pdf.

Jenkins, R. 1997. *Rethinking Ethnicity: Arguments and Explorartions.* Thousand Oaks, CA: Sage Publications.

Johnston, L., and M. Hewstone. 1992. "Cognitive Models of Stereotypes Change." *Journal of Experimental Social Psychology* 28: 360–6.

Jolicoeur, J. et al. 2004. *Sondage sur l'état des relations interculturelles au Québec.* Québec: Ministère de l'Immigration et des Communautés culturelles (Ministry of Immigration and Cultural Communities).

Jou, L. 2002. "El model Català de política lingüística. " Paper presented at the World Congress on Linguistic Politics, Barcelona, 16 April. www.linguax.org/congres/jou.html.

Junne, G., and W. Verkoren, eds. 2005. *Post-conflict Development: Meeting New Challenges.* Boulder, CO: Lynne Rienner Publishers.

Juteau, D. 1993. "The Production of the Québécois Nation." *Humbolt Journal of Social Relations* 19(2): 79–101.

Juteau, D. 1996. "Theorizing Ethnicity and Ethnic Communications at the Margin: From Quebec to the World System." *Nations and Nationalism* 2(1): 45–66.

Juteau, D. 2000a. *L'ethnicité et ses frontières.* Montreal: PUM.

– 2000b. "Du dualisme canadien au pluralisme québécois." In *Relations ethniques et éducation dans les sociétés divisées: Québec, Irlande du*

Nord, Catalogne et Belgique, edited by M. McAndrew and F. Gagnon, 17–38. Montreal: L'Harmattan.

Juteau, D. 2002. "The Citizens Make an Entry: Redefining the National Community in Québec." *Citizenship Studies* 6(4).

– M. McAndrew, and L. Pietrantonio. 1998. "Multiculturalism à la Canadian et intégration à la Québécoise: Transcending their limits." In *Blurred Boundaries: Migration, Ethnicity and Citizenship*, edited by R. Bauboeck and J. Rundell, 95–110. The European Centre, Vienna: Ashgate.

Kanouté, F., and M.-H. Chastenay. 2009. "Pédagogie et diversité culturelle dans l'enseignement universitaire." Conference presented at the Centre d'études et de formation en enseignement supérieur (Centre for Studies and Training in Higher Education), University of Montreal, 8 April.

– and N. Llevot Calvet. 2008. "Les relations école - familles immigrées au Québec et en Catalogne." *Rapport ethniques et Éducation: perspectives nationales et internationales, Éducation et Francophonie*, 36(1): 161–76. Special issue edited by M. McAndrew.

– and M. Vatz Laaroussi. 2008. "Les relations écoles-familles immigrantes: une préoccupation récurrente et pertinente." *Revue des sciences de l'éducation* 34(2) 259–64.

– J. Hohl, and N. Chamlian. 2002. "Les étudiants allophones dans les programmes de premier cycle de la Faculté des sciences de l'éducation de l'Université de Montréal." In *L'intégration des minorités visibles et ethnoculturelles dans la profession enseignante*, edited by D. Mujuwamariya, 183–201. Outremont: Éditions Logiques.

– A. Lavoie, and L. Duong. 2004. "L'interculturel et la formation des enseignants." *Éducation Canada* 44(2): 8–10, 54.

Keating, M. 1996. "Nacions minoritàries en el nou ordre mundial: Quebec, Catalunya i Escòcia." *Nacionalismes I Cięcies Socials*. Barcelona: Fundació Jaume Bofill.

Keulen, M. 2008. "La Flandre vous souhaite la bienvenue!" *Le Soir*, 17 April. www.lesoir.be/forum/cartes_blanches.

Khader, B., M. Martiniello, A. Rea, and C. Timmerman. 2006. *Penser l'immigration et l'intégration autrement*. Brussels: Édition Bruylant.

Kirk, J., C. Mitchell, M. McAndrew, and B. Côté. 2006. "Identity, Experience and Agency: Pre-Service Teachers in a Francophone and an Anglophone Institution in Quebec." *Teaching and Teacher Education*.

Kitson, A. 2007. "History Teaching and Reconciliation in Northern Ireland." In *Teaching the Violent Past: History Education and Reconciliation*, edited by E. Cole, 123–53. Lanham: Rowman and Littlefield.

– and A. McCully. 2005. "You Hear about It for Real in School. Avoiding
   Containing and Risk-Taking in the History Classroom." *Teaching
   History* 120: 32–7.

Koppen, J., B. Distelmans, and R. Janssens. 2002. *Taalfaciliteiten in de
   Rand. Ontwikkelingslijnen Conflictgebieden en Taalpraktijk. Brusselse
   Thema's 9*. Brussels: VUB Press.

Kymlicka, W. 1996. *Multicultural Citizenship*. Oxford: Oxford University
   Press.

La Libre Belgique. 2007. "Comment on se regarde entre voisins. " 16 March.

Labelle, M. 2000. "La politique de la citoyenneté et de l'interculturalisme
   au Québec: défis et enjeux." In *Les identités en débat: intégration ou
   multiculturalisme*, edited by H. Greven and J. Tournon, 269–93. Paris:
   L'Harmattan.

Labio, C. 2002. "The Federalization of Memory." *Yale French Studies* 102:
   1–18.

Laferrière, M. 1983. "L'éducation des groupes minoritaires au Québec: de
   la définition des problèmes par les groupes eux-mêmes à l'intervention
   de l'État." *Sociologie et sociétés* 15(2): 117–32.

Laitin, D.D. 1987. "Linguistic Conflict in Catalonia." *Language Problems
   and Language Planning* 11(2): 129–47.

Lamarre, P. 1997. *A Comparative Analysis of the Development of
   Immersion Program in British Columbia and Québec: Two Divergent
   Socio-political Contexts*. Doctoral dissertation. Vancouver: Faculty of
   Education, University of British Columbia.

– 1999. *Quand le silence parle. Enseignement de la culture dans les pro-
   grammes de langues secondes*. Preliminary research report of the
   Research Group on Ethnicity and Adaptation to Pluralism in Education,
   University of Montreal. Unpublished.

– 2000. "L'éducation et les relations entre anglophones et francophones
   vers un agenda de recherche." In *Relations ethniques et éducation dans
   les sociétés divisées: Québec, Irlande du Nord, Catalogne et Belgique*,
   edited by M. McAndrew and F. Gagnon, 181–90. Montreal/Paris:
   L'Harmattan.

– 2007. "Anglo-Quebec today: Looking at community and schooling issues." *International Journal of the Sociology of Language* 185: 109–32.

– (2008). "English Education in Quebec: Issues and Challenges." In
   *The Vitality of the English-Speaking Communities of Quebec: From
   Community Decline to Revival*, edited by R.Y. Bourhis. Centre d'études
   ethniques des universités montréalaises (CEETUM), Université de
   Montréal.

Lamberts, M.P. De Cuyper, J. Geets, L. Struyven, C. Timmerman, S. Van den Eede, and J. Wets. 2007. *Het Vlaamse inburgeringsbeleid geëvalueerd*. Evaluation report of the civic integration policy, Ministry of the Flemish Community. www.binnenland.vlaanderen.be/inburgering/onderzoek.htm.

Lantheaume, F. 2003. "Solidité et instabilité du curriculum d'histoire en France: accumulation de ressources et allongement des réseaux." Éducation et Société 12(2): 125–42.

Laperrière, A. 1989. "La recherche de l'intégrité dans une société pluriethnique: perceptions de la dynamique des relations interethniques et interraciales dans un quartier mixte de Montréal." *Revue internationale d'action communautaire* 21(61): 109–16.

– et al. (1994. "L'émergence d'une nouvelle génération cosmopolite?" *Revue internationale d'action communautaire* 32(71): 174–84.

– and P. Dumont. 2000. *La citoyenneté chez les jeunes Montréalais: vécu scolaire et représentations de la société*. Report of the Research Group on Ethnicity and Adaptation to Pluralism in Education, University of Montreal.

– and P. Lamarre. 2004. "Crossing Linguistic Boundaries: Perspectives from Parents, Teachers and Youth." Communication presented at a bilateral Québec-Northern Ireland workshop on "Education for Pluralism in Divided Societies." University of Ulster at Coleraine, Unesco Centre for Education, Pluralism, Human Rights and Democracy, 23–26 May.

– 2005. *Franchir les frontières: le cas de parents anglophones et francophones envoyant leurs enfants dans une école franco-anglaise de l'ouest de Montréal*. Research Group on Ethnicity and Adaptation to Pluralism in Education, University of Montreal. Unpublished.

Laville, C. 2004. "Historical Consciousness and Historical Education: What to Expect from the First for the Second." In *Theorizing Historical Conciousness*, edited by P. Seixas, 165–82. Toronto: University of Toronto Press.

– 2006. "Un cours d'histoire pour notre époque." *Le Devoir*, 2 May, A-7.

Le Foyer. 2008. *Enseignement et plurilinguisme*. www.foyer.be.

Le Soir en ligne. 2007. *Face-à-face Nord-Sud*, 22 May.

Lê Than Khoi. 1981. *L'éducation comparée*. Paris: Armand Colin.

Leclerc, J. 2008. "Histoire de la Belgique et ses conséquences linguistiques." www.tlfq.ulaval.ca/axl/europe/belgiqueetat_histoire.htm.

Lefebvre, S. 2007. *Gestion de la diversité religieuse dans l'espace scolaire: nouvelles pratiques*. Report presented to the Secretariat for Religious Affairs, Ministry for Education, Recreation, and Sports (Quebec).

Leman, J. 1991. "The education of immigrant children in Belgium."
    Anthropology and Education Quarterly 22(2): 140–53.

Leman, J. 1997. "School as a socializing and corrective force in inter-
    ethnic urban relations." *Journal of Multilingual and Multicultural
    Development* 18(2): 125–35.

Leman, J. 1999. "Cultural hybridism and self-categorization: trilingually
    and biculturally scholarized adolescents in Brussels." *International
    Journal of Educational Research*[31]: 317–26.

Lennert, M., and J.M. Decroly. 2001. *Flux migratoire de et vers la
    Belgique*. Brussels: Fondation Roi Baudoin, Université libre de Belgique.

Lenoir, Y., and C. Xypas, eds. 2006. *L'éducation à la citoyenneté et divers-
    ité culturelle*. Paris: PUF.

Létourneau, J. 2000. *Passer à l'avenir: histoire, mémoire, identité dans le
    Québec d'aujourd'hui, les Québécois: un parcours historique*. Montreal:
    Fides.

Létourneau, J. 2006. "Un débat mal parti. Rectifications et précisions à
    l'égard d'un texte assassin." *Le Devoir*, 1 May, A-7.

– and S. Moisan. 2004a. "Young People's Assimilation of a Collective
    Historical Memory: A Case Study of Quebeckers of French-Canadian
    Heritage." In *Theorizing Historical Consciousness*, edited by P. Seixas,
    109–28. Toronto: University of Toronto Press.

– 2004b. "Mémoire et récit de l'aventure historique du Québec chez les
    jeunes Québécois d'héritage canadien-français." *The Canadian
    Historical Review* 85(2): 325–56.

Lévesque, S. 2004. "History and Social Studies in Quebec: An Historical
    Perspectives." In *Challenges and Prospects for Canadian Social Studies*,
    edited by A. Sears and I. Wright, chapter 3. Vancouver: Pacific
    Educational Press.

Levine, M.V. ed. 1990. *The Reconquest of Montreal: Language Policy and
    Social Change in a Bilingual City*. Philadelphia: Temple University Press.

Lindemans, L., R. Renard, and J. Vandevelde. 1981. *De taalwetgeving in
    België*. Leuven: Davidsfonds.

Lisée, J.-F. 2007. *Nous*. Montreal: Éditions du Boréal.

Llevot, N. 2004. *Els mediadors interculturals a les institucions educatius
    de Catalunya*. Lleida: Editorial Pagès.

Llobera, J. 1989. "Catalan National Identity: The Dialectic of Past and
    Present." In *History and Ethnicity*, edited by E. Tonkin et al, 247–61.
    London and New York: Taylor & Francis.

Llosada, J., R. Merino, and M.García. 2005. *Itinéraires formatifs des jeun-
    es immigrants après de l'enseignement secondaire obligatoire*. Second

meeting of Youth and Society in Europe and around the Mediterranean, Marseille.

Loobuyck, P., and D. Jacobs. 2006. "The Flemish immigration society: Political challenges on different levels." In *New Citizens, New Policies? Developments in Diversity Policy in Canada and Flanders*, edited by L. D'Haenens, M. Hooghe, D. Vanheule, and H. Gezduci, 105–23. Ghent: Academia Press.

Maclure, J. 2000. *Récits identitaires: le Québec à l'épreuve du pluralisme*. Montreal: Québec/Amérique.

– 2008. "Le malaise relative aux pratiques d'accommodement de la diversité religieuse: une thèse interprétative." In *L'accommodement raisonnable et la diversité religieuse à l'école publique: normes et pratiques*, edited by M. McAndrew, M. Milot, J.S. Imbeault, and P. Eid, 215–42. Montreal: Fides.

Maddens, B., J. Billiet, and R. Beerten. 2000. "National identity and the attitude towards foreigners in multi-national states: the case of Belgium." *Journal of Ethnic and Migration Studies* 26(1): 45–60.

Mallea, J. 1977. *Quebec's Language Policy: Background and Responses*. Québec: CIRB.

Manço, A.A. 1999. *Intégration et identités - Stratégies et positions des jeunes issus de l'immigration*. Brussels/Paris: De Boeck University.

– and D. Crutzen. 1999. "Langues d'origine et langues d'enseignement: un problème de gestion sociolinguistique examiné à travers l'exemple des Turcs et des Marocains en Belgique." In *Moedertaalonderwijs bij allochtonen. Geintegreerd Onderwijs in De Eigen Taal En Cultuur*, edited by J. Leman, 31–46. Leuven: ACCO.

Marois P. 2008. "Non à un Québec bilingue." *Le Devoir*, 13 February. www.ledevoir.com/2008/02/13/175865.html.

Martel, A. 1996. *Official Language Minority Education Rights in Canada: From Instruction to Management*. Ottawa: Office of the Commissioner of Official Languages for Canada.

Martin, J.P. 1994. "Laïcité française, laïcité belge: regards croisés." In *Pluralisme religieux et laïcités*, edited by A. Dierkens, 71–86. Brussels: European Union, Institute for the Study of Religion and Secularity, Université Libre de Bruxelles.

Martineau, R. 1998. "Du patriote au citoyen éclairé…l'histoire comme vecteur d'éducation à la citoyenneté." In À propos de l'histoire nationale, edited by R. Comeau and B. Dionne, 46–56. Sillery: Septentrion.

Martinello, M., and M. Swyngedouw. 1998. *Où va la Belgique? Les soubresauts d'une petite démocratie européenne*. Paris: L'Harmattan.

Masats, D. 2001. "Language awareness: An international project." In *Language Awareness in the Foreign Language Classroom*, edited by A.D. Lasagabaster and J.M. Sierra, 79–97. Zarautz, Spain: Euskal Herriko Unibertsitatea.

Mawet, F., and P. Van Parijs. 2007. "Des écoles de la réussite plurilingue pour tous les enfants bruxellois." Presentation made at the Aula Magna Colloquium, Bruxelles, 2–3 March.

McAndrew, M. 1986. Étude sur l'ethnocentrisme dans les manuels scolaires de langue française au Québec. Montreal: Faculty of Education Publications, University of Montreal.

– 1987. *Le traitement de la diversité raciale, ethnique et culturelle et la valorisation du pluralisme dans le matériel didactique au Québec.* Montreal: Conseil des communautés culturelles et de l'immigration.

– 1996. "Models of Common Schooling and Interethnic Relations: A Comparative Analysis of Policies and Practices in the United States, Israel and Northern Ireland." *Compare* 26(3): 333–45.

– 1999. "Sens et limites du principe de non-discrimination en matière éducative: une réflexion critique." *Revue québécoise de droit international* 12(1): 225–40.

– 2000. "Comparabilité des expériences décrites et perspectives de collaboration." In *Relations ethniques et éducation dans les sociétés divisées: Québec, Irlande du Nord, Catalogne et Belgique,* edited by M. McAndrew and F. Gagnon, 323–45. Montreal: L'Harmattan.

– (2001. *Immigration et diversité à l'école. Le débat québécois dans une perspective comparative.* Montreal: Presses de l'Université de Montréal.

– 2002a. "La loi 101 en milieu scolaire: impacts et résultats." *Revue d'aménagement linguistique,* special issue: 69–83.

– 2002b. "Le remplacement du marqueur linguistique par le marqueur religieux en milieu scolaire." In *Ce qui a changé depuis le 11 septembre 2001: les relations ethniques en question,* edited by J. Renaud, L. Pietrantonio, and G. Bourgeault, 131–48. Montreal: Presses de l'Université de Montréal.

– 2002c. "Ethnic relations and education in divided societies: Belgium, Catalonia, Northern Ireland, Quebec." *Kolor, Journal on Moving Communities* 1: 5–19.

– 2003a. "School Spaces and the Construction of Ethnic Relations: Conceptual and Policy Debates." *Canadian Ethnic Studies/Études ethniques au Canada* 35(2): 14–29.

– 2003b. "L'accommodement raisonnable: atout ou obstacle dans l'accomplissement des mandats de l'école?" *Options* CSQ 22: 131–47.

- 2004. "Éducation interculturelle et éducation à la citoyenneté: regard critique sur la réforme." In *Quelle formation pour l'éducation à la citoyenneté?* edited by F. Ouellet, 27–71. Québec: Presses de l'Université Laval.
- 2006a. "Éducation à la citoyenneté et éducation interculturelle: le cas québécois." In Éducation à la citoyenneté et diversité culturelle, edited by Y. Lenoir and C. Xypas. Paris: PUF.
- 2006b. "L'école et les relations entre francophones et anglophones: un regard sur la réalité régionale." Paper presented in Lennoxvile at the Eastern Townships Resource Centre Colloquium on "Rural Life and Globalization: The Changing Cultural Landscape of the Eastern Townships/Ruralité et mondialisation: mutation des paysages culturels des Cantons de l'Est." May.
- 2006c. "La réussite éducative des élèves issus de l'immigration: enfin au cœur du débat sur l'intégration." *Options CSQ*: 109–28.
- 2006d. "The Hijab Controversies in Western Public Schools: Contrasting Conceptions of Ethnicity and Ethnic Relations." In *The Making of the Islamic Diaspora*, edited by S. Rahnema and H. Moghissi, 151–64. Toronto: University of Toronto Press.
- 2007a. "Québec Immigration, Integration and Intercultural Policy: A Critical Assessment." *Indian Journal of Federal Studies* 15(1): 1–18.
- 2007b. "Pour un débat inclusif sur l'accommodement raisonnable." *Revue Éthique publique* 9(1): 140–51.
- 2007c. "The education of immigrant students in a globalized world: policy debates in a comparative perspective." In *Global Understandings: Learning and Education in Troubled Times*, edited by M. Suarez-Orozco, 232–55. Berkeley/London/New York: University of California Press/Ross Institute.
- 2008a. "Cégeps: des nuances s'imposent. Avant de conclure à l'échec de la Loi 101, il y a tout un pas à ne pas franchir." *La Presse*, 25 January.
- 2008b. "Une réflexion sur la formation des intervenants." In *L'accommodement raisonnable et la diversité religieuse à l'école publique: normes et pratiques*, edited by M. McAndrew, M. Milot, J.S. Imbeault, and P. Eid, 135–58. Montreal: Fides.
- 2009a. "Ensuring proper competency in the host language: contrasting formula and the place of heritage languages." *Teacher College Review* 111(6).
- 2010. "Diversité et éducation au Québec et au Canada: un ou plusieurs modèles?" In *L'École et la diversité: perspectives comparées*, edited by M. McAndrew, M. Milot, and A. Triki-Yamani, 7–20. Québec: Presses de l'Université Laval.

– and C. Cicéri. 1998. "Immigration, ethnocultural diversity and multilingualism in education: The Canadian example." *Zeitschrift für internationale erziehungs- und sozialwissenschaftliche Forschung* 15(2).

– and P. Eid. 2003a. "La traversée des frontières scolaires par les francophones et les anglophones au Québec: 2000–2002." *Cahiers québécois de démographie* 32(2): 223–53.

– 2003b. "Les *ayants droit* qui fréquentent l'école française au Québec: caractéristiques, variations régionales, choix scolaires." *Cahiers québécois de démographie* 32(2): 255–71.

– and F. Gagnon. 2000. *Relations ethniques et éducation dans les sociétés divisées: Québec, Irlande du Nord, Catalogne, Belgique*. Paris: L'Harmattan.

– and R. Janssens. 2004. "The Role of Schooling in the Maintenance and Transformation of Ethnic Boundaries between Linguistic Communities: Contrasting Quebec and Belgium." Études ethniques au Canada/Canadian Ethnic Studies 36(3): 61–83, special issue entitled *Relations ethniques et éducation dans les sociétés divisées: comparaison Belgique-Canada/Ethnic Relations and Education in Divided Societies: Comparing Belgium and Canada*. Edited by G. Bourgeault, M.H. Chastenay et M. Verlot.

– and M. Ledoux. 1995. "La concentration ethnique dans les écoles de langue française de l'île de Montréal: un portrait statistique." *Cahiers québécois de démographie* 24(2): 343–70.

– and F. Lemire. 1994. "Relations interethniques et modèles de scolarisation commune dans des sociétés divisées: une analyse comparative des politiques et pratiques en Israël et en Irlande du Nord." *Interculture* 25–6: 187–222.

– and F. Lemire. 1999. "La concentration ethnique dans les écoles de langue française de l'île de Montréal: Que pouvons-nous apprendre de la recherche américaine sur le 'busing'?" Éducation canadienne et internationale 27(2): 1–24.

– and J.P. Proulx. 2000. "Éducation et ethnicité au Québec: un portrait d'ensemble." In *Relations ethniques et éducation dans les sociétés divisées: Québec, Irlande du Nord, Catalogne et Belgique*, edited by M. McAndrew and F. Gagnon, 123–60. Montreal: L'Harmattan.

– C. Tessier, and G. Bourgeault. 1997. "L'éducation à la citoyenneté en milieu scolaire au Canada, aux États-Unis et en France. Des orientations aux réalisations." *Revue française de pédagogie* 121 (October-November-December): 57–77.

– and A. Triki-Yamani. 2010. "The Muslim Community and Education in Québec: Controversy and Mutual Adaptation." *Journal of International*

Migration and Integration/Revue de l'intégration et de la migration internationale 11(1): 41–58.

– and M. Verlot. 2004. "Diversité culturelle, langue et éducation: que pouvons-nous apprendre d'une comparaison Québec/Flandres?" Études ethniques au Canada/ Canadian Ethnic Studies 36(3): 10–24. Special issue: *Relations ethniques et education dans les sociétés divisées: comparaison Belgique-Canada/Ethnic Relations and Education in Divided Societies: Comparing Belgium and Canada,* edited by G. Bourgeault, M.-H. Chastenay, and M. Verlot.

– and M. Weinfeld. 1997. "L'intégration sociale des immigrants et la réaction des institutions." In *Metropolis. Première conférence internationale,* edited by M. Lombardi, 56–81. Milan: Éditions Quaderni ISMU.

– J. Ledent, and R. Ait-Said. 2008b. *La réussite scolaire des jeunes des communautés noires au secondaire.* Research Report. Quebec Metropolis Centre - Immigration and Metropolis.

– F. Lemire and W. Smith. 2006. "L'éducation et les relations entre les francophones et les anglophones au Québec: les perceptions des directeurs d'école." In *Politiek, Taal, Onderwijs en Samenleving in Beweging. Brusselse Thema's 14,* edited by R. De Groof, R., Janssens, J. Degadt, and E. Witte, 335–59. Brussels: VUB Press.

– M. Pagé, and M. Jodoin. 1997. *Vécu scolaire et social des élèves scolarisés dans les écoles secondaires de langue française de l'île de Montréal.* Research Report. Québec: Ministère des Relations avec les citoyens et de l'Immigration du Québec.

– M. Jodoin, M. Pagé, and J. Rossell. 2000. "L'aptitude au français des élèves montréalais d'origine immigrée: impact de la densité ethnique de l'école, du taux de francisation associé à la langue maternelle et de l'ancienneté d'implantation." *Cahiers québécois de démographie* 29(1): 89–118.

– C. Mitchell, B. Côté, and J. Kirk. 2003a. *Creating Action Spaces for Cultural Collaboration.* Ottawa: Department of Canadian Heritage.

– 2003b. *Exploring Collective Memory: rencontre à Grosse-île, Créer des Espaces de Collaboration.* University of Montreal Research Group on Ethnicity and Adaptation to Pluralism in Education and McGill University.

– C. Veltman, F. Lemire, and J. Rossell. 1999. *Concentration ethnique et usages linguistiques en milieu scolaire.* Research Report presented to the MEQ, MRCI, and CLF.

– B. Garnett, J. Ledent, C. Ungerleider, and M. Adumati-Trache. 2008a. "La réussite scolaire des élèves issus de l'immigration: une question de

classe sociale, de langue ou de culture?" Éducation et Francophonie
  36(1): 177–96. Special issue: *Rapport ethniques et éducation: perspectives nationales et internationales,* edited by M. McAndrew.

McCall, D. 2007. "Reflections on the Teaching of History in Post-Primary
  Schools in Northern Ireland from 1984 to 2006." In *Recent Research on Teaching History in Northern Ireland: Informing Curriculum Change,* edited by E. McCully. Coleraine: Unesco Center Education for
  Pluralism, Human Rights and Democracy.

McClenahan, C., E. Cairns, S. Dunn, and V. Morgan. 1996. "Intergroup
  Friendships. Integrated and Desegregated Schools in Northern Ireland."
  Journal of Social Psychology 136(5): 549–58.

McCombe, J.A. 2006. *School History and the Introduction of Local and
  Global Citizenship into the Northern Ireland Curriculum: The Views of
  History Teachers.* Unpublished doctoral dissertation. Coleraine: School
  of Education, University of Ulster.

McCully, A. 2006. "Practitioner Perceptions of their Role in Facilitating
  the Handling of Controversial Issues in Contested Societies: A Northern
  Irish Experience." *Journal of Cognitive Affective Learning* 3(1): 30–66.

McCully, A.W., K. Barton, and M. Conway. 2003. "History Education and
  National Identity in Northern Ireland." *International Journal of
  Historical Learning, Teaching and Research* 3(1): 31–43.

McCully, A., P. Smith, and M. O'Doherty. 1999. "Exploring Controversial
  Issues in Northern Ireland." *Irish Educational Studies* 18: 49–61.

McCully, A., P. Smith, and M. O'Doherty. 2003. *Speak Your Piece.
  Exploring Controversial Issues in Northern Ireland, A Development
  Project for Teachers and Youth Workers.* Final Report. Coleraine:
  School of Education, University of Ulster.

McCully, A., N. Pilgrim, A., Sutherland, and T. McMinn. 2002. "Don't
  Worry, Mr. Trimble, We Can Handle It: Balancing the Rational with the
  Emotional When Teaching Irish History." *Teaching History* 105: 6–12.

McDonough, K., and W. Feinderg. 2003. *Citizenship and Education in
  Liberal Democratic-Societies: Teaching for Cosmopolitan Values and
  Connective Identities.* Oxford University Press.

McGlynn, C. 2001. *The Impact of Post-Primary Integrated Education in
  Northern Ireland on Past Pupils: A Study.* Ed.D. Thesis. Belfast:
  University of Ulster of Jordanstown.

– 2003. "Integrated Education in Northern Ireland in the Context of
  Critical Multiculturalism." *Irish Educational Studies* 22(3): 11–28.

– 2007. "Rhetoric and Reality: Are Integrated Schools in Northern Ireland
  Really Making a Difference?" *Irish Educational Studies* 26(3): 271–87.

– and Z. Bekerman. 2007. "The management of pupil difference in Catholic-Protestant and Palestinian-Jewish integrated education in Northern Ireland and Israel." *Compare: A Journal of Comparative and International Education* 37(5): 689–705.

– P. Lamarre, A. Montgomery, and A. Laperriere. 2009. "Journeys into the unknown: shared schooling and social change in Quebec and Northern Ireland." *Diaspora, Indigenous and Minority Education* 3(4): 209–25.

– U. Niens, E. Cairns, and M. Hewstone. 2004. "Moving Out of Conflict: The Contribution of Integrated Schools in Northern Ireland to Identity, Attitudes, Forgiveness and Reconciliation." *Journal of Peace Education* 1: 147–63.

McGonigle, J. 2000. *Towards a Culture of Peace: Insight into the Problems and Processes of Integrating Segregated Schools in Northern Ireland.* Doctoral dissertation. University of Oxford.

– A. Smith, and T. Gallagher. 2003. *Integrated Education in Northern Ireland. The Challenge of Transformation.* Coleraine: Unesco Centre, University of Ulster.

McPoilan, A. 1997. *Ultacht Trust. The Irish Language in Education in Northern Ireland.*

Medhoune, A. 2000. "L'ethnicisation des rapports sociaux dans l'espace scolaire: le cas de Bruxelles." In *Relations ethniques et éducation dans les sociétés divisées: Québec, Irlande du Nord, Catalogne et Belgique*, edited by M. McAndrew and F. Gagnon, 309–22. Montreal: L'Harmattan,

Medhoune, A., and M. Lavallée. 2000. "Le système scolaire en Belgique: clivages et pratiques." In *Relations ethniques et éducation dans les sociétés divisées, Québec, Irlande du Nord, Catalogne et Belgique*, edited by M. McAndrew and F. Gagnon, 147–69. Montreal/Paris: L'Harmattan.

Mercadé, F., and F. Hernandez, eds. 1988. *Estructuras sociales e identidades nacionales.* Barcelona: Editorial Ariel.

Merry, M.S. 2005. "Social exclusion of Muslim youth in Flemish- and French-speaking Belgian schools." *Comparative Education Review* 49(11): 1–22.

Mettewie, L. 2003. "Contacthypothese en taalleermotivatie in Nederlandstalige scholen in Brussel." *Toegepaste taalwetenschap in artikelen* 70(2): 79–89.

– 2004. *Attitudes en motivatie van talleerders in België. Een sociaal-psychologisch onderzoek naar het verwerven van de eerste een tweede taal door Nederlandstalige, Franstalige en tweetalige leerlingen in het secundair onderwijs in Brussel.* Doctoral thesis in linguistics. Brussels: Vrije Universiteit Brussel.

– 2007. "Élèves non néerlandophones dans l'enseignement néerlando-phone à Bruxelles: analyse des répercussions éducatives de la traversée de la frontière linguistique." In *L'éducation au-delà des frontières, Apprentissage précoce du néerlandais, apprentissage précoce en néer-landais dans la zone frontalière franco-belge,* edited by L. Puren and S. Babault, 141–78. Paris: L'Harmattan.

– and R. Janssens. 2007. "Language Use and Language Attitudes in Brussels." In *Multilingualism in European Bilingual Contexts,* edited by D. Lasagabaster and A. Hue, 117–43. Clevendon: Multicultural Matters.

Miller, H., and K. Miller. 1996. "Language Policy and Identity: The Case of Catalonia." *International Studies in Sociology of Education* 6(1): 113–28.

Mettewie, L., A. Housen, and M. Pierrard. 2004. "Invloed va contact op taalattitudes en taalleermotivatie in het Nederlandstalig onderwijs in Brussel." In *Taal, Attitudes en Onderwijs in Brussel. Brusselse Thema's 12,* edited by A. Housen, M. Pierrard, and P. Van De Craen, 35–65. Brussels: VUB Press.

Ministère de l'Éducation, du Loisir et du Sport (MELS). 2004. *Québec Education Program: Secondary School Education, Cycle One.* Québec: MELS.

– 2005. *The Establishment of an Ethics Program and Religious Culture: Direction for the Future for All Young People of Quebec.* Québec: MELS.

– 2006a. *Educational Profile of Students from Immigrant Families: 1994–1995 to 2003–2004.* Québec: Gouvernement du Québec.

– 2006b. *Québec Education Program: Secondary Cycle Two. History and Citizenship Education.*

– 2006c. *Rapport d'expérimentation du programme d'anglais langue seconde du premier cycle du primaire – Année 2005–2006.* Program management. www.mels.gouv.qc.ca/DGFJ/dp/experimentationals.htm.

– 2007a. Élèves de langue maternelle anglaise selon le réseau et la langue d'enseignement - Années scolaires 2005–2006 et 2006–2007. Direction de la recherche, des statistiques et des indicateurs. (Directorate for Research, Studies, and Statistics.)

– 2007b. *Québec Education Program: Secondary School Education, Cycle Two.* Applied general training program. Québec: MELS.

– 2007c. *Statistiques de l'éducation: Enseignement primaire, secondaire, collégial et universitaire.* Québec: Government of Québec.

– 2007d. *Répartition (en pourcentage) des nouveaux inscrits à l'enseignement collégial par langue d'enseignement selon la langue maternelle et la langue d'enseignement au secondaire - Automne 1987 à 2006, Tableaux com-mandés par la chercheure.* Direction de la recherche, des statistiques et des indicateurs (Directorate for Research, Studies, and Statistics).

– 2007e. *Supporting Montreal Schools Program: 10 Years of Wishes and Achievements.* Québec: Government of Québec.

– 2007f. *New Approaches, New Solutions.* Québec: Government of Québec. ww.mels.gouv.qc.ca/Agirautrement.

– 2008a. *L'effectif scolaire à temps plein et à temps partiel du secteur des jeunes (2003–2004 à 2007–2008) selon la langue maternelle (regrou-pée) et la langue d'enseignement, par région administrative et sexe, tableau 8.* Québec: Direction de la recherche, des statistiques et des indi-cateurs (Directorate for Research, Studies, and Statistics).

– 2008b. "Exploratory study of the educational paths of students from immigrant backgrounds from the 1994–1995 cohort of secondary school students." *Bulletin statistique de l'éducation* 34.

– 2008c. *La prise en compte de la diversité religieuse et culturelle en mi-lieu scolaire: de la théorie à la pratique.* Training module for school ad-ministrators. Montreal: Direction des services aux communautés culturelles. This publication is in French only.

Ministère de l'Éducation du Québec. 1982. *Proposition de modèles d'implantation des programmes d'enseignement des langues d'origine.* Montreal: Bureau des services aux communautés culturelles.

– 1983. *History of Quebec and Canada. 4e Secondary. General Education and Professional.*

–- 1986. *History of Quebec and Canada. 4e Secondary. General Education and Professional. Teacher's Guide.*

– 1988. *L'école québécoise et les communautés culturelles.* Report of the committee headed by G. Latif. Québec: MEQ. This publication is in French only.

– 1996. *Task Force on the Teaching of History: Learning from the Past.* Québec: MEQ.

– 1997. *Québec Schools on Course: Educational Policy Statement.* Québec: MEQ.

– 1998a. *Overview of the Teaching of Elementary Social Studies and Secondary History within the Anglophone Community of the Province of Québec.* A report prepared by the History Task Force. Québec: MEQ.

– 1998b. *A School for the Future: Educational Integration and Intercultural Education.* Québec: MEQ.

– 2001a. *Québec Education Program. Preschool Education, Elementary Education.* Final version. Québec: MEQ.

– 2001b. *Teacher Training – Orientations – Professional Competencies.* Government of Québec. www.mels.gouv.qc.ca/DFTPS/interieur/forminit. html.

Ministère de l'Immigration et des Communautés culturelles. 1990. *Let's Build Quebec Together: A Policy Statement on Immigration and Integration.*

– 2005. *Plan stratégique 2005–2008.*

– 2008a. *Tableaux sur l'intégration au Québec 2003–2007.*

– 2008b. *To Enrich Québec – Better Integration: Measures to Strengthen Québec's Action with Respect to the Employment Integration of Immigrants.* www.quebecinterculturel.gouv.qc.ca/fr/valeurs-fondements/ index.html.

– 2009. *Tableaux sur l'immigration permanente au Québec.* www.micc. gouv.qc.ca/fr/recherches-statistiques/stats-immigration-recente.html.

Ministère de la Communauté flamande. 1998. *Décret relatif à la politique flamande à l'encontre des minorités ethnoculturelles.* Brussels: Moniteur belge.

– 2002. *Décret relatif à l'égalité des chances en éducation.* Brussels: Moniteur belge.

– 2003a. *Décret relatif à la politique flamande d'intégration civique.* Brussels: Moniteur belge.

– 2003b. *Het Vlaams minderhedenbeleid gewikt en gewogen, Evaluatie van het Vlaams minderhedenbeleid (1996–2002).* Rapport voor de Vlaamse Regering. May.

– 2003c. *Diversiteit als meerwaarde. Engagementsverklaring van de Vlaamse Onderwijswereld.* Commissie Diversiteit en Gelijke Onderwijskansen, Vlaamse Onderwijsraad. www.vlor.be/Sub_Projecten. asp?recordID=18&cat=Projecten&herhaal=neen&subsublink=Gelijke+ onderwijskansen+en+diversiteit&.

– 2004a. *Samenleven in diversiteit, Gedeeld burgeschap en gelijke kansen in een kleurrijk Vlaanderen, Actualisering beleid t.a.v. etnisch-culturele minderheden: strategisch plan minderhedenbeleid 2004–2010.*

– 2004b. *Leerkrachten OKAN en begeleiders GON kunnen eindelijk vast-benoemd worden.* Vlaams Ministerie van Onderwijs en Vorming. www. ond.vlaanderen.be/nieuws/archief/2004/2004pers/0401_okan-gon.htm.

– 2005. *Diversiteit als meerwaarde. Engagementsverklaring van het Vlaams hoger onderwijs.* Commissie Diversiteit en Gelijke Onderwijskansen – Vlaamse Onderwijsraad (Commission for diversity and equality in education – Flemish Education Council). www.vlor.be/ Sub_Activiteiten.asp?recordID=68&cat=Activiteiten&herhaal=neen&su bsublink=Engagementsverklaring+over+diversiteit+in+het+hoger+ onderwijs.

– 2006a. *Égalité des chances en éducation pour chaque enfant… les écoles intensifient leurs efforts!* Brussels: Flemish Authorities, Education and Training Policy Area.

– 2006b. *Onthaalonderwijs voor anderstalige nieuwkomers in het gewoon voltijds secundair onderwijs. Vlaams Ministerie van Onderwijs en Vorming.* Edulex. www.ond.vlaanderen.be/edulex/database/document/document.asp?docid=13123.

– 2006c. *Onthaalonderwijs voor anderstalige nieuwkomers. Vlaams Ministerie van Onderwijs en Vorming.* Edulex. www.ond.vlaanderen.be/edulex/database/document/document.asp?docid=13800.

– 2006d. *Diverse lectoren, diverse studenten? Sluitstuk van een jaar nadenken met lectoren en organisaties over diversiteit in de lerarenopleidingen.* Departement Onderwijs en Vorming. www.ond.vlaanderen.be/publicaties/default.asp?get=ALLE&nr=253.

– 2007a. *Diversiteit in het onderwijs.*

– 2007b. *Databank Diversiteit.* www.ond.vlaanderen.be/diversiteit/databank.

– 2007c. *Flemish Education in Figures.* Education and Training Department. www.ond.vlaanderen.be/publicaties/default.asp?nr=87.

– 2008a. *Inburgering: Integration Courses in Flanders and Brussels.* www.binnenland.vlaanderen.be/inburgering.

– 2008b. *Inburgering in Brussel.* (BON - Brussels Onthaalbureau Nieuwkomers/Brussels Welcome Office for People of Foreign Origin.): www.brussel.inburgering.be.

– 2008c. *Strategy for the European Year of Intercultural Dialogue 2008.* Departement Cultuur, Jeugd, Sport en Media.

– 2008d. *Onthaalonderwijs: Historiek.* Vlaams Ministerie van Onderwijs en Vorming. www.ond.vlaanderen.be/onthaalonderwijs/inhoud/Historiek.

– 2008e. *Vragen en antwoorden over onthaalonderwijs. Vlaams Ministerie van Onderwijs en Vorming.* www.ond.vlaanderen.be/onthaalonderwijs/inhoud/Regelgeving

– (2008f). *Arrêté du Gouvernement flamand relatif aux compétences de base des enseignants du 5 octobre 2007.* Brussels: Moniteur belge.

Ministère de la Communauté française. 1997. *Loi 21557, Décret définissant les missions prioritaires de l'enseignement fondamental et de l'enseignement secondaire et organisant les structures propres à les atteindre.* Administration générale de l'Enseignement et de la Recherche scientifique.

– 1998. *Guide de l'enseignement obligatoire en communauté française.* Administration générale de l'Enseignement et de la Recherche scientifique.

– 1999a. *Compétences terminales et savoirs requis en histoire. Humanités générales et technologiques*, Administration générale de l'Enseignement et de la Recherche scientifique.

– 1999b. *Socles de compétences. Éveil. Formation historique et géographique comprenant la formation à la vie sociale et économique.* Administration générale de l'Enseignement et de la Recherche scientifique, Enseignement fondamental et premier degré de l'enseignement secondaire.

– 2002. *Programmes des études. Enseignement fondamental.* Administration générale de l'Enseignement et de la Recherche scientifique.

Ministère des Affaires internationales, de l'Immigration et des Communautés culturelles. 1994. *Actes du séminaire sur les indicateurs d'intégration des immigrants.* Government of Québec.

Ministère des Communautés culturelles et de l'Immigration. 1990a. *Au Québec pour bâtir ensemble.* Policy statement on immigration and integration. Québec: Direction des communications.

– 1990b. *Profil de la population immigrée recensée au Québec en 1986.* Québec: Direction des communications.

Ministère des Relations avec les Citoyens et de l'Immigration. 1997. *Le Québec en mouvement: statistiques sur l'immigration.* Québec.

Ministerio de Educación y Ciencia. 2004. *Una Educación de Calidad para Todos y Entre Todos.* Madrid.

Ministry of the Flemish Community, Education Department. 1997. *Secondary Education in Flanders Core Curriculum, Final Objectives on Developmental Aims of the First Cycle of Regular Secondary Education. Text of the Government of Flanders Act and Starting Points.*

– 2001. *Cross-Curricular Teams in Flemish Secondary Education.*

– 2002a. *Core Curriculum, Final Objectives of the Mainstream Primary Education, Cross-Curricular Final Objectives of Social Skills.*

– 2002b. *Core Curriculum, Final Objectives of the First Grade Secondary Education, History.*

– 2002c. *Final Objectives of the Second Grade of Mainstream Secondary Education, History.*

– 2002d. *Final Objectives of the Third Grade of Mainstream Secondary Education, History.*

Mitchell, C. 2003. "From Victims to Equals? Catholic Identification in Northern Ireland after the Agreement." *Irish Political Studies* 17(1): 51–71.

Montés, R.V. 1999. "De los manuales de historia a la historia de la disciplina escolar: nuevos enfoques en los estudios sobre la historigrafía escolar española." *Historia de la Educación, Revista interuniversitaria* 18: 169–90.

Montés, R.V. 2004. "La Enseñanza de la Historia. Entre polémicas interesadas y problemas reales." In *Miradas a la Historia: Reflexiones Historiográficas en recuerdo*, edited by E.N. Marin and J.A. Gómez-Hernandez, 141–54. Murcia: Universidad de Murcia.

Montmongomery, A., G. Fraser, C. McGlynn, A, Smith, and T. Gallagher. 2003. *Integrated Education in Northern Ireland. Integration in Practice.* Coleraine: Unesco Centre, University of Ulster.

Montreuil, A., and R.Y. Bourhis. 2004. "Acculturation Orientations of Competing Host Communities towards Valued and Devalued Immigrants." *International Journal of Intercultural Relations* 28(6): 507–32.

Morgan, V. 2000. "L'évolution récente des structures et des programmes scolaires en Irlande du Nord." In *Relations ethniques et éducation dans les sociétés divisées: Québec, Irlande du Nord, Catalogne et Belgique*, edited by M. McAndrew and F. Gagnon, 309–22. Montreal: L'Harmattan,

– and G. Fraser. 1999. *Integrated Education in Northern Ireland – The Implications of Expansion.* Coleraine: Centre for the Study of Conflict, University of Ulster.

– S. Dunn, E. Cairns, and G. Fraser. 1992. *Breaking the Mould: The Role of Parents and Teachers in the Integrated Schools in Northern Ireland.* Coleraine: Centre for the Study of Conflict, University of Ulster.

– 1993. "How Do Parents Choose a School for their Child? An Example of the Exercise of Parental Choice." *Educational Research* 32(12): 139–48.

Murray, D. 1985. *Worlds Apart: Segregated Schools in Northern Ireland.* Belfast: Appletree.

Nagel, T. 1994. Égalité et partialité. Translated by C. Beauvillard. Paris: PUF.

Niens, U., and M.-H. Chastenay. 2005. "Citizenship Education in Divided Society: Comparing Conceptualization and Research from Quebec and Northern Ireland." Paper presented at the annual congress of the American Educational Research Association (AERA). Montreal, 11–15 April.

Normand, M., and J. Hohl. 2000. *Les droits à l'école et l'école des droits. Vers des pratiques de la citoyenneté en classe.* Research Group on Ethnicity and Adaptation to Pluralism in Education, Faculty of Education, University of Montreal. Unpublished report.

Northern Ireland Council for Integrated Education (NICIE). 2006. *A Reply to Independent Strategic Review of Education.* NICIE, July.

O'Connor, U., B. Hartop, and A. McCully. 2002. *A Review of the Schools Community Relations Programme*. Coleraine: Unesco Centre, School of Education, University of Ulster.

– 2003. *A Research Study of Pupil Perceptions of the Schools Community Relations Programme*. Coleraine: Unesco Centre, School of Education, University of Ulster.

O'Murchei, H. 1999. *L'Irlandais face à l'avenir*. Brussels: European Bureau for Lesser-Used Languages.

Office of the First Minister and Deputy First Minister for Northern Ireland (OFMDFMNI). 2005a. *A Racial Equality Strategy for Northern Ireland (2005–2010)*.

– 2005b: *A Shard Future, Policy and Strategic Framework for Good Relations in Northern Ireland*. March. OFMDFMNI.

Office québécois de la langue française. (2008). *Rapport sur l'évolution de la situation linguistique au Québec*. Government of Québec. www.olf. gouv.qc.ca/ressources/sociolinguistique/index_indic.html.

Organisation for Economic co-operation and development. 2006. *Where Immigrant Students Succeed: A Comparative Review of Performance and Engagement in PISA 2003*. Edited by C. Shewbridge, and A. Schleicher.

Ouellet, M. 2008. "Accommodements raisonnables et liberté religieuse au Québec." Statement presented to the Commission de consultation sur les pratiques d'accommodement reliées aux différences culturelles. www.accommodements.qc.ca/documentation/quebec.html.

Oueslati, B., M. McAndrew, A. Triki-Yamani, and D. Helly. 2008. "The Evolution of the Coverage of Islam and Muslim Cultures in Québec French-Language Textbooks since the 1980s." Paper presented at the colloquium on *Islam and Education in Pluralistic Societies: Integration and Transformation*, Montreal, 8 May.

– M. McAndrew, and D. Helly. 2004. *Le traitement de l'islam et des musulmans dans les manuels scolaires de langue française du secondaire québécois (histoire, géographie, éducation économique, formation personnelle et sociale)*. Research report. Montreal: Chair in Ethnic Relations, University of Montreal.

Paelman, F. 2005. "CLIM in Flanders: a success story." In *CLIEC: A Report on the Methodology of Cooperative Learning and its Implementation in Different European Educational Settings*, edited by A. Joos and V. Ernalsteen, 56–71. Ghent: Steunpunt Intercultureell Onderwijs (Centre for Diversity and Learning), University of Ghent.

Pagé, M., and M.H. Chastenay. 2002. *Jeunes citoyens du Québec et du Nouveau-Brunswick*. Ottawa: Department of Canadian Heritage.

– and B. Côté. 2006. "Les contacts entre jeunes francophones ou anglophones: heureux ou malheureux?" Paper presented at the colloquium on "De la diversité linguistique à l'école et en société: nouveaux enjeux pour la recherche." Montreal: Centre d'études ethniques des universités montréalaises.

– and F. Gagnon. 1999. *Les approches de la citoyenneté dans six démocraties libérales*. Ottawa: Department of Canadian Heritage.

– Côté, B., and C. Lasry. 2007. *Les contacts entre jeunes francophones et anglophones dans l'Île de Montréal*. Montreal: Centre d'études ethniques des universités montréalaises. Unpublished.

– M. McAndrew, and M. Jodoin. 1997. *Vécu scolaire et social des élèves scolarisés dans les écoles secondaires de langue française de l'île de Montréal*. Montreal: Ministère des Relations avec les Citoyens et de l'Immigration du Québec.

Pagès, J. 1999a. "Las representaciones previas de los estudiantes de maestro de ciencias sociales, geografía e historia." *Teoría y Didáctica de las Ciencias Sociales* 4: 161–78.

– 2001. "¿Hacia dónde va la enseñanza de la historia y de las ciencias sociales? Apuntes para la comprensíon de un debate." *Éndoxa* 14: 261–88.

Pagès, J. 2003a. "Ausencias olvidos e interpretaciones interesadas en los contenidos de la historia escolar en España (1970–2003)." *Le Cartable de Clio* 3, 59–71.

– 2003b. "La Història de Catalunya al nou Curriculum." *Materials d'Història de Catalunya* 5.

– 2004a. "L'histoire de la Catalogne dans le nouveau programme d'enseignement obligatoire." Lyon: Presentation at the Institut de Formation des Maîtres de Lyon, May 2004.

– 2004b. "Enseñar a enseñar historia: La formación didáctica de los futuros profesores de Historia." In *Miradas a la historia: Reflexiones historiográficas en recuerdo*, edited by E.N. Marin and J.A. Gómez-Hernandez, 155–78. Murcia: Universidad de Murcia

– 2005. "Educación cívica, formación politica y enseñenza de las Ciencias Sociales, de la Geografia y de la Historia." *Didáctica de las Ciencias Sociales, Geografia e Historia* 44: 45–55.

Paillé, M. 2002. "L'enseignement en français au primaire et au secondaire pour les enfants d'immigrants: un dénombrement démographique." *Revue d'aménagement linguistique*. Special issue: *L'aménagement linguistique au Québec: 25 ans d'application de la Charte de la langue française*, 51–67.

Palaudàrias, J.M. 2008. "Trajectoires de continuation et d'abandon entre le secondaire obligatoire et le post-obligatoire en Catalogne." Seminar on immigration, social cohesion, and the school. Montreal: Immigration et métropoles.

– and J. Garreta. 2008. "La acogida del alumnado de origen inmigrante: un análisis comparado desde la situación en Cataluña." *Revista Española de Educación Comparada* 14: 49–78.

– and C. Serra, eds. 2007. *La migración extranjera en España: balance y perspectivas*. Girone: CGC Ediciones.

Parlement belge. 1963. Loi du 30 juillet 1963 concernant le régime linguistique dans l'enseignement. Brussels: Moniteur belge, 8210.

Pascual, J. 1998. *Discursos d'etnicitat en l'escolarització*. Doctoral dissertation. Barcelona: Department of Sociology, Universitat Autònomia de Barcelona.

Pettigrew, T.F. 1998. "Intergroup Contact Theory." *Annual Review of Psychology* 49: 65–85.

Phalet, K., and M. Swyngedow. 2002. "National identities and representations of citizenship." *Ethnicities* 2(1): 5–30.

– P. Deboosere, and V. Bastiaenssen. 2007. "Old and new inequalities in educational attainment: ethnic minorities in the Belgian Census 1991–2001." *Ethnicities* 7(3): 390.

Phillips, R. 1998. *History Teaching, Nationhood and the State: A Study in Educational Politics*. London: Cassell.

– P. Goalen, A. McCully, and S. Wood. 1999. "Four Histories, One Nation? History Teaching, Nationhood and a British Identity." *Compare* 29(2): 153–69.

Plourde, M. 1988. *La politique linguistique du Québec 1977–1988*. Montreal: IQRC.

Ponjaert-Kristoffersen, I., J. Van Braak, and P. Lambrecht. 1998. "Mogelijkheden om een taalbeleid te ontwikkelen binnen het Brussels Nederlandstalig basisonderwijs." In *Twintig jaar onderzoek over Brussel. Brusselse Thema's 6*, edited by E. Witte and A. Mares, 169–93. Brussels: VUB Press.

Potvin, M. 2008. *Crise des accommodements raisonnables: Une fiction médiatique?* Outremont, QC: Athéna Éditions.

– and P.R. Crarr. 2008. "La 'valeur ajoutée' de l'éducation antiraciste: conceptualisation, et mise en œuvre au Québec, et en Ontario." *Éducation et francophonie* 36(1): 197–216.

- M. McAndrew, and F. Kanouté. 2006. *L'éducation antiraciste en milieu scolaire francophone à Montréal: diagnostic et prospectives*. Research report. Université de Montréal, Chaire en relations ethniques.
- A. Morelli, and L. Mettewie. 2004. "Du racisme dans les rapports entre groupes nationaux au Canada et en Belgique?" *Canadian Ethnic Studies/Études ethniques au Canada* 36(3): 25–60. Special issue. *Ethnic Relations and Education in Divided Societies: Comparing Belgium and Canada*. Edited by G. Bourgeault, M.H. Chastenay, and M. Verlot

Prats, J. 1999. "La Enseñanza de la Historia y el Debate de las Humanidades." *Tarbiya, Revista de Investigación e innovación educativa* 21(May). Madrid: ICE, Universidad Autónoma de Madrid.
- 2000. "La Enseñanza de la Historia: Reflexiones para un Debate." *La Vanguardia*, 7 July.

Proulx, J.P. 1998. "Restructuration scolaire: la concurrence des valeurs religieuses et linguistiques." In *Transformation des enjeux démocratiques en éducation*, edited by L. Corriveau and M. Saint-Martin, 165–203. Montreal: Éditions Logiques.
- 1999. *Laïcité et religions. Perspective nouvelle pour l'école québécoise: Rapport du Groupe de travail sur la place de la religion à l'école*. Québec: MEQ.
- and J. Woerling. 1997. "La restructuration du système scolaire québécois et la modification de l'article 93 de la Loi constitutionnelle de 1867." *Revue juridique Thémis* 31(2): 399–510.

Pueyo, M. 2007. "La politique linguistique en tant que politique sociale. Le rôle des langues dans une société ouverte. " Paper presented at the Reial Acadèmia de Bones Lletres, Barcelone, 12 June.

Puig Rovira, J., J. Gómez Andres, J. Gómez-Bruguera, A. Pla Pi, and L.S. Ylla Janer. 2005. "Desenvolupament Personal i Ciutadania." In *Pacte Curricular per a l'Educació Debat Curricular. Reflexions i Propostes.* Barcelona: Generalitat de Catalunya.

Puig Salellas, J.M. 2000. "La legislació lingüística a Catalunya. Llei de 1983 a la de 1998." *Direcció General de Politika Lingüística*: 53–70.

Pujol, J. 1976. *La immigració, problema i esperança de Catalunya* Barcelona: Editorial Nova Terra.

Pulinx, R. 2008. *Vivre ensemble dans la diversité. L'intégration linguistique en Flandre*. Conseil de l'Europe: Division des politiques linguistiques.

Querol, E. 2001. "Evolució dels usos i de les representacions socials de les llengües a Catalunya (1993–2000)." *Noves SL*.

Racine, J. 2008. "Vers la laïcité de l'école." In *L'accommodement raisonnable et la diversité religieuse à l'école publique. Normes et pratiques,* edited by M. McAndrew, M. Milot, J.S. Imbeault, and P. Eid, 15–26. Montreal: Fides.

Rea, A. 1999. "La reconnaissance et la représentation de l'Islam." *L'année sociale*: 269–75.

Real Academia de la Historia. 2000. *Informe sobre los textos y cursos de Historia en los centros de Enseñanza Media*. Madrid.

Rees, E.L. 1996. "Spain's liguistic normalization in the educational system of Catalonia." *International Review of Education* 37(1): 87–98.

Ricoeur, P. 2000. *La mémoire, l'histoire et l'oubli*. Paris: Seuil.

Robitaille, A. 2006. "Cours d'histoire épurés au secondaire. Québec songe à un enseignement moins 'politique.'" *Le Devoir*, 27 April, A-1, A-8.

Roekens, F. 2008. *Données sur l'enseignement dans la langue d'origine (OETC) en communauté flamande – Année 2002*. Correspondence with F. Roekens, Instellingen en leerlingen Secundair onderwijs en Volwassenenonderwijs.

Romani, J. 1999. *Els joves i el Català: Resultats d'une enquesta*. Barcelona: Institut de Sociolingüistica Catalana.

Roosens, E. 2007. "First-language and -culture learning in light of globalization: the case of Muslims in Flanders and in the Brussels area, Belgium." In *Global Understandings: Learning and Education in Troubled Times*, edited by M. Suarez-Orozco, 256–71. Berkeley/London/New York: University of California Press/Ross Institute.

Rossell, J. 2005. "Los usos lingüísticos de los jóvenes en las escuelas secundarias de Montreal." Paper presented at the Centre Universitari de Sociolingüística i Comunicació (CUSC), Barcelona, 18 May.

– 2006. "Les usages linguistiques des jeunes fréquentant les écoles secondaires de Montréal." Paper presented at the colloquium on *La diversité linguistique à l'école et en société: nouveaux enjeux pour la recherche*, during a symposium organized by CEETUM, 17 February.

Rothbart, M., and O.P. John. 1985. "Social Categorisation and Behavioral Episodes: A Cognitive Analysis of the Effects of Intergroup Contact." *Journal of Social Issues* 41(3): 81–104.

Rüsen, J. 2005. *History, Narration, Interpretation, Orientation*. New York: Berghan Books.

Rust, V.D., A. Soumaré, O. Pescador, and M. Shibuya. 1999. "Research Strategies in Comparative Education." *Comparative Education Review* 4(1): 86–109.

Salée, D. 2007. "The Quebec State and the Management of Ethnocultural Diversity: Perspectives on an Ambiguous Record." In *Belonging?*

Diversity, Recognition and Shared Citizenship in Canada, edited by K. Banting, T.J. Courchesne, and F.L. Seidle. Montreal: The Art of the State.

Samper, L. 1996. "Etnicidad y curriculum oculto: la construcción social del otro por los futuros educadores." In *Racismo, etnicidad y educación intercultural*, edited by C. Solé, 63–100. Lleida: Universitat de Lleida

– and J. Garreta. 2007. "Educación e inmigración en España: debates en torno a la acción del profesorado." In *Educación e inmigración: nuevos retos para España en una perspectiva comparada*, edited by M.A. Alegre and J. Subirats, 361–83. Madrid: Centro de Investigaciones Sociológicas

– 2008. "Muslims in Catalan schools: presences and absences." Paper presented at the workshop on *Islam and Education in Pluralistic Societies: Integration and Transformation*, University of Montreal, 6–9 May.

– J. Garreta, and N. Llevot. 2001. "Les enjeux de la diversité culturelle dans l'école catalane." *Revue des sciences de l'éducation* 27(3): 543–68.

– N. Llevot, J. Garreta, and M.H. Chastenay. 2000. "Éducation et ethnicité: le cas catalan." In *Relations ethniques et éducation dans les sociétés divisées: Québec, Irlande du Nord, Catalogne et Belgique*, edited by M. McAndrew and F. Gagnon, 183–210. Montreal: L'Harmattan

Schermerhorn, R.A. 1970. *Comparative Ethnic Relations: A Framework for Theory and Research*. New York: Random House.

Schleicher, A. 2006. "És il·limitat el rendiment educatiu? La importància d'avaluar l'educació amb una perspectiva internacional." *Debats d'Educació* 5: 5–27.

Schmit, A. 2003. "Citizenship Education in Northern Ireland: Beyond National Identity?" *Cambridge Journal of Education* 33(1): 15–31.

Schrauwen, W., and J. Van Braak. 2000. "Het opzetten van plannen voor taalbeleid in Brusselse scholen en elders." In *Retoriek en praktijk van het schoolvak Nederlands*, edited by A. Mottart, 238–88. Brussels: Academia Press.

Secretaría de Estado de Inmigración y emigración. 2008. *Extranjeros con certificado de registro o tarjeta de residencia en vigor según provincia y nacionalidad*. Government of Spain. extranjeros.mtas.es/es/InformacionEstadistica/Informes.

Segura, A., P. Comes, S. Cucurella, A. Mayayo, and F. Roca. 2000. *Sobre L'Ensenyament de la Història i Altres Històries: Reposta a l'Informe de la Real Academia de la Historia*. Barcelona: Fundació Jaume Bofill.

Segura, A., P. Comes, S. Cucurella, A. Mayayo, and F. Roca. 2001. *Els Llibres d'Història, l'Ensenyament de la Història i Altres Històries*. Barcelona: Fundació Jaume Bofill.

Seixas, P. 2004. "Introduction." In *Theorizing Historical Consciousness*, edited by P. Seixas, 3–20. Toronto: University of Toronto Press.

Sept sur Sept Canal Infos. 2007. *Les médias alimentent les stéréotypes Wallons-Flamands*, 16 May.

Serra, C. 1997. *Immersió lingüística, rendiment acadèmic i classe social*. Barcelona: ICE-Horsori.

Sévigny, D. 2008. *Portrait socioculturel des élèves inscrits dans les écoles publiques de l'île de Montréal*. Montreal: Comité de gestion de la taxe scolaire de l'Île de Montréal. www.cgtsim.qc.ca/pls/ htmldb/f?p=105:34:3952723807278821].

Siguan, M. 1984. "Language and Education in Catalonia." *Quarterly Review of Education* 14(1): 111–24.

Simon, R.I. 2004. "The Pedagogical Insistence of Public Memory." In *Theorizing Historical Consciousness*, edited by P. Seixas. University of Toronto Press.

Sinn Féin. 2009. Website of Sinn Féin. *Education*. www.ardfheis. com/?page_id=364.

Smith A., and A. Robinson. 1996. *Education for Mutual Understanding: The Initial Statutory Years*. Coleraine: Centre for the Study of Conflict, University of Ulster.

Smith, A. 2001. "Religious Segregation and the Emergence of Integrated Schools in Northern Ireland." *Oxford Review of Education* 27(4): 559–75.

– 2003. "Citizenship Education in Northern Ireland: Beyond National identity?" *Cambridge Journal of Education* 33(1): 15–31.

– and S. Dunn. 1990. *Extending Inner School Links: An Evaluation of Contact between Protestant and Catholic Pupils in Northern Ireland*. Coleraine: Centre for the Study of Conflict, University of Ulster.

Smith, M. 2005. *Reckoning with the Past: Teaching History in Northern Ireland*. Lanham: Lexington Book.

Smith, W.J., M. McAndrew, and F. Lemire. 2003. *L'école et les relations entre les francophones et les anglphones au Québec: les perceptions des directeurs d'école - Rapport d'analyse*. Research report by the Groupe de recherche sur l'ethnicité et l'adaptation au pluralisme en éducation, www.ceetum.umontreal.ca/pdf/Conferences/Fr-An_Rap.pdf.

Smyth, M., and M. Scott. 2000. *YouthQuest 2000 Survey: A Report on Young People's Views and Experiences in Northern Ireland* Derry: INCORE, University of Ulster.

Soetart, R., and K. van Heule. 1999. "Teacher education in Belgium, Flemish and French communities – the situation at the end of the 1990s." *TNTEE Publications* 2(2): 43–70.

Solé, C. 1982. *Los inmigrantes en la sociedad y en la cultura catalanas.* Barcelona: Ediciones Peninsula.

– 2000. "L'identité nationale et régionale en Espagne." In *Relations ethniques et éducation dans les sociétés divisées: Québec, Irlande du Nord, Catalogne et Belgique,* edited by M. McAndrew and F. Gagnon, 63–88. Montreal: L'Harmattan.

Somers, W. 2005. "Immigratie: vijf na twaalf!" *Breuklijn, Vormingsblad van de Vlaams Belang Jongeren* December. www.vlaamsbelang.org/3/11.

Speak Your Piece. 1995. *Speak Your Piece: Exploring Controversial Issues through Youth Work.* Belfast: University of Ulster, the Youth Council for Northern Ireland, and Channel Four BBC.

Spotti, M. 2008. "Exploring the construction of immigrant minority pupils' identities in a Flemish primary classroom." *Linguistics and Education* 19: 20–36.

Statistics Canada. 2007. *The Evolving Linguistic Portrait, 2006 Census: Findings.* www12.statcan.ca/english/census06/analysis/language/allo_lang.cfm.

Statistique Canada. 2008. *Notes moyennes en lecture et en mathématiques selon la province, la langue du système scolaire et le statut d'immigrant, issu des résultats canadiens de l'étude PISA de l'OCDE (2006).* Tables requested by author.

Stephan, W.G., and C.W. Stephan. 1985. "Intergroup Anxiety." *Journal of Social Issues* 41(3): 157–75.

Steunpunt Gelijke Onderwijskansen (GOK). 2009. "School en ouders." www.steunpuntgok.be/volwassenen/materiaal/school_en_ouders/index.aspx.

Stevens, A.J. 2008. "Exploring pupil's perceptions of teacher racism in their context: a case study of Turkish and Belgian vocational education pupils in a Belgian school." *British Journal of Sociology of Education* 29(2): 175–87.

Straub, J. 2005. "Telling Stories, Making History: Toward a Narrative Psychology of the Historical Construction of Meaning." In *Narration, Identity, and Historical Consciousness,* edited by J. Straub, 44–98. New York: Berghahn Books.

Stringer, M., R. Wilson, P. Irwing, M. Giles, C. McClenahan, and L. Curtis. 2003. *The Impact of Schooling on the Social Attitudes of Children.* Belfast: The Integrated Education Fund.

Strubell, M. 1996. "Language Planning and Bilingual Education in Catalonia [and] a Response." *Journal of Multilingual and Multicultural Development* 17(2): 262–79.

Suárez-Orozco, M.M. 2007. *Learning in the Global Era: International Perspectives on Globalization and Education*. Berkeley, CA and East Hampton, NY: University of California Press and Ross Institute.

Subirats, J., and R. Gallego. 2003. *Les propostes sobre educació dels partits polítics catalans per a les eleccions autonòmiques de 2003*. Universitat Autònoma de Barcelona, Institut de Govern i Polítiques Públiques.

Subirats, M. 2002. "Els trets lingüístics." In *Enquesta de la regió de Barcelona. Condisions de vida i hàbits de la població*, edited by S. Giner, 180–7. Barcelona: Diputació de Barcelona.

Tajfel, H. 1982. *Human Groups and Social Categories*. Cambridge: Cambridge University Press.

Tajfel, H., and J.C. Turner. 1986. "The Social Identity Theory of Intergroup Behavior." In *Psychology of Intergroup Relations*, edited by S. Worchel and W.A. Austin, 7–24. Chicago: Nelson-Hall Publisher.

Taylor, C. 2001. "The Politics of Recognition." In *Multiculturalism*, edited by C. Taylor, 25–74. Princeton University Press.

Tessier, C., and M. McAndrew. 2001. "Citoyenneté en milieu scolaire et conseils étudiants: une étude exploratoire dans quatre écoles montréalaises." In *L'éducation à la citoyenneté*, edited by M. Pagé, F. Ouellet, and L. Cortesao, 187–200. Sherbrooke: CRP, Université de Sherbrooke,

Thompson, C. 2007. "Presenting the Past or Shaping the Future: An Investigation into Current Issues in Post-Primary History Education." In *Recent Research on Teaching History in Northern Ireland: Informing Curriculum Change*, edited by E. McCully, 30–2. Coleraine: Unesco Centre, University of Ulster.

Thornberry, P., and D. Gibbons. 1997. "Education and Minority Rights: A Short Survey of International Standard." *International Journal on Minority and Group Rights* 4(2): 115–52.

Timmerman, C. 2000. "Secular and religious nationalism among young Turkish women in Belgium: education may make the difference." *Anthropology & Education Quarterly* 31(3): 333–54.

Timmerman, C., J. Geets, and K. Van Der Heyden. 2006. "Les nouveaux arrivants en Flandre." In *Penser l'immigration et l'intégration autrement. Une initiative belge interuniversitaire*, edited by B. Khader, M. Martiniello, A. Rea, and C. Timmerman. Brussels: Bruyant.

Tomlinson, S. 1997. "Diversity, choice and ethnicity: The effects of educational markets on ethnic minorities." *Oxford Review of Education* 23(1).

Tonkin, E., M. McDonald, and M. Chapman, eds. 1989. *Ethnicity and History* London and New York: Routledge.

Torres, J. 2006. "El coneixement de català dels nats a l'estranger residents a Catalunya l'any 1996." In *Integrar, des de la fragilitat? Societats plurilingües davant els reptes de les immigracions multilingües: Suïssa, Brusselles, Luxembruge, Quebec i Catalunya*, edited by F.X. Vila i Moreno, E. Boix, and N. Alturo. Barcelona: Institute of Catalan Studies.

– 2005. "Üs familiar i transmissió lingüística." In *Estadística sobre els usos lingüístics a Catalunya 2003. Llengua i societat a Catalunya en els inicis del segle XXI,* edited by A.J. Torres. Barcelona: Generalitat de Catalunya, Secretaria General de Política Lingüística.

Trudel, M., and G. Jain. 1970. *L'histoire du Canada: enquête sur les manuels*. Ottawa: Commission royale sur le bilinguisme et le biculturalisme.

Vallcorba, J. 2008. "Plan Langue, Interculturalité et Cohésion sociale - Plan interdépartemental de la citoyenneté et de l'immigration." Paper presented at the seminar on immigration, social cohesion and the school at Lleida University, Catalonia, 24 November.

– 2009. "Dades referides a l'evolució dels cursos de les llengües d'origen." Email correspondence. May.

Valls, R. 2005. "La dimension multiculturelle de l'enseignement de l'histoire et de la géographie dans le contexte espagnol: un décalage entre intentions éducatives et pratiques scolaires." *Le cartable de Clio* 5: 1501–9.

Van Avermaet, P., and J. Klatter-Folmer. 1998. "The role of L$_2$ self-assessment in language choice behavior: immigrant shift to Dutch in Flanders and the Netherlands." *Te Reo* 41: 137–52.

Van Dam, D., and J. Nizet. 2002. *Wallonie. Flandres. Des regards croisés*. Brussels: De Boeck Université.

Van de Craen, P., and A.S. D'Hondt. 1997. *Anderstaligen in Brusselse Nederlandstalige Scholen*. Eindrapport voor Minister Grijp en de Vlaamse Gemeenschapscommissie. Brussels: VUB.

Van den Braembussche, A. 2002. "The silence of Belgium: Taboo and trauma in Belgian memory." *Yale French Studies* 102: 34–52.

Van den Branden, K., and K. Van Gorp. 2002. "How to evaluate CLIM in terms of intercultural education." *Intercultural Education,* 11: 42–51.

– and M. Verhelst, eds. 2006. *Tasks in Action: Task-Based Language Education from a Classroom-Based Perspective*. Cambridge Scholars Publishing.

Van Mensel, L., A. Housen, L. Mettewie, and M. Pierrard. 2005. "Multilinguisme dans l'enseignement néerlandophone à Bruxelles: résultats d'une étude pilote." In *Language, Attitudes and Education in Multilingual Cities*, edited by E. Witte, L. Van Mensel, M. Pierrard, L.

Mettewie, A. Housen, and R. De Groof, 133–42. Brussels: Koninklijke Vlaamse Academie van België voor Wetenschappen en Kunsten.

Van Parijs, P. 2005. "Language use and linguistic compétence in the Brussels Capital Region." *Aula Magna*, 29 November. Université libre de Bruxelles.

Van Parys, J., and S. Wauters. 2006. *Les connaissances linguistiques en Belgique*. Center for Research in Economics. centres.fusl.ac.be/CEREC/document/cahiers.html.

Van Robaeys, B., and N. Perrin. 2006. *La pauvreté chez les personnes d'origine étrangère en Belgique: un réel problème*. Liège: University of Liège, Fondation Roi Baudoin.

Van Velthoven, H. 1981. "Taal en onderwijspolitiek te Brussel, 1878–1914." *Taal en Sociale Integratie*. 4: 203–11.

Vanoverbeke, D. 2008. "Le Nord veut exporter son modèle." *Le Soir*, 24 June.

Vázquez, R.H. 2004. "Entre historias y experiencias: conciencia histórica e identidades en construcción en jóvenes inmigrantes en Catalunya." In *Formación de la ciudadanía: las TICs y los nuevos problemas*, edited by María Isabel Vera Muñoz and David Pérez i Pérez, 1–13. Alicante: Asociación Universitaria de Profesores de Didáctica de las Ciencias Sociales.

Verhelst, M. 2005. *Circus kiekeboe succeeds in promoting literacy/reading in multilingual kindergartens*. Paper and poster presented at The Fifth International Conference of the International Association for the Improvement of Mother Tongue Education: The Learning and Teaching of Language and Literature, 10–15 May. Albi, France: Centre for Language and Migration.

Verhoeven, M. 2006. *Politiques éducatives et intégration des jeunes issus de l'immigration en Communauté française de Belgique: état des lieux et modèle d'analyse*. Paper presented at international workshop on "Educating immigrant pupils: approaches and policies challenging educational integration and equal opportunities for all." February. Barcelona.

Verlot, M. 1998. "De la politique de non-discrimination à l'action positive." *Agenda interculturel* 169 (December): 16–21.

– 2000a. "Chaque enfant est-il le même devant la loi? L'inconsistance cohérente dans les politiques de discriminations positives dans l'enseignement en Belgique." In *Affirmative action: des discours, des politiques et des pratiques en débat*, edited by M. Martiniello and A. Rea, chapter 8. Louvain-la-Neuve: Academia Bruylant.

– 2000b. "Implementing Intercultural Education in Flanders, Belgium. Patterns and Ambiguities." Presentation at the 5th International Metropolis Conference, 13–17 November, Vancouver.

- 2002. "Resistance, complexity and the need for rethinking intercultural education." *Kolor, Journal of Moving Communities* 1: 5–19.
- and K. Delrue. 2004. "Multilingualism in Brussels." In *Urban Multilingualism in Europe: Immigrant Minority Languages at Home and School,* edited by G. Extra and K. Yagmur, 221–50. Clevedon: Multilingual Matters.
- and M. McAndrew. 2004. "Diversité culturelle, langue et éducation: que pouvons-nous apprendre d'une comparaison Québec/Flandres?" *Canadian Ethnic Studies/ Études ethniques au Canada* 36(3): 10–24. Special issue: *Relations ethniques et éducation dans les sociétés divisées: comparaison Belgique-Canada/Ethnic Relations and Education in Divided Societies: Comparing Belgium and Canada.* Edited by G. Bourgeault, M.H. Chastenay, and M. Verlot.
- and R. Pinxten. 2000. "Intercultural education and complex instruction. Some remarks and questions from an anthropolocial perspective on learning." *Intercultural Education* 11(Suppl. 1): 7–14.
- and S. Suijs. 2000. "L'apprentissage pragmatique de l'interculturel." *VEI Enjeux* 120: 111–20.
- K. Delrue, G. Extra, and K. Yagmur. 2003. *Meertaligheid in Brusselse: De status van allochtone talen thuis en op school.* Amsterdam: European Cultural Foundation.
- S. Sierens, R. Soenen, and S. Suijs. 2000. *Intercultureel onderwijs: leren in verscheidenheid* Ghent: Steunpunt Intercutureel Onderwijs (Centre for Diversity and Learning).
Verstraete, E. 2006. *Flemish Teaching Resources under the Magnifying Glass: In Search of Intercultural Content.* Ghent: Steunpunt Intercutureel Onderwijs (Centre for Diversity and Learning).
Vickers, E. 2005. "I Want to Use my Subject Matter to ... The Role of Purpose in One Secondary US History Teacher's Instructional Decision-Making." Paper presented at the annual congress of the American Educational Research Association (AERA), Montreal, 11–15 April.
Vila, I., ed. 1995. *El català i el castellà en el sistema educatiu de Catalunya.* Barcelona: Horsori.
- 2004. "Diversidad, escuela e inmigración." *Aula de innovación educativa* 131: 62–6.
- 2006. "Immersion linguistique en Catalogne, identité et image." Presentation at the colloquium on *Diversité linguistique à l'école et en société: nouveaux enjeux pour la recherche,* 15–16 February, Montreal.
- and S. Perera. 1997. "Immersió linguística a Catalunya, identitat i imatge." *Caplletra* 21: 95–104.

– C. Siqués, E. Serrat, C. Serra, and P. Monreal. 1997. *Lengua propia, lengua de la escuela y escolarización.* Universitat de Girona, Facultat d'Educació i Psicologia.

Vila i Moreno, F.X. 2004a. "Barcelona (Catalonia): Language, education and ideology in an integrationist society." In *Language, Attitudes and Education in Multiculingual Cities*, edited by E. Witte, L. Van Mensel, M. Pierrard, L. Mettewie, A. Housen, and R. De Groof, 53–86. Koninklijke Vlaamse Academie van Belgie voor eetenschappen en Kunstein.

– 2004b. "Català i el castellà a començament del mil-lenni a Catalunya: condicionants i tendències." In *Les llengües a Catalunya, Aula de Ciència i Cultura 15*, edited by L. Payarató and F.X. Vila, 29–51. Barcelona: Fundació Caixa Sabadell.

– 2004c. "Ora heur de fer balanç? Elements per valorar les polítique lingüístique a Catalunya en el període constitutional." *Revista de Llingua i Dret* 41: 243–86.

– and M. Galindo. 2006. "Els usos lingüístics en l'educació primària a Catalunya: situació, tendéncies i perspectives." In *Quaderns d'Avaluació 6*, edited by F.X. Vila i Moreno and M. Galindo. Generalitat de Catalunya: Departament d'Educació i Universitat.

– E. Boix-Fuster, and N. Alturo i Monné. 2006. *Integrar, des de la fragilitat? Societats plurilingües davant els reptes de les immigracions multilingües: Suïssa, Brussel-les, Luxembruge, Quebec i Catalunya.* Barcelona: Institute of Catalan Studies.

Vlaamse Gemeenschapscommissie. 2008. Statistics on the teaching of the Flemish language in Brussels at the primary and secondary levels. www.vgc.be/Onderwijs/Onderwijsbeleid+van+de+VGC/Over+het+Brussels+Nederlandstalig+onderwijs/cijfers.htm.

– 2009. *Description du Voorrangsbeleid Brussel.* www.vgc.be/Onderwijs/Initiatieven/pedagogisch-didactische+ondersteuning/VBB.htm.

Walford, G. 1996. "Diversity and Choice in School Education: An Alternative View." *Oxford Review of Education* 22(2).

Wicklow, C. 1997. *Integrated Education in Northern Ireland: The Lagan Experience* Glasgow: University of Glasgow.

Wilder, D.A. 1984. "Intergroup Contact: The Typical Member and the Social Identity." *Journal of Personality and Social Psychology* 47(2): 342–8.

Wils, K. 2003. "Les paradoxes d'un renouvellement ralenti: réflexions sur l'enseignement de l'histoire en Flandre et aux Pays-Bas." *Le cartable de Clio* 3: 144–54.

Witte, E., and H. Van Velthoven. 1998. *Taal en Politiek: de Belgische casus in een historisch perspectief.* Brussels: VUB Press.

- 1999. *Langue et politique: la situation en Belgique dans une perspective historique.* Brussels: VUB Press.

Witte, E., A. Alen, H. Dumont, and R. Ergec, eds. 1999. *Het Statuut van Brussel/Bruxelles et son statut.* Brussels: De Boeck and Larcier.

Woehrling, J. 2008. "Les fondements et les limites de l'accommodement raisonnable en milieu scolaire." In *L'accommodement raisonnable et la diversité religieuse à l'école publique. Normes et pratiques*, edited by M. McAndrew, M. Milot, J.S. Imbeault, and P. Eid, 43–56. Montreal: Fides.

Zanazanian, P. 2005. *Teaching the History of Quebec and Canada: Perspectives of Anglophone and Francophone Teachers.* Research report. University of Montreal: Chair in Ethnic Relations.

- 2008. "Historical Consciousness and the 'French-English' Divide among Quebec History Teachers." *Revue canadienne d'études ethniques/ Canadian Ethnic Studies* 40(3): 109–30.

Zapata, R. 2004. *Multiculturalidad e inmigración.* Madrid: Editorial Síntesis.

- R. Requijo, and A. Giménez. 2005. *La immigració en estats plurinacionals: El cas de Catalunya en perspectiva.* Research report. Barcelona: Universitat Pompeu Fabra, Fundació Trias Fargas.

Index

Action Plan for Language and Social
Cohesion in the School (Catalonia,
2003), 129
Action Week against Racism, 162
Advisory Committee on Integration
and Reasonable Accommodation
in the Schools, 161. *See also*
Bouchard-Taylor Commission
anti-racism: Action Week against
Racism, 162; and Complex
Instruction, 188; and education,
112, 124, 156; and interventions,
163; and school activities, 162; in
school curriculum, 157–60; and
teachers, 177, 187
Aula Intercultural (Catalonia), 173

Belgium, 26; and academic success of
immigrant students, 144–6; and
adaptation to diversity, 179–92;
and ambiguity of ethnic dominance, 8–9; Catholic heritage of,
10; and crossing school boundaries, 57–8; educational segregation
in, 29–32; educational systems and
ethnic relations in, 25–9; and immigrant migratory patterns, 135–7;

and *Inburgering* policy, 136; and
language marker, 9; language programs and interventions in, 139–
44; linguistic integration in, 137–9;
and teaching of history, 87–91
bilingualism, 19, 26, 28, 34; and
anglophones in Quebec, 23; in
Brussels, 29, 31, 137, 141, 143;
in Catalan schools, 41–2; 100;
in Catalonia, 40, 41, 100; and
Dutch schools, 137; and ethnic
boundaries, 9; in Flanders, 28;
in Flemish schools, 26, 30; in
Northern Ireland, 34; objective of
immigrant families, 149; in Quebec
schools, 22, 56; Royal Commission
on, 91; and social mobility, 113;
and trilingualism, 113; in Walloon
schools, 27
Bill 101, 17, 18, 19, 20, 92, 98, 115,
116, 117, 119, 153; attitudes of
children of, 164–5, 167; innovative aspects of, 116. *See also*
Charter of the French Language
Blacks: and contact theory, 49; in
Quebec, 123–4; and Whites, 49, 50
Bofill Foundation, 173